Unless Recalled Earlier
Date Due

The Theory of Free Banking

Co-published with the
Cato Institute

THE THEORY OF
FREE BANKING

Money Supply under Competitive Note Issue

George A. Selgin

Hong Kong University

CATO
INSTITUTE

Rowman & Littlefield
PUBLISHERS

ROWMAN & LITTLEFIELD

Published in the United States of America in 1988
by Rowman & Littlefield, Publishers
(a division of Littlefield, Adams & Company)
81 Adams Drive, Totowa, New Jersey 07512

Copyright © 1988 by Rowman & Littlefield

Co-published by arrangement with the Cato Institute

Library of Congress Cataloging-in-Publication Data

Selgin, George A., 1957–
     The theory of free banking: money supply under competitive note
issue / George A. Selgin.

     Revision of the author's thesis (doctoral—New York University).
     Bibliography: p. 201
     Includes index.
     ISBN 0-8476-7578-5
     1. Banks and banking. 2. Money supply. 3. Monetary policy.
4. Banks and banking, Central. I. Title. II. Title: Free banking:
Money supply under competitive note issue.
HG1586.S38   1987
332.4—dc19   87-20012

90 89 88
 6   5   4   3   2   1

Printed in the United States of America

To My Parents

Contents

Preface

M OST ECONOMISTS BELIEVE that "money will not manage itself." In this book I challenge that belief. In doing so I also try to add a few reinforcing-rods to the so-called microfoundations of monetary theory.

Like most contemporary investigators of free banking, I became interested in the subject after reading F. A. Hayek's *Denationalisation of Money* (1978). The argument of that monograph, that competition in the issue of money would result in greater monetary stability and order than central banks can achieve, contradicted both traditional interpretations of history (including especially American history) and conventional theory. Challenged by Hayek, I decided to review the development of money and banking institutions in the United States. I became convinced that unwise regulations, rather than the absence of a central bank, could explain most of the shortcomings—past and present—of our monetary system. In the course of investigating this issue I was exposed to some manuscript chapters of Lawrence White's *Free Banking in Britain* (1984d). One chapter described the successful performance of an unregulated banking system in 19th-century Scotland; this was further evidence against the view that past unregulated systems had failed. Another chapter presented an abbreviated theory of free banking, explaining how competition could result in a smoothly operating system of money supply. White's study caused my interest in free banking to blossom. It also suggested the need for a more comprehensive, theoretical work—one that would evaluate free banking both as a system that might have been permitted in the past and as one that might be adopted in the future. I was eventually able to undertake this project as my doctoral dissertation for the Department of Economics at New York University. This book is a substantially revised version of that dissertation.

I am grateful to Professor White, not only for having inspired the present study, but also for helping to see it through to completion as chairman of my dissertation committee. I also owe a great intellectual debt to Kurt Schuler, whose research on free banking has uncovered many useful facts, which he has generously shared with me, and whose enthusiasm for the subject has been a constant source of encouragement. Finally, for their scholarly input I would like to thank Richard H. Timberlake, Jr., of the University of Georgia; Richard Ebeling, of the University of Dallas; and the members of my dissertation committee: Jesse Benhabib, Clive Bull, and Jonas Prager, all of New York University, and Anna J. Schwartz, of the National Bureau of Economic Research.

I have received financial support from several sources, including the Austrian Economics Program at New York University, which provided fellowship support for all of my three and one-half years at N.Y.U. I would like to thank in particular Israel M. Kirzner for his role in securing my participation in the program. The Mises Institute of Auburn University provided me a summer fellowship in 1984, and I owe thanks for this to its Director, Llewellyn Rockwell, Jr. Finally, The Institute for Humane Studies at George Mason University has assisted me by various means, including a Summer Non-Resident Fellowship Award offered to me in 1981, and an in-residence fellowship for the summer of 1985. Most of the present work was composed during the latter summer and also in the spring of 1985, when I was an employee of the Institute, and I am grateful to the staff of the Institute, and to Walter Grinder especially, for turning what might have been a painful task of composition into a pleasant undertaking.

In addition to intellectual and financial assistance I have received other help of various sorts from a number of people and institutions. I wish to thank in particular: Karen Cash and Colleen Morreta of the Center for the Study of Market Processes at George Mason University, and Mary Blackwell and Jean Berry of the George Mason Word Processing Center, for assistance in completion of the final draft of this study; Paula Jescavage, of the Interlibrary Loan Office at Bobst Memorial Library at N.Y.U., for supplying me with hundreds of obscure articles and books; and my brother, Peter Selgin, for his thoughtful editorial advice.

Finally, for their companionship and moral support, which sustained me through four difficult years of graduate work, I wish to thank my parents, Paul and Pinuccia Selgin, and my friends Mark Brady, Roy Childs, Charles Fowler, Andrea and Howie Rich, Chris Rowland, and Barbra Schwartz.

Foreword

THIS BOOK is an important work in monetary theory. As such it brings to mind a statement by the learned John Hicks in an essay that I always assign to my graduate students in Monetary Theory: "Monetary theory is less abstract than most economic theory; it cannot avoid a relation to reality, which in other economic theory is sometimes missing. It belongs to monetary history, in a way that economic theory does not always belong to economic history." This is so, Hicks continues, for two reasons. First, the best work in monetary theory is often topical, aimed at understanding a monetary problem of the times. Second, monetary institutions are continually evolving, and with them the appropriate theoretical apparatus.*

The present work bears out Hicks's generalization both by being topical and by being attuned to institutional evolution. It is topical because the outstanding monetary problem of our time is the failure of central banking to deliver the macroeconomic stability its adherents have promised. The Federal Reserve System, in particular, has not carried its own weight. This book offers a promising alternative. It is attuned to the evolutionary institutional developments not only of the recent past—the increasing competitiveness and partial deregulation of banking and financial markets—but also of the foreseeable future. A system of free banking of the sort analyzed here is plausibly the logical culmination of movements in the direction of monetary laissez-faire.

Not long ago the debate over government's role in the monetary system was largely confined to conflicting sets of advice to the monetary authorities concerning their day-by-day activities. A few voices raised the broader issue of constitutional rules to restrain the monetary authorities. Happily, the professional and even political discus-

*John Hicks, "Monetary Theory and History—An Attempt at Perspective," in *Critical Essays in Monetary Theory* (Oxford: Clarendon Press, 1967), pp. 156–57.

sion of monetary policy options has broadened in recent years to include possibilities for doing without monetary authorities. The question now on the table is which ideal is more feasible: the ideal of a monetary bureaucracy that is mechanically apolitical and selflessly efficiency-minded, or the ideal of a purely private and market-disciplined monetary system.

Historical evidence on past monetary systems free of central banking is naturally important to this discussion. The first chapter of this book contributes a useful summary of such evidence. But empirical evidence must be interpreted in the light of theory. It is to the theoretical understanding of free banking that this work primarily and excellently contributes. The need for clarification and development of the theory of free banking is plainly acute. Free banking has gotten undeserved short shrift even from open-minded economists keenly interested in alternative monetary regimes because, to quote Robert J. Barro as a case in point, "the workings of a private, noncommodity monetary system are not well understood (at least by me)."*

The standard money-supply model of undergraduate textbooks assumes a central bank monopoly of currency and binding reserve requirements against demand deposits. Selgin reconstructs and extends the theory of money supply under free banking conditions, that is, where competing private banks are legally unrestricted in creating currency and demand deposits (and are compelled by market forces to make their liabilities redeemable for an outside money). There has been surprisingly little work on this topic, despite the recent growth of professional interest in alternative monetary systems. Happily my own modest theoretical effort† is now succeeded by Selgin's several longer steps in the direction of a modern theory of free banking.

The theoretical excellence of this study lies not in developing high-powered mathematical techniques, but in deriving surprising results from the thoughtful and novel application of familiar money-and-banking ideas. The central results show that the standard "rule of excess reserves"—that a competitive bank cannot safely expand its liabilities by more than the size of its excess reserves—applies to note-issuing as well as to the more familiar deposit-creating banks, provided that money-holders do not accept various brands of notes

---

*Robert J. Barro, "United States Inflation and the Choice of a Monetary Standard," in Robert E. Hall, ed., *Inflation: Causes and Effects* (Chicago: University of Chicago Press for the National Bureau of Economic Research, 1982), p. 110 n. 2.

†Lawrence H. White, *Free Banking in Britain: Theory, Experience, and Debate, 1800–1845* (Cambridge: Cambridge University Press, 1984), ch. 1.

indiscriminately. The rule does not, however, apply to a monopoly issuer.

What is more provocative, we learn that the limits to note issue expand when the demand to hold inside money increases, and that the consequent expansion of bank liabilities and assets is warranted by considerations of credit-market equilibrium. A bank is able to vary its liabilities in response to demand shifts even if its reserves are unchanging, because an increase in holding demand implies a fall in the rate of turnover, hence in the optimal reserve ratio. The theory of optimal reserves elaborated by Selgin undermines the mechanistic textbook view of the reserve ratio as constant, and links changes in desired bank reserve ratios to changes in the money multiplier. A further surprising and novel extension is the refutation of the standard view that no economic forces check a concerted expansion by banks.

Later chapters usefully compare the problems facing free banking and central banking systems. A central bank that wants to behave neutrally is shown to lack the market feedback mechanism that informs competitive banks in supplying money. A equilibrium mix of deposits and currency in particular is more difficult to maintain under central banking. Various disfunctions that have been ascribed to a free banking system are either not compelling or are more severe under central banking.

The final chapter offers a proposal for monetary reform based on Selgin's conclusions regarding the stability and efficiency of free banking. The case is compelling, and there is no need for me to argue its merits here. But I might note optimistically that the Selgin proposal holds out the hope of uniting the advocates of various programs (who are sometimes prone to overemphasize their variety) for the denationalization of money, a laissez-faire approach to monetary stability, the abolition of legal restrictions against private money, free banking, and (as the strictest of monetarist rules) the freezing of the monetary base.*

Given my personal involvement with this work, as the advisor of the New York University doctoral dissertation on which it is based, some comments of a more personal nature will perhaps be excused. In an interview recorded in Arjo Klamer's *Conversations with Economists*, the

---

*I have in mind such economists as F. A. Hayek, Roland Vaubel, Leland B. Yeager, Gerald P. O'Driscoll, Jr., Neil Wallace, myself, and Milton Friedman. All but Wallace are represented in chapters 13–18 of James A. Dorn and Anna J. Schwartz, eds., *The Search for Stable Money* (Chicago: University of Chicago Press, 1987).

macroeconomist Thomas J. Sargent observes that the most rewarding experience he has had as an economist is to see his students surpass what he has done: "A guy you remember, who first came to class and didn't know anything, is now inventing new stuff that you have a hard time understanding, arguments that in general you couldn't have thought of. What's also nice is that some of them got the message, they are building on our shoulders."* I would say that Sargent's statement captures very well the way I feel about the present work by George Selgin, whom I am certainly proud to claim as a former student.

The statement fails to fit in a few ways, however. To begin with, I never actually instructed Selgin in a classroom. More important, he did know something when he "first came to class." In fact, he arrived at NYU in fall 1981 already knowing that the topic of his dissertation was to be free banking. Although he did not already know everything he was to write (and thus there is still room to think that I had some input into this work—opportunities for such self-flattery are among the leading rewards of an academic career), I cannot claim that he "got the message" primarily from me. I cannot even claim that Selgin is building largely on my shoulders—one shoulder at most. The breadth and depth of his self-directed reading in monetary theory is evident throughout this work and is perhaps its most impressive aspect. From the outset we have been colleagues pursuing complimentary lines of research rather than teacher and student. To see this work by my colleague in print is a pleasure indeed.

Lawrence H. White

New York
June 1987

---

*Arjo Klamer, *Conversations with Economists: New Classical Economists and Opponents Speak Out on the Current Controversy in Macroeconomics* (Totowa, N.J.: Rowman & Allanheld, 1984), p. 78.

PART ONE

Setting the Stage

1

Overview

THAT COMPETITION IN production serves the interests of consumers, and that monopoly in production is opposed to those
interests, is a maxim which has guided mainstream economic thought
and policy since the days of Adam Smith. Most enterprises have been
influenced by it. One exception, though, is the issue of currency. Only
a handful of theorists objected to governments setting up privileged
banks, with monopolies or quasi-monopolies in note issue, during the
17th, 18th, and 19th centuries, and fewer still took exception later on,
as central banking—a supposedly conscientious version of monopolized currency supply—came to be viewed as an indispensable part of
national monetary policy.

As a consequence of these developments, the theory and implications of unregulated and decentralized currency supply have been
largely ignored. Indeed, central banking has been taken so much for
granted that for many years no effort was made to examine alternative systems, even to show why they must fail. Lately, though, a new
interest in unregulated or "free" banking with decentralized currency
supply has surfaced, spurred on by the poor performance of central
banks. F. A. Hayek's pioneering work on *Choice in Currency* (1976) and
his later monograph on *Denationalisation of Money* (1978) challenged
the view that governments are more fit to provide media of exchange
than private firms. This opened the gate to an entire new field of
inquiry, to which there have already been numerous contributions.
Most have been studies of the history of decentralized banking
systems. The studies show that, of past systems involving decentralized currency issue, those that were least regulated actually worked
rather well, whereas those that worked poorly were also not free from
inhibiting regulations.[1] By questioning the claim that free banking has
failed in the past these studies justify renewed theoretical inquiry into
its operational characteristics compared to those of central banking.

3

Purpose and Plan of This Study

The purpose of this study is threefold. Its principal aim is to advance the theoretical understanding of free banking. Despite recent and excellent empirical work, the *theory* of free banking is still more or less where it was when Vera Smith (1936) reviewed the literature on it. Second, it seeks to employ the theory of free banking in a critique of banking systems with monopolized currency supply, including all central banking systems. Finally, the study will suggest practical means for improving existing monetary and banking arrangements.

The sequence of chapters reflects this tripartite purpose. Chapters 2 through 6 offer a positive theory of free banking. The purpose of chapter 2, "The Evolution of a Free Banking System," is to motivate and justify assumptions concerning the institutional make-up of free banking. These assumptions provide the framework for the rest of the study. Chapter 3 considers the limits to the expansion of free bank liabilities (inside money) when the demand to hold them is unchanging; it also discusses the special status of monopoly suppliers of currency that places them beyond the pale of the usual forces of control. Chapter 4 defends a particular view of monetary equilibrium, which serves as a criterion for evaluating the response (discussed in chapters 5 and 6) of a free banking system to changes in the demand for inside money. Chapters 7 and 8 contrast free banking to central banking, with a focus on their abilities to keep the quantity of money and currency at their equilibrium levels. Chapters 9 and 10 complete this comparison by examining some alleged shortcomings of free banking that central banking is supposed to avoid. Finally, chapter 11 looks at free banking as a practical alternative to other means of monetary reform; the chapter ends with a sketch of a plan for deregulating and decentralizing the existing mechanism of currency supply.

Throughout the study emphasis is placed on the distinctive, *macroeconomic* implications of free banking. Its microeconomic consequences, though not unimportant, are less controversial. In fact, the emphasis is even more narrow: as the subtitle indicates, the study concentrates on the macroeconomic implications of competitive note issue, free banking's most distinct and unconventional feature. Other features, such as deregulated deposit banking (with payment of interest on checkable accounts), branch banking, use of special electronic means for transfer of funds, etc., have not only been extensively dealt with elsewhere but are currently being put to practice in existing banking systems around the world. Moreover, scholarly opinion decidedly favors deregulation in these areas.² The competitive issue of currency—and of redeemable bank notes in particular—is, on the other hand, a relatively unfamiliar and unexplored possibility, and one that most economists dismiss. The reason for this is not far to seek: monopolization of the supply of currency is essential to modern central banking operations. Therefore, to consider this form of deregulation is to consider a radical restructuring or abandonment of conventional views on the conduct and necessity of centralized monetary policy. Such revisionism is far removed from the everyday concerns of money and banking theorists, who need to study arrangements as they find them. But it is precisely what the present investigation undertakes.

The argument is straightforward: nothing about free banking requires it to be approached with technical sophistication beyond what might be found in a graduate money and banking textbook. Money and banking professors might even assign this book to their students as a complement to standard theory. In fact, many of the theoretical arguments that appear in these pages should be familiar: what is new is the effort to put old concepts to work in examining a banking system with different institutional features. The reader needs to realize this. If he pays attention only to particular arguments (the trees), he might think little of what is being said is new or controversial. If, instead, he only pays attention to the conclusions (the forest), he might think that what is being said is not merely new but also the product of some new and bizarre reasoning.

The reader should also note that this book does not attempt to discuss the relative *political* merits of free versus central banking. There is much to be said in favor of deregulation and choice in currency as means for freeing the monetary system from political manipulation. Nevertheless this study seeks to explore the theoretical merits and demerits of free banking quite apart from any political considerations. Therefore, in discussing the operations of central banks, it generally assumes that they are governed solely in the interest of consumers. As a result, the argument must be somewhat biased in favor of centralized control, since it is assumed that free banks operate only for the sake of private profit.

The Historical Background

Although this study will look at free banking from a theoretical point of view, it will help to sketch briefly the history of central banking in various leading nations. Conventional wisdom holds that central banks were established, at least in large part, in response to defects of unregulated banking. Recent works that contradict this view have already been mentioned. The following survey highlights historical evidence from these and other sources.[3]

The Bank of England was established by King William III in 1694. It was designed to secure "certain recompenses and advantages . . . to such persons as shall voluntarily advance the sum of fifteen hundred thousand pounds towards carrying on the war with France." In the age of mercantilism the granting of special privileges to business firms in exchange for financial assistance to the state, especially during wartime, was common. Yet in banking this pattern continued even into the twentieth century. The Bank of England followed it faithfully until 1826, routinely securing for itself additional monopoly privileges in addition to extensions of its charter. In 1697, in exchange for a loan of £ 1,001,071, it was given a monopoly of chartered banking, limiting competition to private bankers. In 1708, in return for a loan of £ 2,500,000, the Bank's owners were rewarded by an act prohibiting joint-stock banks (private banks of six partners or more) from issuing notes. To extend its privileges through the remainder of the century the Bank made further, large loans to the government in 1742, 1781, and 1799. In 1826 it suffered its first setback: a campaign led by Thomas Joplin gained for joint-stock banks the right to engage in note issue and redemption outside a circle with its radius extending 65 miles from the center of London, where the Bank of England was headquartered. But this threat of competition was made up for in 1833 by a law officially sanctioning the use of Bank of England notes by "country" banks as part of their legal reserves and for use instead of specie for redeeming their own notes. This encouraged country banks to use Bank of England notes as high-powered money (a role the notes were already playing to a limited extent as a result of the Bank's monopoly of London circulation), expanding the Bank's power to manipulate the English money supply.

In the meantime the reputation of all note-issuing banks suffered as a result of the suspension of 1793–1821. It was further eroded by a crisis in 1826. The authorities clamoured for restrictions upon note issue, making no effort to distinguish the powers of the Bank of England from those of other less privileged note-issuing banks. The country banks thus shared the blame for overissues that originated in the policies of the Bank of England. The consequence was Peel's Bank Act of 1844, which prohibited further extension of country-bank note issues while placing a 100 percent marginal specie-reserve requirement on the note issues of the Bank of England. The Bank Act eventually gave the Bank of England a monopoly of note issue, as the Bank assumed the authorized circulation of country banks when they closed. It also added to the rigidity of the system by increasing the dependence of country banks on the Bank of England for meeting their depositors' increased demands for currency. Since the Bank of England was itself restricted in its ability to issue notes, the system was incapable of meeting any substantial increase in demand for currency relative to the demand for checkable deposits. For this reason the Bank Act had to be repeatedly suspended until the desirability of having the Bank of England free to function as a "lender of last resort" during "internal drains" of currency was made conspicuous in Bagehot's *Lombard Street* (1874). When it formally acknowledged its special responsibilities the Bank of England became the first true central bank, the prototype for other central banks that would be established in nearly every nation on the globe.

If England's was a model central banking system, then Scotland's was its antithesis. From 1792 to 1845, Scotland had no central bank, allowed unrestricted competition in the business of note issue, and imposed almost no regulations on its banking firms. Yet the Scottish system was thought to be superior by nearly everyone who was aware of it. Its decline after 1845 was caused, not by any shortcoming, but in consequence of the unprovoked extension of Peel's Act, which ended new entry into the note issue business in Scotland as well as England.[4]

From 1831 to 1902 Sweden also had a nearly unregulated free banking system (Jonung 1985). At the end of this period there were 26 note issuing private banks with a total of 157 branches. The note issues of these private banks competed successfully with those of the Riksbank (the bank of the Swedish Parliament) despite taxes and other restrictions imposed upon private notes and despite the fact that Riksbank notes alone were legal tender. One measure of the success of the Swedish private note-issuing banks is that, throughout their existence, none failed even though the government had an explicit policy of not assisting private banks in financial trouble. The system was also orderly in that there was an organized system of note exchange, with all notes accepted at par by the various banks. Finally, the absence of banking regulations in Sweden was crucial to its exceptionally rapid economic growth during the second half of the 19th century.[5] In this private note issue played a major role, both as an instrument for marshalling loanable funds and as a means for promoting overall development and sophistication of the Swedish financial system. Still, despite its success, Swedish free banking was dismantled in stages beginning in 1901 when the government, resenting the loss of state revenue from reduced circulation of Riksbank notes, sought by means of regulations and offers of subsidies to restore to the Riksbank a monopoly of note issue. The private banks' right to issue notes was formally abrogated in 1904.

Still another free-banking episode took place in Foochow, the capital of Fukien province, in mainland China.[6] China went through numerous, disastrous experiences with reckless issues of government paper money, starting as early as the 9th century. At last the Ch'ing dynasty (1644–1911) decided to let note issue be an exclusively private undertaking, except for two brief, unsuccessful government issues during the 1650s and 1850s. In Foochow (and also in some other cities) local banks prospered under the Manchus, issuing paper notes redeemable (usually on demand) in copper cash and free from all government regulation.

Unlike government issues this private paper currency, which grew greatly in importance during the 19th century, was highly successful. Typically it did not depreciate, and it was widely preferred to bulky and non-uniform copper cash. Notes of larger banks circulated throughout Foochow at par, thanks to an efficient note-clearing system. Though smaller banks often failed, only one large local bank did so in the entire history of the industry. The large banks (of which there were 45 in the system's last decades) commanded a high level of public confidence and respect.

The downfall of free banking in Foochow following the Republican revolution of 1911 was caused by the new central government's restrictive regulations. These favored several very large, non-local or "modern style" banks which had given financial support to the revolutionaries. The Nationalists, when they gained power in 1927, were especially beholden to the modern banks (which issued silver-based monies) and favored them by prohibiting the issue of copper notes. At last, in 1935, the Nationalist government made notes of the three largest modern banks legal tender. The government eventually intended to give its greatest financial benefactor, the Central Bank of China, a monopoly of note issue. But its program was interrupted by the Japanese invasion of 1937, which caused it to concentrate on maximizing revenues from increased issues of legal tender. The consequence was yet another instance of paper money issued by the Chinese government becoming absolutely worthless.

Centralization of note issue in China was finally accomplished during the 1950s by the Communists, whose People's Bank took over the branches of the Central Bank of China as well as offices of many remaining local banks. Though little information exists concerning the performance of the People's Bank, what there is suggests that China continued long after the war to suffer from hidden inflation, disguised by an extensive system of official prices. Despite the general superabundance of money that this inflation implied, local communities also suffered from a *shortage* of convenient, small-denomination exchange media,[7] such as had been well provided in Foochow during the non-inflationary, free-banking era.

In France merchants' attempts to establish banking on a sound, competitive basis were repeatedly frustrated by the government's desire to borrow money that it could not, or would not, repay. The spectacular failure of John Law's Banque Royale in 1721, which had become a government bank three years before, prevented for half a century the establishment of any new bank of issue. In 1776 a new bank, the Caisse d'Escompte, was established to engage in commercial lending, but soon became involved in large loans to the state that caused it to suffer a liquidity crisis. The bank appealed to the Treasury to repay its most recent loan, but instead the government authorized a suspension of specie payments. The bank remained solvent, however, and when the government loan was repaid it resumed specie payments. After this, repeated forced loans to the state so entwined the bank with the government that it became, in effect, a branch of the Treasury. Its notes were made redeemable in Treasury *assignats*, which were made legal tender in 1790. The government soon sank into bankruptcy under a torrent of assignats, dragging the Caisse d'Escompte down with it.

Renewed attempts to establish banks of issue in the 1790s were defeated by Napoleon, who reacted to private banks' refusal to discount government paper by establishing a rival institution, the Bank of France, in which he was also a shareholder. Support for the new bank, at first unimpressive, improved when one of the private banks decided to consolidate with it. Nonetheless Napoleon remained dissatisfied, and in 1803 he passed a law giving the Bank of France the exclusive privilege of issuing bank notes at Paris and forbidding the establishment of banks in other regions without official approval. This forced the Bank of France's principal rival, the second Caisse d'Escompte, into merger with it. Finally, in 1806, the Bank of France was placed under formal government control, and in 1808 it was given an exclusive right of note issue in every town in which it established branches.

The fall of Napoleon led to the establishment, throughout the country, of local banks of issue. These defied the monopoly of the Bank of France, although the latter remained the sole nationwide supplier of currency.[8] After 1840 the government refused to grant any more charters for new note-issuing banks, and in 1848 those already in existence were absorbed by the Bank of France. Thus the period of limited competition was short lived. But its end gave rise to a prolonged debate between the champions of free banking and defenders of the Bank of France, with the majority of French economists on the former side.[9] The French free banking theorists were again active in 1857, when the charter of the Bank of France came up for renewal. The 1860 annexation of Savoy, which had its own note-issuing bank, generated the most intense discussion of all, but soon their repeated failure to win any practical victory for their beliefs caused the free bankers to abandon their cause. The close of the decade marked the end of significant anti-monopoly agitation.

Unlike France, Spain had a relatively liberal banking policy in the years just prior to 1873. It had many note-issuing banks, most of which were monopolies solely in their province of establishment. The exception was the Bank of Spain which, although begun as a financially conservative enterprise, became involved in large-scale loans to the government that eventually made it fiscal agent to the state. In return for this it was eventually given exclusive rights to interprovincial branching. Then, in 1874, six years after the overthrow of the Bourbon monarchy, in return for a loan of 125 million pesetas the new republican government gave the Bank a monopoly of note issue.[10] The government also offered generous concessions to other banks in return for their becoming branches of the Bank of Spain. Most of the smaller banks accepted.

During the first decades of its independence, Italy, too, had a plurality of note-issuing banks. But the risorgimento left the new state with an immense debt, in which several of the banks, and the National Bank of the Kingdom in particular, were involved. As an alternative to retrenchment the Italian government sought further help from the note-issuing banks.[11] It secured this help by allowing the notes of the Bank of the Kingdom issued in connection with loans to the state to pass as inconvertible (forced) currency, while at the same time awarding limited legal tender status to the notes of other issuing banks. This arrangement continued until 1874, when all Italian banks were placed on an equal footing, in that all were allowed to participate in the issue of irredeemable paper for the purpose of monetizing the national debt. This reform also prohibited further entry into the business of note issue. In consequence of these reforms the Italian money supply became extremely unstable. Its growth followed the growth of government expenditures. In 1883 gold convertibility was officially restored, but lack of strict enforcement, including severe limitations placed on the exchange of bank notes and settlement of clearings between competing banks, caused the system to remain in a state of de facto inconvertibility. Ten years later, a scandal erupted when several banks made unauthorized issues of legal tender notes.[12] This gave rise to reforms leading to the establishment of the Bank of Italy, which had a monopoly of note issue conferred upon it in 1926.

Francesco Ferrara, the leading Italian economist of the era of the risorgimento, argued vehemently against the forced currency laws and other legislation that limited banks' obligations to redeem their notes (Ferrara 1866). Ferrara also objected to the limitation of entry into the note-issue business, arguing that free competition among issuers of convertible currency was the best means for ensuring monetary stability (Ferrara 1933). These opinions were seconded by Guiseppe Di Nardi in his definitive study of this era in Italian banking (Di Nardi 1953).[13] The findings of these writers suggest strongly that interference by the Italian government ruined what might otherwise have been a successful example of free banking.

Canadian experience also contradicts the view that free banking is inferior to central banking. During the 19th century Canada had a much more liberal banking policy than the U.S., and its banking system performed much better than the U.S. banking system of the same era. Canadian laws allowed plural note issue, permitted branch banking, and encouraged the growth of an elaborate clearing system.[14] After 1841 the only serious restrictions on banking freedom had to do with capital and note issue. To receive a charter and limited-liability status a bank had to have $500,000 (Canadian) or more of paid-in capital soon after opening. Note issue was limited to the amount of this paid-in capital, but this restriction had no effect until the severe currency drain of 1907.[15] In 1908 the law was changed to allow an emergency circulation exceeding capital by 15 percent during crop moving season. The government also monopolized the issue of notes under five dollars, but government note issues were restricted by a 100 percent marginal reserve requirement modeled after Peel's Act. For this reason government note issue did not become a source of inflation until World War I, when Canada joined Britain and the other Dominion nations in going off the gold standard. It was then that the government allowed, even pressured, the chartered banks to suspend payment, which they did. Meanwhile government (Dominion) notes were made legal tender and issued in large denominations to encourage their use for the settlement of clearings among the chartered banks. Since neither the government nor the banks were paying out gold, this was in effect a fiat-money central banking system, with the Treasury acting as the issuer of high-powered money. Though the war ended, the government did not retire the large Dominion notes, nor did it abolish the legal tender laws which made them high-powered money, and so the Treasury retained its power to manipulate the money supply.

Although Canada returned to the gold standard in the 1920s, it went off it again (once more in sympathy with Britain) in 1931. Canadian monetary experts soon became disenchanted with the "half-way house" measures affecting note issue, in which the Treasury was able to manipulate the money supply like a central bank but was not guided by any set policy. This fact, together with the desire of the government to escape permanently from the confines of private finance, led to demands for the creation of a true central bank.[16] To satisfy these demands the Bank of Canada was established in 1935. It secured a monopoly in note issue shortly thereafter.

The Canadian banking system was an example of a well working free banking system which suffered few crises and included some of the world's most prestigious banking firms. It was frequently referred to by American writers anxious to correct the defects of their own system but, unfortunately, equally anxious in most cases to find the answer in some piece of legislation. At the beginning of the Great Depression (several years before the Bank of Canada was established), when thousands of banks in the United States went out of business, the Canadian system proved its worth by not suffering a single bank failure.

Three other Dominion nations, South Africa, Australia, and New Zealand, also had plural note-issue systems and also adopted central banking in the wake of wartime financial measures. (The experience of Australia is discussed below in chapter 3.) In these cases also it is not clear that central banking was adopted because of any inherent defects of unregulated banking. The desire of these governments to borrow money on favorable terms, together with theorists' recognition that wartime legislation had undermined natural checks against monetary expansion, were the most obvious reasons for the creation of central banks in these places.[17] Other Dominion nations were urged by the Home Government to follow suit on the grounds that there was need for "intra-imperial co-operation."[18] By this time central banking had become a matter of national pride, and the opinion developed that "no country could be considered to have attained maturity until it had given birth to a central bank."[19]

The U.S. Experience

More than any other nation the United States has bolstered the myth of free banking as an historic failure. It cannot be said that central banking emerged in the U.S. in direct response to the government's quest for funds. The Federal Reserve System was the end result of a long monetary reform effort, aimed at correcting real problems of the previous system—a system that involved plural note issue. The new institution also commanded the approval of an overwhelming majority of economists.

Nevertheless, U.S. experience does not demonstrate the failure of unregulated banking, for the simple reason that banks have been heavily regulated throughout American history. As Bray Hammond notes (1957, 186), legislators in the early years of the republic never applied the principle of laissez faire to the banking business. "The issue was between prohibition and state control, with no thought of free enterprise." Banks were outlawed except when specifically authorized by state legislatures, and permission to set up a bank was usually accompanied by numerous restrictions, including especially required loans to the state. The situation after 1837—when the charter of the Second Bank of the United States expired—has been aptly referred to as involving "decentralism without freedom";[20] many note-issuing banks were established, but all were subjected to inhibiting regulations by the State governments that chartered them, and entry into the business was tightly restricted. Many western states and territories, including Wisconsin, Iowa, Oregon, Arkansas, and Texas, for a time allowed no note-issuing banks whatsoever. Other states restricted the business to a single, privileged firm. In most places branching was also outlawed.

1837 was, however, also the year in which increased public dissatisfaction with the charter or spoils system of bank establishment led to the adoption of "free banking" laws in Michigan and New York. These laws, later adopted in other states as well, brought banking into the domain of general incorporation procedures, so that a special charter no longer had to be secured in order for a new bank to open. This was an important step toward truly free banking, but it stopped well short of it. State governments, having relied for years on financial assistance they had received from privileged banks, sought to retain such assistance while still allowing free entry into the banking business. To accomplish this they included "bond-deposit" provisions in their free-banking laws. These provisions required banks to secure their note issues with government bonds, including bonds of the state in which they were incorporated. Typically, a bank desiring to issue 90 dollars in notes would first have to purchase 100 dollars (face value) of specified state bonds, which could then be deposited with the state comptroller in exchange for certified currency.

Though bond-deposit requirements were ostensibly aimed at providing security to note holders, they only served this function if the required bond collateral was more liquid and secure in value than other assets that banks might profitably invest in. In reality, the opposite was often true, particularly in free banking states in the west and midwest. In these places, "banks" emerged whose sole business was to speculate in junk bonds—especially heavily discounted government bonds. Bond-collateral, purchased on credit, was duly deposited with state officials in exchange for bank notes equal to the better part of the *face value* of the bonds. The notes were then used to finance further rounds of bond speculation, with any increase in the market value of purchased bonds (which remained the property of their buyers) representing, along with interest earnings, a clear gain to the bankers. The infamous "wildcat" banks were mainly of this species, most of their issues being used to monetize state and local government debt.[21]

Even the more responsible examples of bond-deposit banking had a critical flaw: they linked the potential growth of the currency component of the money stock to the value of government debt. This flaw became evident when, with the onset of the Civil War and the tremendous financial burden brought by it, Treasury Secretary Chase decided to employ bond-deposit finance on a national scale. Thus arose the National Banking System, in which the supply of currency varied with conditions in the market for federal bonds. The new system first revealed its incompatibility with monetary stability in the years after 1865, when state bank notes were taxed out of existence. After 1882, when surpluses began to be used to contract the federal debt, the system's shortcomings were magnified: as the supply of federal securities declined, their market values increased. The national banks found it increasingly difficult and costly to acquire the collateral needed for note issue. This precluded secular growth of the currency supply.[22] It also meant that cyclical increases in the demand for currency relative to total money demand could not be met, except by paying out limited reserves of high-powered money which caused the money supply as a whole to contract by a multiple of the lost reserves.

These conditions set the stage for the great money panics of 1873, 1884, 1893, and 1907. Each of these crises came at the height of the harvest season, in October, when it was usual for large amounts of currency to be withdrawn from interior banks to finance the movement of crops. The crises provided the principal motive for creating the Federal Reserve System, which ended the era of plural note issue. Yet the crises would never have occurred (or would have been less severe) had it not been for government regulations that restricted banks' powers of note issue in the first place.[23]

The United States did have one experience with more or less unregulated, plural note issue. This was the New England Suffolk system of the antebellum period. New England had been more generous than other regions in granting charters to note-issuing banks. But prohibition of branch banking slowed the evolution of an efficient system of note exchange and clearing, thwarting normal competitive checks against overissue. Eventually the Suffolk Bank of Boston, in an effort to improve its note circulation by reducing the Boston circulation of country bank notes, set up an innovative system of note exchange which eventually formed the heart of America's most praised banking system.[24] The Suffolk is sometimes said to have performed as a free-market central bank. This is misleading. Unlike central banks the Suffolk did not have even a local monopoly of note issue; rival banks did not reissue its notes, and they held only such minimum deposits with it as it required as a condition for par acceptance of their notes. Thus the liabilities of the Suffolk Bank were not high-powered money. It could restrict the issues of other banks by promptly redeeming their notes, but it could not cause a general expansion of bank money by increasing its own issues. The Suffolk's position was, in this crucial sense, more like that of contemporary commercial banks competing among co-equal rivals than like that of a privileged bank of issue.

Obviously these brief remarks do not add up to an historical argument for free banking. Nor do they adequately describe the complex political and intellectual forces responsible for the universal adoption of central banking.[25] The reason for mentioning them here is to show the reader that the historical record does not provide any clear evidence of the failure—except politically—of free banking. Since past experience provides no motive for the rejection of free banking, we are justified in examining its theoretical and practical implications.

2

The Evolution of a Free Banking System

I N RECENT YEARS several studies have been made of the properties of hypothetical, unregulated payment systems.[1] The value of these studies is limited, however, by their authors' use of ad hoc assumptions, ranging from the proliferation of competing fiat currencies at one extreme to the complete absence of money at the other. To be really useful in interpreting the effects of regulation in the past, or in predicting the consequences of deregulation in the future, a theory of unregulated banking should be based on *realistic* assumptions drawn, if possible, from actual experience.

Unfortunately, there have been few free banking episodes in the past, none of which realized it in a pure form. Thus history furnishes an inadequate basis for drawing theoretical conclusions about free banking. To rely exclusively on it would invite generalizing from features unique to a single episode or from features attributable to regulation.

Another approach, which also helps in interpreting historical evidence, is to base assumptions on a logical (but also conjectural) story of the evolution of a "typical" free banking system, as it might occur in an imaginary, unregulated society called Ruritania. The story can be supported along the way by illustrations from actual history. But it only accounts for features of past banking systems that were predictable (though perhaps unintended) consequences of self interested, individual acts, uninfluenced by legislation.

Our story involves four stages: First, the warehousing or bailment of idle commodity money; second, the transition of money custodians from bailees to investors of deposited funds (and the corresponding change in the function of banks from bailment to intermediation); third, the development of assignable and negotiable instruments of

16

credit (inside money); and fourth, the development of arrangements for the routine exchange (clearing) of inside monies of rival banks. The historical time that separates these stages is not crucial. Also, innovation, rather than consisting of steady progress as pictured here, is likely to involve many dead ends and much "creative destruction." What matters is that each stage is a logical outgrowth of the preceding stage. Moreover, though every step is a result of individuals finding new ways to promote their self-interest, the final outcome is a set of institutions far more complex and important than any individual could have contemplated, and one which was not consciously aimed at by anyone.

Commodity Money

Since the use of money logically precedes the emergence of banks, we begin by considering how money evolves in Ruritania. Carl Menger (1892, 250) showed that money, rather than being invented or adopted by legislative act, emerges as "the spontaneous outcome . . . of particular, individual efforts of members of society."[2] Menger's method serves as a prototype for our look at events in Ruritania, which will show how complex banking procedures, devices, and institutions—including some still present in regulated and centralized banking systems—can also evolve spontaneously.

Early in Ruritania's history persons relying upon barter offer goods in exchange only for other goods directly useful to them. The number of bargains struck this way is very small, owing to the infrequency of what Jevons (1882, 3) called a "double coincidence" of wants. In time, some frustrated Ruritanian barterer realizes that, by trading his goods or services for some more saleable good regardless of its use value to him, he can increase his chances for profitable exchange. Ruritania's earliest media of exchange are therefore simply its most barterable goods. Other traders, noticing the gains achieved by persons using indirect exchange, emulate them, despite their lack of awareness of all the advantages from using a small number of exchange media (such as the fact that it may eventually lead to the emergence of a unified price system). This further enhances the saleability of the most widely accepted media. In time, the chasm separating these more saleable goods from all others grows wider and wider. This snowballing of saleability results in the spontaneous appearance of generally accepted media of exchange. Eventually, traders throughout Ruritania converge on some single good as their most generally accepted medium of exchange, i.e., money.

Historically cattle were often the most frequently exchanged commodity. Yet, owing to their lack of transportability and their nonuniformity, cows left much to be desired as a general medium of exchange (Burns 1927a, 286–88). Their chief contribution to the evolution of money seems to have been as a unit of account (Menger 1981, 263–66; Ridgeway 1892, 6–11). It was the discovery of methods for working metals which finally allowed money to displace barter on a widespread basis.[3] So we assume that Ruritania's first money is some metallic medium.

Like that of money itself the idea of coinage does not "flash out upon" Ruritania or in the mind of one of its rulers (Burns 1927a, 285). Rather, it is the unplanned result of Ruritanian merchants' attempts to minimize the necessity for weighing and assessing amounts of crude commodity money (e.g., gold or silver) received in exchange. The earliest surviving historical coins—the famous electrum coins of Lydia—were, according to Ridgeway (1892, 203ff) probably in use throughout the Aegean before the reign of Pheidon of Argus, who is often credited as the inventor of coinage.[4] The merchants of Lydia at first marked shapeless electrum blobs after assessing their value. A merchant recognizing his own mark or the mark of a fellow merchant could thereby avoid the trouble and cost of reassessment. Marking led to stamping or punching, which eventually gave way to specialists making coins in their modern form (Burns 1927a, 297ff). Techniques for covering coins entirely with type safeguarded them against clipping and sweating, assuring their weight as well as their quality (Burns 1927b, 59).

States monopolized their coinage early in history. But this does not mean that they were the best makers of coin or that coinage is a natural monopoly.[5] Rather, state coinage monopolies were established by force. Once rulers had set up their own mints they prohibited private issues, making their coins both a symbol of their rule and a source of profits from shaving, clipping, and seignorage. By the end of the 7th century such motives had caused coinage to become a state function throughout the Greek world (Burns 1927b, chaps. 3 and 4; and 1927a, 308).

In Ruritania, however, since state interference is absent, coinage is entirely private. It includes various competing brands, with less reliable, more "diluted" coins first circulating at discount and eventually forced out of circulation entirely. This appears to contradict Gresham's Law, which states that "bad money drives good money out of circulation." Yet, properly understood, Gresham's Law applies only where legal tender laws force the par acceptance of inferior coins.[6] In contrast, Ruritania's free market promotes the emergence of coins of standard weights and fineness, valued according to their bullion content plus a premium equal to the marginal cost of mintage.

The Development of Banks

Under Ruritania's pure commodity-money regime traders who frequently undertake large or distant exchanges find it convenient to keep some of their coin (and bullion) with foreign-exchange brokers who can then settle debts by means of less costly ledger-account transfers.[7] Money-transfer services also develop in connection with deposits initially made, not for the purpose of trade, but for safekeeping. Wealthy Ruritanians who are not active in commerce begin placing temporarily idle sums of commodity money in the strong-boxes of bill brokers, moneychangers, scriveners, goldsmiths, mint-masters, and other tradespeople accustomed to having and protecting valuable property and with a reputation for trustworthiness.[8] Coin and bullion thus lodged for safekeeping must at first be physically withdrawn by its owners for making payments. These payments may sometimes result in the redeposit of coin in the same vault from which it was withdrawn. This is especially likely in exchanges involving money changers and bill brokers. Such being the case, it is possible for more payments to be arranged, without any actual withdrawal of money, at the sight of the vault, or better still by simply notifying the vault's custodian to make a transfer in his books. Such transfer banking was first practiced by English goldsmiths during the 17th century, when they began to keep a "running cash" account for the convenience of merchants and country gentlemen (De Roover, 183–84).

In transfer banking of this kind money on deposit is meant to be "warehoused" only. The custodian is not supposed to lend deposited money at interest, and receipts given by the "banker" for it are regular warehouse dockets.[9] Thus, primitive Ruritanian bankers are bailees rather than debtors to their depositors, and their compensation comes in the form of depositors' service payments.

Of course, Ruritania's primitive bankers may also engage in lending; but their loans are originally made out of their personal wealth and revenues. The lending of depositors' balances is a significant innovation: it taps a vast new source of loanable funds and fundamentally alters the relationship between Ruritanian bankers and their depositors. "The . . . bailee develops into the debtor of the depositor; and the depositor becomes an investor who loans his money . . . for a consideration" (Richards 1965, 223). Money "warehouse receipts" or bailee notes become IOUs or promissory notes, representing sums still called deposits but placed at the disposal of the banker to be reclaimed upon demand (ibid., 225).

W. R. Bisschop reports (1910, 50fn) that during the time of Charles

II goldsmiths had already begun to function as savings-investment intermediaries: "they made no charge for their services . . . but any deposit made in any other shape than ornament was looked upon by them as a free loan. The cash left in their hands remained at call." Soon afterwards, however, the practice of paying interest on deposits began. This led to a substantial increase in business: by 1672 the custom of depositing had become widespread among all ranks of people.[10] It is significant that throughout this entire period, despite wars and internal disturbances, no goldsmith banker suspended payment (ibid.).

The ability of bankers, in Ruritania and elsewhere, to lend out depositors' balances rests upon two important facts. The first is the fungibility of money, which makes it possible for depositors to be repaid in coin or bullion other than the coin or bullion that they originally handed to the banker. The second is the law of large numbers, which ensures a continuing (though perhaps volatile) supply of loanable funds even though single accounts may be withdrawn without advance notice. In his 1691 *Discourse upon Trade*, Sir Dudley North, an observer of developments in English banking, commented on the ability of the law of large numbers to render England's effective money supply greater than what the existing stock of specie could alone account for:

> The Merchants and Gentlemen keep their Money for the most part with Goldsmiths and Scriveners, and they, instead of having Ten Thousand Pounds in cash by them as their Accounts show they should have of other Mens Money, to be paid at sight, have seldom One Thousand in Specie; but depend upon a course of trade whereby Money comes in as fast as it is taken out.[11]

Assignability and Negotiability

Up to this point Ruritania's most important banking procedures and devices have yet to emerge. Since purchases must still be made with actual coin, substantial savings remain locked up in circulation. Bank depositors, in order to satisfy changing needs for transactions balances, have to make frequent cash withdrawals from their balances. Though the withdrawals might largely offset one another, they still contribute to the banks' need for precautionary commodity-money reserves. What is lacking is some negotiable alternative to standard IOUs which can pass easily in exchange from one person to another, replacing coin in transactions balances. Lacking also are efficient means for reassigning deposit credits represented, not by IOUs, but by ledger entries, which could also reduce the need for coin in circulation.

The development of such assignable and negotiable bank instruments proceeds through several steps. At first, deposited money (whether warehoused or entrusted to the banker for lending at interest) is assigned by the depositor to another party by oral transfer. This requires the presence of all three parties to the exchange or their attorneys,[12] as standard money IOUs or promissory notes cannot be assigned by their owner without the banker acting as witness. The first important innovation, therefore, is a bank-issued promissory note transferable by endorsement; a parallel development is that of nonnegotiable checks for use in transferring deposits represented in book entries rather than by outstanding promissory notes. Nonnegotiable checks open the way to negotiable ones, while assignable promissory notes open the way to negotiable bank notes.[13] What distinguishes the latter is that they are not assigned to any one in particular, but are instead made payable to the bearer on demand.

Thus Ruritania would evolve the presently known forms of inside money—redeemable bank notes and checkable deposits. With these forms of inside money at hand all that remains for Ruritania's bankers to conceive is what Hartley Withers (1930, 24) called "the epoch-making notion" of giving inside money, not only to depositors of coin or bullion, but also to those who come to borrow it.

The use of inside money is not just convenient to bank customers. It also makes for greater banking profits, so that only the reluctance of Ruritania's courts to enforce obligations represented by assigned or negotiable paper stands in its way.[14] In England bearer notes were first recognized by the courts during the reign of Charles II, about the time when warehouse banking was beginning to give way to true banking (Richards 1966, 225). At first, the courts grudgingly approved the growing practice of repeated endorsement of promissory notes (ibid., 46). Then, after some controversy, fully negotiable notes were recognized by an Act of Parliament. In France, Holland, and Italy during the 16th century, merchants' checks drawn in blank and circulated within limited groups may have cleared the way for the appearance of bank notes (Usher 1943, 189).

Benefits of Fiduciary Substitution

Aside from its immediate benefits to Ruritania's bankers and their customers, the use of inside money has wider, social consequences. Obviously it reduces the demand for coin in circulation, while generating a much smaller increase in the demand for coin in bank reserves. The net fall in demand creates a surplus of coin and bullion, which Ruritania may export or employ in some nonmonetary use. The result is an increased fulfillment of Ruritania's nonmonetary desires with no sacrifice of its monetary needs. This causes a fall in the value of money, which in turn "acts as a brake" on the production of commodity money and directs factors of production to more urgent purposes (Wicksell 1935, 124).

Of even greater significance than Ruritania's one time savings from fiduciary substitution (the replacement of commodity money with unbacked inside money) is its continuing gain from using additional issues of fiduciary media to meet increased demands for money balances. By this means every increase in real money demand becomes a source of loanable funds to be invested by banks, whereas under a pure commodity-money regime an increase in money demand either leads to further investments in the production of commodity money, or, if the supply of commodity money is inelastic, to a permanent, general reduction in prices. The latter result involves the granting of a pure consumption loan by money holders to their contemporaries.[15] Thus, fiduciary issues made in response to demands for increased money balances allow Ruritania to enjoy greater capitalistic production than it could under a pure commodity-money regime.[16]

According to Harry Miskimim (1979, 283–89), the growth of private credit made possible by fiduciary substitution in actual history began to aid economic progress as early as the 16th century. The benefits in more recent times from the use of fiduciary media in place of commodity money have been outlined by J. Carl Poindexter (1946, 137):

> It is highly probable that the phenomenal industrial progress of the last century would have been greatly reduced had institutions not developed through which the monetary use of the limited supply of precious metals could be economized . . . The evolution of fractional reserve banking permitted the substitution of a highly convenient and more economical money medium whose supply could be expanded by a multiple of the available quantity of monetary gold . . . [H]istory and theory support the view that the real value of the expanding bank credit pyramid has actually borne a reasonably close secular relationship to the real value of voluntary savings of depositors. If this be the correct view, it also follows that the pyramiding of credit was the fortuitous factor by virtue of which secular deflation and involuntary dissaving were avoided or minimized.

Two questions must be asked in light of these potential benefits: First, what economic forces exist in Ruritania to sponsor more complete fiduciary substitution; and second, what forces exist to prevent *excessive* use of the power of fiduciary issue? The rest of this chapter concentrates on the first question, since it is relatively easy to show how bankers and other persons in Ruritania, left to pursue their own interests, are led to improve the acceptability of inside money and the efficiency of banking operations. This is the essence of the story of Ruritania's organized note-exchange and clearinghouse institutions. The second question, concerning whether adequate forces exist to *limit* issues of bank money, is addressed at length in later chapters.

Regular Note-Exchange

The progress of fiduciary substitution in Ruritania requires more complete use of inside money as well as more complete development of bank note and check clearing facilities that reduce the need for commodity money reserves. When inside money first emerges, although bank notes are less cumbersome than coin, and checkable deposits (in Ruritania) are both convenient for certain transactions and interest paying, some coin might still remain in circulation. Ruritanian consumers trust notes of local banks more than those of distant banks because they know more about the likelihood of local banks honoring their notes and also because they are more familiar with the appearance of these notes (and hence less prone to accept forgeries).[17] It follows that the cost to a bank of building a reputation for its notes in some market is higher the further away the market is from where the notes are issued and redeemed. On the other hand, the building of a network of branch offices for more widespread note issue and redemption is limited by transportation and communication costs. Therefore, in the early stages of Ruritania's free-banking development the par circulation of each bank's notes is geographically relatively limited. Those holding the inside money of a local bank, but wishing to do business in distant towns, must either redeem some of their holdings for gold (and suffer the inconvenience of transporting coin), or suffer a loss in the value of their notes by taking them where they are accepted only at a discount, if at all.[18] In general, every brand of inside money is at first used only for local transactions, with coin remaining in circulation alongside notes of like denomination. The continued use of coin for non-local exchange also forces banks to hold commodity-money reserves greater than those required by the transfer of inside money. This is because the withdrawal of commodity money for spending generates more volatile reserve outflows than does the spending of notes and deposits.

Given that Ruritania's banks have limited resources to devote to confidence- or branch-building, how can their need for commodity money be further reduced? Can individuals benefit privately from their actions that promote more widespread use of inside money in place of coin, or is some form of collective action needed to achieve further economies by use of fiduciary media?

The answer is that profit opportunities exist to promote a more general use of particular inside monies. The discounting of notes outside the neighborhood of the issuing bank's office provides an opportunity for arbitrage when the par value of notes exceeds the price at which they can be purchased for commodity money or local issues in a distant town, plus transaction and transportation costs. With the growth of interlocal trade, note brokers with specialized knowledge of distant banks can make a business, just as retail foreign currency brokers do today, of buying discounted non-local notes and transporting them to their par-circulation areas (or reselling them to travelers bound for those areas). Competition eventually reduces note discounts to the value of transaction and transportation costs, plus an amount reflecting redemption risk. In accepting the notes of unfamiliar banks at minimal commission rates, brokers unintentionally increase the general acceptability of all notes, promoting their use in place of commodity money.

So far it has been taken for granted that Ruritania's free banks refuse to accept one another's notes. This is not an unreasonable assumption, since the banks have as many reasons as individuals do to refuse unfamiliar and difficult-to-redeem notes. They also have a further reason, which is that by doing so they limit the acceptability of rival banks' notes and enhance the demand for their own issues. To cite just one historical illustration of this, in Edinburgh in the 1770s the Bank of Scotland and the Royal Bank of Scotland, the two then existing chartered banks of issue, refused to accept the notes of unchartered, provincial banks of issue for a number of years (Checkland 1975, 126).

Nonetheless, note brokerage presents opportunities for profit to Ruritania's bankers. Moreover, because they can issue their own notes (or deposit balances) to purchase "foreign" notes and therefore need not hold costly till money, banks can out-compete other brokers. Still another incentive exists for banks to accept rival notes: larger interest earnings. If a bank redeems notes it acquires sooner than other banks redeem the first bank's notes issued in place of theirs, it can, in the interim, purchase and hold interest-earning assets. The resulting profit from "float" can be continually renewed. In other words, a bank's earnings from replacing other notes with its own may be due, not just to profits from arbitrage, but also to enhanced loans and investments. If transaction and transportation costs and risk are low enough, competition for circulation reduces brokerage fees to zero, reflecting the elimination of profits from arbitrage. This leads Ruritanian banks to accept each other's notes at par.

It is important to see that the development of par acceptance of notes does not require that Ruritania's banks get together to explicitly agree on such a policy. It only takes a single bank acting without the consent or cooperation of other banks to nudge the rest toward par acceptance as a defensive measure on their part to maintain their reserves and circulation. This has also been the case historically. In New England at the beginning of the 19th century it was the Boston banks that gave the nudge that put the whole region, with its multitude of "country" banks lacking branches and with offices far removed from the city, on a par-acceptance basis.[19] In Scotland it was the Royal Bank of Scotland which, when it opened for business in 1727, immediately began accepting at par notes from the Bank of Scotland, at that time its only rival (Checkland 1975). In both New England and Scotland established banks that were accepting each other's notes at par sometimes refused to take the notes of newly entering banks. But they soon had to change their policies, because new banks that accepted their notes were draining their reserves, whereas the established banks were not offsetting this by engaging in the same practice in reverse.

In the long run, banks that accept other banks' notes at par improve the market both for their own notes and, unintentionally, for the notes that they accept. Statistics from Boston illustrate this dramatically: from 1824 to 1833 the note circulation of Boston banks increased 57 percent, but the Boston circulation of country banks increased 148 percent, despite the Boston banks' intent to drive the country banks out of business.[20]

The rivalrous behavior of banks in Ruritania causes inside money to become even more attractive to hold relative to commodity money. Because notes from one town come to be accepted in a distant town at par, there is little reason to lug around commodity money any more. This, too, can be seen in history. As par note acceptance developed during the 19th century in Scotland, Canada, and New England—places where note issue was least restricted—gold virtually disappeared from circulation.[21] In England and in the rest of the United States where banking (and note issue in particular) were less free, considerable amounts of gold remained in circulation.

Even complete displacement of commodity money in circulation by inside money does not, however, necessarily mean increased fiduciary substitution. Commodity money, formerly used in circulation to settle exchanges outside Ruritania's banks, might now be used to settle clearings among them. To really economize on commodity money rival banks have to exchange notes frequently enough to allow their mutual obligations to be offset. Then only net clearings, rather than gross clearings, need to be settled in commodity money. Thus banks can take further advantage of the law of large numbers, and more commodity money becomes available for nonmonetary uses.

Initially there might not be much movement towards rationalization of note exchange. That Ruritania's banks accept one another's notes at par does not mean that they exchange notes regularly. In Scotland par acceptance without regular note exchange was present before 1771. During that period, banks' sought to bankrupt their rivals by "note dueling"—aggressively buying large amounts of their rival's notes and presenting them for redemption all at once.[22] For a bank to stay solvent during such raids it has to keep substantial reserves, so that its contribution to the process of fiduciary substitution is small. Charles Munn reports that one Scottish provincial bank at one point kept reserves equal to 61.2 percent of its inside-money liabilities to protect itself against raids by its rivals. More typically, reserves during Scotland's note-dueling era were in the neighborhood of 10 percent of total liabilities (Munn 1981, 23–24). Yet even this smaller figure contrasts greatly with reserve ratios of around 2 percent which were typical under the Scottish free banking system after note clearings became routine (ibid., 141).

Though it does not catch on immediately in Ruritania, regular note exchange has advantages that guarantee that it will eventually be adopted, as it was in every historical instance of relatively unregulated plural note issue. Note dueling ceases to be advantageous to any bank as all of them learn how to protect themselves in response to it by holding large reserves. Because of this, Ruritania's banks soon find it more convenient to accept their rival's notes only as they are brought to them for deposit or exchange. They do not continue actively to buy notes in the marketplace since this is both costly and unreliable as a means for expanding circulation. Also, instead of being accumulated in large sums, rivals' notes are immediately returned at once to their issuers for redemption in commodity-money reserves, which can be profitably employed. Finally, as banks in Ruritania realize the savings to be had by offsetting note debits with one another, they may *formally* agree to engage in regular note exchange and to refrain from purchasing rivals' notes except as they are brought to them for deposit or exchange.[23]

Clearinghouses

Suppose Ruritania has three banks, A, B, and C. A has $20,000 of B's notes, B has $20,000 of C's notes, and C has $10,000 of A's notes.[24] If they settle their obligations bilaterally, they need to have $20,000 to $40,000 of commodity-money reserves on hand among them, depending on the chronological sequence of their exchange.[25] On the other hand, if they settle their balances multilaterally, they need only $10,000 of reserves among them: A's net balance to B and C combined is +$10,000; B's net balance to A and C combined is $0; and C's net balance to A and B combined is −$10,000. Hence all three balances can be settled by a transfer of $10,000 from C to A. Apart from reducing reserve needs, multilateral clearing also allows savings in operating costs by allowing all debts to be settled in one place rather than in numerous, scattered places.

Such advantages impel Ruritania's banks to establish clearing-houses—organizations devoted to the multilateral settlement of bank obligations—which help to further unify the banking system. The clearinghouses do not, however, have to spring into existence full blown. Instead, they may gradually evolve from simpler note-exchange arrangements. The history of the earliest and most well known clearinghouses, in London, Edinburgh, and New York, illustrates this. All of them were products of human action but not of human design or, as Adam Smith would say, they were instances of the invisible hand at work.

Geographical, economic, and legislative differences in each of those cities affected the shape their clearinghouses took. Nevertheless the clearinghouses shared a common pattern of development. The circumstances leading to the establishment of the New York Clearinghouse in 1853, as reported by Gibbons (1858, 292–93), were typical. The first improvements were due to note porters anxious to save shoe leather:

> The porters crossed and re-crossed each other's footsteps constantly; they often met in companies of five or six at the same counter, and retarded each other, and they were fortunate to reach their respective banks at the end of one or two hours. This threw the counting of the exchanges into the middle and after part of the day, when the other business of the bank was becoming urgent.

The porters finally hit upon the idea of meeting at a convenient spot, outside of any bank, to combine and reconcile their claims.

Approximately three-quarters of a century earlier nearly identical events took place in London, though here checks rather than notes were being exchanged, the Bank of England being the only note-issuing bank in the region. As later happened in New York, the porters first traveled among the banks to settle accounts bilaterally:

> The majority of them belonged to offices which were situated in Lombard Street. . . . Soon . . . occasional encounters developed into daily meetings at a certain fixed place. At length the bankers themselves resolved to organize these meetings on a regular basis in a room specially reserved for this purpose [Bisschop 1910, 160].

And so the London clearinghouse came into being.[26]

Whenever a clearinghouse is set up in Ruritania, all banks within the region feel compelled to join it due to the advantages membership brings. However, banks suspected of being ill managed or unsound may be denied membership. Also, where there are several clearinghouses within a region that clear with each other, a bank would only need to join one of them to partake of the full advantages of multilateral clearing.[27]

The principal purpose of Ruritania's clearinghouses is the economical exchange and settlement of banks' obligations to each other. Once established for this purpose, however, the clearinghouses serve a variety of other uses, becoming "instruments for united action among the banks in ways that did not exist even in the imagination of those who were instrumental in [their] inception" (Cannon 1908, 97).

One of the more common tasks the clearinghouses take on is to serve as a credit information bureaus for their members. By pooling their records, Ruritania's banks can discover whether people have had bad debts in the past or are presently overextended to other banks. This allows them to take appropriate precautions (Cannon 1900, 135).[28] Through a clearinghouse banks can also share information concerning forgeries, bounced checks, and the like. Clearinghouses may also conduct independent audits of member banks to assure each member bank that the others are worthy clearing partners. For example, beginning in 1884 the New York Clearinghouse carried out comprehensive audits to determine its members' financial condition (ibid.). Others, such as the Suffolk Bank and the Edinburgh clearinghouse, took their bearings mainly from the trends of members' clearing balances and the traditional canons of sound banking practice. Those two clearinghouses enjoyed such high repute that to be taken off their lists of members in good standing was a black mark for the offending bank (Trivoli 1979, 20; Graham 1911, 59).

Another task Ruritania's clearinghouses may undertake is to set common reserve ratios, interest rates, exchange rates, and fee schedules for their members. However, inasmuch as common rates on reserve ratios are not consistent with profit-maximizing strategies of individual banks, they tend to break down. Those that prevail are in most instances merely formally agreed upon confirmations of results that rivalrous competition would also have established informally but no less firmly. There is an excellent example of this from Scottish experience. In order to formalize certain banking practices, the Edinburgh banks set up a General Managers' Committee in 1828. In 1836 the Glasgow banks joined the committee, which then represented the preponderance of Scottish banks in number as well as in total assets. Though not itself a clearinghouse association, the committee had much the same membership as the Edinburgh clearinghouse. If ever there was an opportunity to cartellize Scottish banking, this was it. Yet in spite of repeated attempts the banks could not agree on a common reserve ratio. Though they gave the appearance of having agreed on common interest rates, in reality the General Manager's Committee was full of dissent even on this matter. The moment any course other than that recommended by the Committee appeared profitable to any of its members, interest-rate agreements would collapse (Checkland 1975, 391).

Perhaps the most interesting of all roles clearinghouses in Ruritania may perform is aiding members in times of crisis.[29] If a bank or group of banks is temporarily unable to pay its clearing balances, or should it experience a run on its commodity-money reserves, a clearinghouse can serve as a medium through which the troubled bank borrows from more liquid banks. It provides the framework for an intermittent, short-term credit market similar to the continuous Federal Funds market to which reserve-deficient banks resort in the present U.S. banking system.

Related to their role in assisting illiquid members is clearinghouses' role as note issuers. This function has been exercised by historical clearinghouses where member banks have had their own rights to issue notes artificially restricted, preventing them from independently filling all of their customers' requests for currency. It is *not*, however, a function that clearinghouses would be likely to perform in Ruritania, where bank-note issue is unregulated. This is not the place to discuss the causes and consequences of currency shortages, which are treated at length later in chapter 8. It will suffice to note that currency shortages occurred frequently in the United States during the 19th century, and that clearinghouses helped to fill the void caused by deficient note issues of the National banks.[30]

So far the most important of the unintended effects of Ruritania's clearinghouses has not been mentioned. This is their ability to regulate strictly the issues of their members through the automatic mechanism of adverse clearings. Together with free note issue, the existence of an efficient clearing arrangement gives Ruritania's banking system special money-supply properties, to be examined in detail in later chapters.

The Mature Free Banking System

We have now described the mature stage of Ruritania's free banking system, insofar as consideration of self-interested actions allows us to predict its development. Historical evidence on industry structure from Scotland, Canada, Sweden, China, and elsewhere suggests that Ruritania would possess, not a natural monopoly in currency supply, but an industry consisting of numerous competing note-issuing banks, most having widespread branches, all of which are joined through one or more clearinghouses. In Scotland's final year of free entry, 1844, there were 19 banks of issue. The largest four banks supplied 46.7 percent of the note circulation. These banks also had 363 branch offices, 43.5 percent of which were owned by the largest (measured by note issue) four banks (L. White 1984d, 37).

Banks in Ruritania issue inside money in the shape of paper notes and demand deposit accounts (debited either by check or electronically) transferred routinely at par. Each bank's notes and tokens bear distinct brand-name identification marks and are issued in denominations most desired by the public. Because of computational costs involved in each transfer, interest is generally not paid on commonly used denominations of bank notes or tokens.[31] Checkable accounts, however, pay competitive interest rates reflecting rates available on interest-earning assets issued outside the banking system.

Outside of Ruritania the most familiar kind of checkable bank accounts are demand deposits which have a predetermined payoff payable on demand. One important reason for their popularity is that, historically, debt contracts have been easier for depositors to monitor and enforce than equity contracts, which tie the account's payoff to the performance of costly-to-observe asset portfolios. This predetermined payoff feature of demand deposits does, however, raise the possibility of insolvency and, consequently, of a run: bank depositors may fear that, by being late in line, they will receive less than a full payoff.

One way Ruritania's banks can prevent runs is to advertise having large equity cushions, either on their books or off them, in the form of extended liability for bank shareholders.[32] A second solution is to link checkability to equity or mutual-fund type accounts with post-determined, rather than predetermined, payoffs. Former obstacles to such accounts in actual history—such as asset-monitoring and enforcement costs—have eroded over time due to the emergence of easy to observe assets (namely: publicly traded securities) and may be presumed absent in Ruritania also. For a balance sheet without debt liabilities, insolvency is ruled out and the incentive to redeem ahead of other account holders is eliminated.

A Ruritanian bank that linked checkability to equity accounts would operate like a contemporary money-market mutual fund, except that it would be directly tied to the clearing system instead of having to clear through a deposit bank. Its optimal reserve holdings would be determined in the same way as those of a standard bank (see chapter 6).

The assets of Ruritania's banks include short-term commercial paper, corporate and government bonds and loans on various types of collateral. The structure of asset portfolios cannot be predicted in detail without particular information on the assets available in Ruritania as a whole, except to say that Ruritania's banks, like banks elsewhere, strive to maximize the present value of their interest earnings, net of operating and liquidity costs, discounted at risk-adjusted rates. The declining probability of larger liquidity needs, and the trade-off at the margin between liquidity and interest yield, suggest that the banks hold a spectrum of assets ranging from perfectly liquid reserves to highly liquid interest-earning investments (which serve as a "secondary reserve"), to less liquid, higher-earning assets. Because the focus in this book is on monetary arrangements, the only bank liabilities discussed are notes and checking accounts. Nonetheless, free banks would almost certainly diversify on the liability side by offering several kinds of time deposits as well as traveler's checks. Some banks would probably also get involved in the production of bullion and token fractional coins, the issue of credit cards, and management of mutual funds. Such banks would fulfill the contemporary ideal of the "financial supermarket," but with the additional feature of issuing bank notes.

In a mature free-banking system, such as Ruritania's, commodity money seldom if ever appears in circulation, most of it (outside numismatic collections) having been offered to the banks in exchange for inside money. Some commodity money continues to be held by individual banks or clearinghouses so long as it remains the ultimate settlement asset among them. Since no statutory reserve requirements exist, reserves are held only to meet banks' profit-maximizing liquidity needs, which vary according to the average size and variability of clearing balances to be settled after routine (e.g. daily) note and check exchanges.

The holding of reserve accounts at one or more clearinghouses results in significant savings in the use of commodity money.[33] In the limit, if inter-clearinghouse settlements are made entirely with other assets (perhaps claims on a super-clearinghouse which itself holds negligible amounts of commodity money), and if the public is weaned completely from holding commodity money, the only active demand for the old-fashioned money commodity is nonmonetary: the flow supply formerly sent to the mints is devoted to industrial and other uses. Markets for these uses then determine the relative price of the money commodity. Nonetheless, the purchasing power of monetary instruments continues to be fixed by the holders' contractual right (even if never exercised) to redeem them for physically specified quantities of commodity money. The special difficulty of meeting any significant redemption request or run on a bank in such a system can be contractually handled, as it was historically during note-dueling episodes, by invoking an "option clause" allowing the bank a specified amount of time to gather the needed commodity money while compensating the redeeming party for the delay. The clause need not (and, historically, did not) impair the par circulation of bank liabilities.

Our image of an unregulated banking in Ruritania differs significantly from visions presented in some recent literature on competitive payments systems. The Ruritanian system has assets fitting standard definitions of money. Its banks and clearinghouses are contractually obligated to provide at request high-powered reserve money. They also issue debt liabilities (inside money) with which payments are generally made. These features contrast sharply with the situation envisioned by Fischer Black and Eugene Fama, in which banks hold no reserve assets and the payments mechanism operates by transferring equities or mutual fund shares *unlinked to any money*.

In the evolution of Ruritania's free banking system, bank reserves do not entirely disappear, since the existence of bank liabilities that are promises to pay continues to presuppose some more fundamental money that is the thing promised. Ruritanians forego actual redemption of promises, preferring to hold them instead of commodity money, so long as they believe that they will receive money if they ask for it. Banks, on the other hand, have a competitive incentive to redeem each other's liabilities regularly. As long as net clearing balances are sometimes greater than zero, some kind of reserve, either commodity money itself or secondary reserves priced in terms of the commodity money unit of account, has to be held.

The scarcity of the money commodity, and the costliness of holding reserves, also serves to pin down Ruritania's price level and to limit its stock of inside money. In a moneyless system, on the other hand, it is not clear what would be used to settle clearing balances. Hence, it is not clear what forces would limit the expansion of payment media or what would pin down the price level. Nor are these things clear, at the other extreme, in a model of multiple competing fiat monies.[34]

Our story suggests that a commodity-based money would persist in Ruritania because its supreme saleability is self reinforcing. This contradicts recent suppositions that complete deregulation would lead to the replacement of monetary exchange by a sophisticated form of barter.[35] In a commodity-based money economy prices are stated in terms of a unit of the money commodity, so that the need to use an abstract unit of account does not arise as it does in a sophisticated barter setting.[36] Even if actual commodity money disappears entirely from reserves and circulation, media of exchange are not divorced from the commodity unit of account. Rather, they continue to be linked to it by redeemability contracts. Nor is renunciation of commodity-redemption obligations compelled by economization of reserves, as Warren Woolsey predicts (1985). There is, therefore, no reason to expect deregulation to lead to the spontaneous emergence of a multi-commodity monetary standard or of any pure fiat monetary standard, as is suggested in works by Robert Hall, Warren Woolsey, Benjamin Klein, and F. A. Hayek.[37] In few words, unregulated banking is likely to be far less radically unconventional, and much more like existing financial arrangements, than recent writings on the subject suggest.

One important contemporary financial institution is nonetheless absent from the Ruritanian system: to wit, the central bank. This is because market forces at work in Ruritania do not lead to the natural emergence of a monopoly bank of issue capable of willfully manipulating the money supply.[38] As was shown in chapter 1, the historical emergence of central banks was typically a consequence of monopoly privileges respecting note issue being conferred on some state-owned or state-chartered bank. Legal restrictions imposed on commercial banks directly or indirectly promoting unit (instead of branch) banking have also played an important part in the historical emergence of central banks. Where legislation did not inhibit the growth of plural note issue and branch banking, as in Scotland, Sweden and Canada in the 19th century, there was not any movement toward monopolized note issue or toward spontaneous emergence of a central bank.[39]

Long-Run Equilibrium

A free bank adds to its gross income by enlarging its holdings of interest-earning assets. But it can only do this by either attracting more depositors and note holders or by losing some of its reserves.[40] Thus its costs include not only operating costs but also liquidity costs and costs that arise from its efforts to maintain a demand for its liabilities, such as interest payments to depositors. Assuming that these costs—liquidity costs in particular—are increasing at the margin, there is a limit to the bank's accumulations of interest-earning assets and hence to its overall size. Individual free banks compete for shares in the market for checkable deposit accounts and currency just as commercial banks today compete for shares of deposits alone.[41]

Assuming that free-bank liability issues run up against increasing marginal costs (an assumption to be defended in the next chapter), the conditions for long-run equilibrium of a free banking industry can be stated. As the public holds only inside money, with commodity money used only in bank reserves to settle clearing balances, these conditions are as follows: First, the demand for reserves and the available stock of commodity money must be equal. Second, the real supply of inside money must be equal to the real demand for it. Once the first (reserve-equilibrium) condition is met, the tendency is for any disequilibrium in the money supply to be corrected by adjustments in the nominal supply of inside money. An excess supply increases, and an excess demand reduces, the liquidity requirements (reserve demand) of the system. This is shown in chapters 5 and 6 below. On the other hand, if the reserve-equilibrium condition is not satisfied, the system is still immature. An excess supply of reserves then causes an expansion of the supply of inside money. If this leads to an excess supply of inside money, it will promote an increase in both reserve demand and prices, causing both the nominal demand for money and the demand for reserves to rise.

There must be one price level at which both equilibrium conditions are met. When this price level is achieved, the system is in a long-run equilibrium. For the sake of simplicity, the analysis that follows starts with a free banking system (similar to Ruritania's) in long-run equilibrium and assumes an unchanging supply of bank reserves. It may be thought of as involving a closed banking system in which production of commodity money is limited by rising average costs.

Thus we have our hypothetical free banking system, painted in bold brush strokes that permit us to regard it as typical. Though much detail is lacking in this picture, it will, in due course and with some filling in of additional details as we proceed, allow us to derive far-reaching theoretical results.

PART TWO

Free Banking and Monetary Equilibrium

3

Credit Expansion with Constant Money Demand

T HE PREVIOUS CHAPTER ended with a description of long-run
equilibrium in a free banking industry. It assumed that note
issue and deposit granting under free banking involve increasing
marginal costs, especially liquidity costs. This chapter attempts to
justify this assumption, showing that it applies *only* to free banking.
Throughout the chapter it is assumed that the public's total demand
for inside-money balances, and the division of this demand between
the two forms of inside money (currency and demand deposits) are
constant. The effects of changes in the demand for inside money
balances will be examined later, in chapter 5; those of changes in the
public's desired currency-deposit mixture will be the subject of chapter 8.

The Rule of Excess Reserves

A well-known principle of money and banking is that, in a system
with monopolized currency supply, an individual bank cannot increase its loans and investments unless it has reserves in excess of what
it needs to meet currency demands of its customers as well as clearing
balances it owes to other banks.[1] If a bank has reserves in excess of its
liquidity needs and there are no statutory reserve requirements it can
expand credit by the amount of the excess, but no more. This "rule of
excess reserves" assumes that bank borrowers generally secure loans
from banks only when they have purchases to make, implying that the
demand for inside money balances does not increase. When a bank
makes a loan to a client, the client writes checks against the new
balance made out to people who are mainly clients of other banks.
The checks are soon deposited, and the banks that acquire the checks
waste no time returning them for payment to the bank on which they

were drawn. Consequently, the bank that expands credit suffers a clearing drain practically equal to the amount of new credit it grants: its reserves are reduced "just as effectively as if each individual borrower had elected to take cash in the first place" (Rodkey 1928, 41). If the bank lacks excess reserves at least equal to this drain, it has to borrow emergency reserves. Otherwise it has to liquidate some of its investments or contract its loans to restore its reserve/liability ratio to a sustainable level.

The rule of excess reserves is usually applied to the circumstance of a small bank with many, equally small competitors. Nonetheless the rule also applies to a group of banks so long as the demand for inside money is stationary. Consider a system of five banks, each with an equal amount of fully employed reserves and having equal shares of the market for deposit balances. Suppose Bank A grants a loan of $50,000, a net increase in its outstanding liabilities, to John Smith. On average, four-fifths of the checks drawn by Smith on the new balance will be paid to persons having deposits at Banks B through E. This causes Bank A to suffer an immediate clearing drain of $40,000. The other checks end up with persons who are depositors at Bank A, so that the bank is temporarily spared from a further reserve drain of $10,000. However, the persons who temporarily add $10,000 to their accounts at Bank A also, by assumption, do not intend to increase their average money holdings. Therefore, in the next round of spending they write checks for $10,000 (beyond what they would usually spend) to keep their balances at their original levels. Once again Bank A suffers an immediate clearing drain equal to four-fifths of the amount withdrawn, or $8,000, and so on. The schedule of clearing losses would therefore be as follows:

Spending round	Reserve drain
1	$40,000
2	8,000
3	1,600
4	320
5	64
	Total: $49,984

After five rounds of spending Bank A suffers clearing drains equal to all save $16 of its initial expansion. Assuming that each round of spending and clearing takes five days, this loss is suffered during a twenty-five day period, which is almost certainly less than the time required for the maturation of the loan on which the credit was issued. In any event, the greater part of any reserve drain occurs in the first few spending rounds and hence well before an expanding bank can expect to recover any part of its latest loans or investments.[2]

The rule of excess reserves also assumes that banks face a determinate demand schedule for their deposit balances (a schedule of quantity demanded for various deposit rates of interest), so that they cannot profit from expansionary policies that increase their loans while simultaneously increasing the public's demand to hold deposit liabilities. The assumption is justified because, although an expanding bank might offset its reserve losses by attracting an equal sum of new deposits, it can only do so (other things being equal) by raising its marginal deposit rate of interest. On the other hand, the bank can only expand credit by marginally lowering the interest rates it charges to borrowers (or by buying assets with lower risk-adjusted interest yields). It follows that, in its attempts to generate deposit demand sufficient to cover reserve drains from its new loans, an expanding bank, operating in a competitive environment, would incur interest and operating expenses in excess of what the new loans would themselves bring in. Then, although the bank does not lose reserves to its rivals, it still suffers a reduction of net revenues, so that its expansion is unprofitable.[3]

Finally, the rule of excess reserves requires that, although one or a few banks may try to expand credit beyond their customers' willingness to hold deposit credits, other banks are not induced by this to engage in sympathetic overexpansion: if all banks expand in unison their behavior will not be checked by individual banks' suffering net clearing debits. It is easily shown, though, that profit-maximizing banks are not likely to overexpand in sympathy with their overexpanding rivals. If overexpansion by one bank or group of banks has any effect at all on conditions influencing other banks it is the reduction of the rate of interest on new loans, which makes further lending by them seem *less* desirable.[4]

The rule of excess reserves demonstrates clearly that, if *all* deposit banks in a system are fully loaned up, aggregate credit expansion can only take place if the banks get additional reserves from outside their own ranks:

> It is evident that such increased reserves must come from outside the system since otherwise as one bank succeeded in increasing its reserves such increase would be at the expense of some other bank whose reserves were being correspondingly diminished. The expansion of loans by the bank with the increasing reserves would be offset by the contraction necessary in the bank whose reserves were being drawn away, with no net change in the volume of loans for the system as a whole [Rodkey 1928, 185].

If new reserves are added to the system each bank is able to expand, in the first instance, by the amount of new reserves it receives. Loan expansion for the system as a whole, however, will be several times greater than the combined first-round expansion of the first banks to receive the new reserves. "The new reserve, split into small fragments, becomes dispersed among the banks of the system. Through the process of dispersion it comes to constitute the basis of a manifold loan expansion" (Phillips 1920, 40). Expansion continues until all of the new reserve media is absorbed in the economically required balances of the banks (see below, chapter 6).[5]

The Principle of Adverse Clearings

There is nothing controversial about the rule of excess reserves, applied to a conventional system of deposit banks. What is controversial is whether a similar rule restricts the granting of credit in the form of competitively-issued bank notes. The generalization of the rule of excess reserves involved here will be referred to as the "principle of adverse clearings." Early upholders of this principle include Sir Henry Parnell (1827), Lord Peter King (1804), and G. Poulett Scrope (1832). More recently, Ludwig von Mises has stated the principle as follows:

> If several banks of issue, each enjoying equal rights, existed side by side, and if some of them sought to expand the volume of circulation credit while others did not alter their conduct, then at every bank clearing, demand balances would regularly appear in favor of the conservative enterprise. As a result of the presentation of notes for redemption and withdrawal of their cash balances, the expanding banks would very quickly be compelled to limit the scale of their emissions.[6]

Still more recent is Hayek's allusion to the principle in his *Denationalisation of Money* (1978, 59):

> There will of course always be a strong temptation for any bank to try and expand the circulation of its currency by lending cheaper than competing banks; but it would soon discover that, insofar as the additional lending is not based on a corresponding increase of saving, such attempts would inevitably rebound and hurt the bank that over-issued.

According to Alex N. McLeod (1984, 202), adverse clearings "not only limit the total note issue" in a system of competing banks of issue but also "limit the share [of circulation] accruing to each individual bank. A disproportionate expansion of one bank's issues will deplete its reserves just as surely as if its competitors returned them directly, though perhaps somewhat more sluggishly."

To prove that the principle of adverse clearings is valid, one must demonstrate that the rule of excess reserves applies to lending and investment of competitively issued notes. The rule assumes that banks extend credit in the shape of checkable deposits. It also assumes that there is a determinate demand for deposit balances, that checks are drawn against unwanted balances, and that these checks rapidly find their way to other banks and thence to their issuers for collection, either directly or through a clearinghouse. The principle of adverse clearings rests on similar assumptions. These are (a) that the total demand for bank notes is determinate, and that surplus notes are parted with; (b) that most of these surplus notes end up in possession of banks other than their own issuers; (c) that banks return their rivals' notes for redemption; and (d) that a preponderance of the notes that enter the clearing mechanism following overexpansion by any bank will be notes of the overexpanding bank. This implies that the *division* of the public's demand for note balances among the issues of various banks is also determinate.

Let us examine these assumptions one by one. The first is straightforward. A note-issuing bank faces a market where the *total* demand for the combined note balances of issuing banks is given in the short run. This means that any note issue not in response to an increased demand for note balances causes an aggregate excess supply of notes. That surplus notes when spent eventually find their way into possession of rival banks (assumption b) is less obvious because, unlike checks, notes are not necessarily cashed or deposited immediately upon their receipt. They might be used to make additional purchases and so remain in circulation for an extended period. Still the assumption is justified. Consider the typical fate of a bank note not wanted in anyone's average holdings. If the note is not immediately deposited at some bank, it will probably be used to purchase goods from a retail merchant.[7] Merchants receive much more money in the form of notes in the course of a typical business day or week than they require for making change. They bring the excess notes to their banks in exchange for checkable deposits, a form of inside money more useful than notes for paying rent and insurance and making wholesale purchases, and one that can earn interest as well. Thus the majority of notes received by retail merchants is deposited: the deposit accounts of merchants act as "note filtering" devices, helping surplus notes find their way rapidly into banks that are (for the same reason as in the case of checks) mainly not the banks that created the note surplus to begin with. The farther a note travels up the ladder of production (from retail tradesmen to distributors to manufacturers of higher-order goods), the greater its chances of being exchanged for a deposit credit, and the greater its chances of entering the clearing system.

Assumption (c) is also not difficult to defend. Notes received by banks other than those responsible for their issue are immediately sent for redemption directly or through a clearinghouse. This is the strategy most consistent with the maximum profits and safety of the recipient banks. Some reasons for this were given in the previous chapter. By returning its rivals' notes a bank gives up only assets (notes of other banks) that do not earn interest, in return for which it receives either its own notes held by other banks (which reduces its outstanding liabilities that could be employed to drain off its reserves) or, alternatively, more liquid and risk-free commodity money.

Note-Brand Discrimination

Hence, if, starting in a situation where no excess demand for bank-note balances exists, some bank adds $100,000 of notes to the total quantity of notes in circulation, the result would be an excess supply of notes of $100,000, which amount (if not redeemed or deposited directly) would be added to the stream of expenditure and income. As a consequence $100,000 of surplus notes would eventually enter the clearing mechanism, to be sent to their issuers for redemption. This brings us to assumption (d). Is it reasonable to assume that, of the $100,000 of notes returned for redemption, a preponderance will belong to the bank that caused the note surplus to begin with? If the banks initially had (on average) zero net clearing balances with one another, how would net balances due be altered by the additional $100,000 of clearing debits and credits? Would the expanding bank suffer adverse clearings after creating a note surplus, or would it emerge unscathed, even victorious, because other banks are forced to share the burden of a note reflux?

The answer depends on which notes are spent off when consumers first find themselves holding more notes than they want, and this in turn depends on how strong the note-brand preferences of consumers are. If consumers practice 100 percent note-brand discrimination—that is, if besides knowing the total quantity of notes they desire they have strict preferences about what brands or mixture of brands they will hold—then any bank that causes an aggregate note surplus in the face of unchanged preferences cannot expect consumers to substitute its notes for notes of other banks in their holdings. Such being the case, the expanding bank would bear the full burden of clearing debits caused by the note surplus it creates, just as if it had created a surplus of checkable deposits.

On the other hand, if consumers do not at all discriminate among note brands they are not likely to select for spending the notes of a bank that causes an excess aggregate supply of notes. Then the principle of adverse clearings would not be valid and note issue, from the perspective of the individual bank, would not be subject to increasing marginal liquidity costs. This means that there might be a tendency for banks to try to out-issue their competitors. Such "predatory overexpansion" could continually push the system as a whole beyond sustainable limits of expansion as determined by the supply of reserves. (On the demand for precautionary reserves as an ultimate check on expansion see below, chapter 6.)

Notice that there is no reason to doubt that consumers are discriminating when it comes to checkable deposit accounts. Were this not so, someone who receives a check written on any bank would be as likely to deposit it into that bank as into any other. If his total accounts became excessive, he might withdraw some part of each (or withdraw from one account chosen at random). The result would be that people would on average have accounts at scores of banks. Obviously such is not the case.

That consumers would discriminate among note brands is not so obvious, though. The inconvenience of holding an everchanging mixture of bank notes is not so apparent as is the inconvenience of holding deposit accounts at numerous, continually changing, banks. If all note brands are equally acceptable to merchants and to banks, why should consumers care which brand they use?

The answer is that, although many note brands may be equally receivable, people may still prefer to *hold on* to particular brands. Banks, like manufacturers of light bulbs, razor blades, and gasoline, have every reason to establish brandname reputations for their products so that individuals do not, at least in their holding behavior, treat all brands as equals.[8] A bank profits if note holders discriminate in favor of its issues since their holdings of its notes constitute an interest-free loan to it. Since, however, some may doubt that this is so, the reasonableness of assuming note-brand discrimination can be more decisively demonstrated by showing the counterfactual implications of nondiscrimination among bank notes. Under nondiscrimination, consumers return excess notes in proportion to the banks' shares of total circulation after the excess is created.[9] This would be tantamount to consumers shedding excess notes while blindfolded. Thus, for example, suppose there are two banks, A and B, each with a starting note circulation of $1 million and commodity-money reserves of $100,000. Their combined circulation of $2 million is just what consumers want to hold. Suppose A decides to issue an additional $100,000, which consumers do not want to hold. The consumers shed the excess by depositing it in the proportion $11 of A's notes for every $10 of B's notes, or $52,381 of A's notes and $47,619 of B's notes.[10] Taking into account assumption b (discussed above), that all returned notes fall into the hands of banks other than their issuer, A loses $4,762 of reserves to B at their next clearing. This is much less than the entire amount of A's overissue. Although A would be deterred from overissuing if it lacked excess reserves, if A *did* have excess reserves it could expand credit (in the form of notes) in amounts greater than the excess, suffering only a partial reserve drain.

For an expanding bank, expansion is more costly the greater the number of other banks in the system, assuming the bank overissues by the same amount and that all banks begin with equal shares of the original ($2 million) circulation. Thus, if there are four banks beginning with $500,000 circulation each, and one overexpands $100,000, it will lose approximately $5,720 of reserves to one or several of the other banks, instead of losing $4,762 as in the previous example.[11] Furthermore, if an expanding bank begins with a greater than average share of total circulation, this also causes it to suffer greater clearing debits relative to the total note surplus, other things being equal. Even so, the principle of adverse clearings does not apply with full force.

Even more troublesome is a situation where there are few banks and the expanding bank is smaller than the rest. Suppose there are three banks, where Bank A has $1 million of notes in circulation and $100,000 of commodity-money reserves, Bank B has $2 million of circulation and $200,000 of reserves, and Bank C has $3 million of circulation and $300,000 of reserves. If Bank A overissues $100,000 of notes again, consumers return $11 of A's notes for every $20 of B's notes and every $30 of C's notes, or $18,033 of A's notes, $32,787 of B's notes, and $49,180 of C's notes. Bank A does not lose any reserves at all; instead, Banks B and C, which did not overissue, lose reserves to it; furthermore, Bank C loses reserves to Bank B! Since the proportions in which consumers return the notes of one bank to the other banks makes a difference in the amounts of the net clearing balances, let us assume in accordance with the previous example that consumers return the notes of each bank to its rivals in proportion to the rivals' relative shares of total circulation.[12] They return the $18,033 of A's notes in the proportion of $20 to Bank B for every $30 to Bank C, or $7,213 to B and $10,820 to C. They return the $32,787 of B's notes in the proportion $11 to A for every $30 to C, or $8,797 to A and $23,990 to C. They return the $49,180 of C's notes in the proportion $11 to A for every $20 to B, or $17,429 to A and $31,729 to B. The net clearing balances are:

$$B \text{ loses } \$\ 8,797 - \$\ 7,213 = \$1,584 \text{ to A;}$$
$$C \text{ loses } \$17,429 - \$10,820 = \$6,609 \text{ to A; and}$$
$$C \text{ loses } \$31,729 - \$23,990 = \$7,739 \text{ to B.}$$

Bank C suffers a net reserve loss of $14,348, whereas banks A and B gain $8,193 and $6,155 of reserves, respectively. These results are summarized in Table 3.1 below. They imply that Bank A can continue to engage in predatory overexpansion without losing any reserves until its circulation is as big as Bank B's; Bank C will continue to lose reserves to Banks A and B until Bank A's circulation is as big as its own.

Table 3.1 **Consequences of Excessive Note Issue Under the Assumption of Note-brand Indiscrimination**

	Initial circula- tion	Initial reserves	Additions to circu- lation	Notes returned	Reserves after note exchange	Reserve gain (+) or loss (−)
Bank A	1,000,000	100,000	100,000	18,033	108,193	+ 8,193
Bank B	2,000,000	200,000	——	32,787	206,155	+ 6,155
Bank C	3,000,000	300,000	——	49,180	285,652	− 14,348

Note: all figures are $.

Thus the absence of note-brand loyalty would make it especially profitable for "undersized" banks to overissue, while forcing larger than average banks to suffer the consequences. Notice, however, that this circumstance would *not* encourage any *general* overexpansion, since larger banks would not have any profitable opportunities to expand, much less to overexpand; their best strategy would be to stand pat while their smaller rivals whittle away their circulation. The assumption of note-brand indiscrimination is, in other words, equivalent to an assumption of diseconomies of scale in note issue.

Here, then, is the rub, for the assumption of diseconomies of scale in competitive note issue has empirical implications which are clearly counterfactual, namely, that a banking system with competitive note issue should tend toward large numbers (if not an infinite number) of banks each having a minuscule share of total note circulation. Nothing of the kind appears to have been the case anywhere where competitive note issue took place. In Scottish, Canadian, and Swedish experience there was considerable diversity of market shares of circulation of various banks, with no evidence that banks with larger shares were at a disadvantage.[13] Indeed, in the various historical cases of free banking there seems to have been nothing at all that corresponds to the sequence of events one would expect were consumers indiscriminate among note brands. The Scottish, Canadian, Swedish, and Suffolk systems were all remarkably stable; prudent banks did not appear to suffer at all from overexpansion of their rivals, including smaller ones. During the months leading up to the failure of the Ayr Bank, for instance, the larger Scottish banks did not experience abnormal reserve drains. In fact, their reserves increased because they consistently enjoyed favorable net clearing balances with the Ayr Bank thanks to the latter's overissue. So historical experience confirms that consumers do discriminate between note brands and, hence, that competitive note issue, like deposit creation, is subject to increasing marginal costs.

To reject the hypothesis of note-brand indiscrimination is, however, not to say that all persons have rigid note-brand preferences (as the 100 percent note-brand discrimination hypothesis would suggest). What *can* be said is that a significant number of money holders do exhibit brand loyalty. It is these people's choices that determine the relative market shares of the various note issuers. Ultimately, the presence of a stratum of nondiscriminating individuals, if it has any influence whatsoever, merely increases the amount of precautionary reserves each bank has to hold relative to its total outstanding note liabilities. Banks may find that they do not always suffer reserve drains equal to the full amount of the expansion of their note liabilities. But this temporary reprieve will be offset at other times when the lack of note-brand discrimination works in favor of other banks. On the whole, fluctuations in the flow of clearing balances are random, so that no systematic opportunities for overexpansion result from the presence of nondiscriminating note holders. In other words, as long as note-brand discrimination is not rare, the principle of adverse clearings can be assumed to govern credit expansion in a system with competing banks of issue. It follows that there is no reason to expect competitively issued note liabilities to be more prone to overexpansion than competitively issued checkable deposit liabilities.

This result has other important implications. It means that a solitary bank in a free banking system cannot pursue an independent loan-pricing policy. A "cheap-money" policy in particular would only cause it to lose reserves to rival banks. Also, no bank would be able, by overissuing, to influence the level of prices or nominal income to any significant degree, since the clearing mechanism rapidly absorbs issues in excess of aggregate demand, punishing the responsible bank. Consequently, the structure of nominal prices would not be indeterminate. Assuming stationary conditions of production, free banks face a *determinate* schedule of nominal money demand which strictly limits the extent of their issues.

These conclusions are precisely opposite those reached by John G. Gurley and Edward S. Shaw in *Money in a Theory of Finance* (1960, 253ff). Gurley and Shaw claim that a laissez-faire banking system will lead to an indeterminate price level, with the nominal supply of money "subject to no rational rule and . . . free of guidance by any hand, visible or invisible" (ibid., 256). A (minimal) solution to this problem of price-level indeterminacy, according to these authors, requires the presence of a central bank able to create nominal private-bank reserve balances in the form of claims on itself (ibid., 257). The central bank must limit its issues of such reserves while also paying a fixed rate of interest on them:

> Nominal money and the price level are determined when the Central Bank sets nominal reserves and the reserve-balance rate, given a reserve-demand function (liquidity-preference function) that defines the optimal portfolio between reserves and primary securities at alternative combinations of bond rate, reserve-balance rate, deposit rate, and real stock of money [ibid., 266–67].

Gurley and Shaw note that this solution does *not* depend on a legally-specified, minimum ratio of reserves to private banks' liabilities.

What Gurley and Shaw overlook in their analysis is that private banks in an unregulated setting already have a well-defined demand for reserves (determinants of which are discussed below, in chapter 6). This demand does not rest on the existence of a central bank capable of augmenting or otherwise influencing the supply of reserve media. Rather, it stems directly from the fact, noted by Gurley and Shaw (ibid., 256) that "the individual bank [in a laissez-faire system] is not permitted to run up an indefinite amount of clearinghouse debt to its competitors." Thus a market for reserves will exist under laissez faire, where reserves consist of some asset which, though not issued by a central bank, is acceptable to private banks in the settlement of clearinghouse balances. If the reserve asset is an outside commodity-money such as gold, which is costly to produce and which does not bear interest (or, in other words, bears interest at a fixed rate of zero percent), its use satisfies the conditions given by Gurley and Shaw for a determinate price level and nominal money supply. Hence their rejection of laissez-faire banking in favor of central banking is unwarranted. Indeed, as we shall see in the next section, their belief that a central bank is helpful for tying down the price level and nominal supply of money is in a sense the opposite of the truth.

Monopolized Note Issue

Now let us consider a centralized system, based on commodity money, where deposit banking is entirely free but where one bank has sole right of note issue. It has been shown that the rule of excess reserves limits the ability of deposit banks in such a system to expand credit. A monopoly bank of issue is under no similar restraint. This bank is the sole source of currency, apart from commodity money, for the entire system. When holders of deposit accounts want to convert parts of their balances into a form useful in hand-to-hand payments where checks are less acceptable, they will demand conversion of their deposits into the notes of the monopoly issuer (or, perhaps, into commodity money). If public confidence in the notes of the monopoly issuer is high, its notes will be preferred to commodity money, which is more cumbersome. For their part the deposit banks, stripped of the ability to issue their own notes to supply their depositors with currency, rely upon notes of the monopoly bank of issue, or upon deposit credits at the monopoly bank (which they can convert into its notes). As all deposit banks share a common motive for holding liabilities of the monopoly bank of issue, a general demand for these liabilities develops. As Charles Rist notes in his *History of Monetary and Credit Theory* ([1940] 1966, 208), the liabilities of the monopoly bank of issue come to be treated by the deposit banks much as commodity-money is treated by banks in a system with competitive note issue:

> In countries where there is a central bank of issue, which has the exclusive right of issuing bank-notes . . . the deposit banks have come to regard bank-notes, and not coin, as the currency which they must use for payments . . . banks settle their accounts with each other by means of notes or by transfer through the central bank, and their chief concern is to be able at any moment to repay in these notes the deposits entrusted to them.

Commodity money, instead of being held by the deposit banks, may (to a large extent) be deposited with the bank of issue, possibly at interest, in exchange for liabilities of that bank which, besides being useful in settling clearing balances, are at least as useful as commodity money for supplying the public's currency needs.[14]

Thus as a consequence (perhaps unintended) of monopolized note issue, the liabilities of the privileged bank acquire a special status in the banking system; they become a kind of reserve media, supplementing and even superseding reserves of commodity money. Unlike deposit liabilities of non-note-issuing banks and unlike any of the bank liabilities in a system with competing note-issuers, the liabilities of a monopoly bank of issue are a form of high-powered money. Issues of such liabilities add to the base money of the system. This means, in effect, that a monopoly bank of issue is, in the short run at least, exempt from the principle of adverse clearings. The liabilities it issues not employed as currency in circulation become lodged in the reserves of deposit banks, where they cause a multiplicative expansion of credit. In general (assuming a closed economy) these liabilities will *not* be returned to their issuer for redemption even though their issue, and the multiplicative expansion of credit caused by it, is not justified by any prior excess demand for inside money. In other words, in a closed system a monopoly bank of issue can cause an inflationary increase in the money supply—raising the level of nominal income and prices—without suffering any negative consequences.[15] Unless some external short-run control is imposed on it, a monopoly bank of issue *even when its issues are convertible into commodity money* can for some time at least pursue any loan-pricing policy it desires, arbitrarily expanding or contracting the money supply and causing widespread changes in nominal income and prices.

Of course, in an open system, an increase in the level of domestic prices (due to monetary overexpansion) eventually reduces exports relative to imports, causing an outflow of commodity-money reserves to foreign banking systems. This belatedly checks overexpansion by the domestic bank of issue. Also, inflation usually involves a decline in the relative price of commodity money, encouraging its withdrawal, for industrial and other nonmonetary uses, from the monopoly bank. This last effect checks overexpansion by a monopoly bank of issue even in a closed economy. Still it is a long-term corrective, which takes place after overexpansion has done the larger part of its damage. (On the effects of short-run monetary disequilibrium see below, chapter 4.) Long-term checks on overissue differ significantly from the short-run adjustments that come into play when the principle of adverse clearings operates.

Because of the special character of its liabilities, a monopoly bank of issue is able to influence the money supply like a central bank. Indeed, it is no coincidence that all central banks—that is, banks responsible for carrying out some government-directed monetary policy—have either a monopoly or a virtual monopoly of currency supply. Such a monopoly "gives them the power to dictate terms to banks which are in need of notes for deposit conversion" (Whitney 1934, 17). By controlling the issue of currency, a central bank also controls deposit expansion by non note-issuing banks:

> Deposits must always have at the back of them a sufficient reserve of currency, and therefore the total amount of currency must be a major factor in the determination of the total volume of deposits that can be created through the lending operations of the banks. Thus, if a central banking authority controls the issue of notes, it also controls, though less rigidly, the volume of credit [V. Smith 1936, 7].

From this one may be tempted to conclude that legislators, realizing some of the consequences of monopolized note issue, saw fit to impose it as a means for rational monetary control. In reality, however, monopolized note issue is much older than the idea of central-ized, "rational" money management. The Bank of England has had a monopoly or quasi monopoly of the London note issue since its establishment in 1694. Yet the idea that it should be held responsible for preventing undesirable fluctuations in England's money supply was not adopted as public policy until the latter half of the 19th century. Before this, the Bank of England was essentially a profit-maximizing firm the directors of which vigorously denied any respon-sibility for fluctuations in the money supply. In English experience, which served as the model for all subsequent central-banking re-forms, it was not a demand for rational, centralized monetary control that caused note issue to be monopolized. Rather, it was the existence of a partial note-issue monopoly that inspired demands for more rational, centralized control. When monopolization of note issue awards, to a single bank, the power to "control" the money supply, it also gives that bank power to over- and underexpand credit that it would not possess were it one of a system of competing note issuers.

Illustration: The Post–1910 Australian Inflation

Some of the conclusions reached in this chapter are strikingly illustrated by the experience of Australia in the years surrounding World War I.[16] Before 1910 Australia had several note-issuing banks all adhering to a gold standard. The banks settled clearings with one another in specie, since this was the only form of high-powered money in the system at the time. Under this arrangement prices were fairly stable, and the principle of adverse clearings insured that no single bank could step out of line with its competitors. If by chance the entire system went out of line, adjustment would come as a conse-quence of gold losses abroad.

In 1910 the Australian government passed a law authorizing a limited issue of legal-tender Australian government notes, and a year later the Commonwealth Bank was set up as an agent for issuing these notes. Soon afterwards a prohibitive 10 percent tax was imposed on all private bank note issues, and restrictions on the issue of legal-tender notes were relaxed. This gave the Australian government and its agent, the Commonwealth Bank, a virtual monopoly in note issue. The result was that the Australian notes became a new kind of high-powered money. Almost immediately the government increased its issues, and a general expansion of credit followed. So as to thwart the corrective influence of the international price-specie-flow mechanism, the government declared a gold export embargo. In the space of two or three years what had been an open system with plural note issuers was transformed into a closed system with monopolized note issue.

More consequences, all in accord with the predictions of theory, followed. In September 1914, the private banks formally abandoned their regular procedure of settling clearings in specie, giving priority to acquisition of notes from the monopoly bank of issue. By this time Australian credit expansion was entirely unleashed from normal sources of control. The Treasury and the Commonwealth Bank were free to manipulate the money supply, by altering the supply of high-powered money, in any direction they desired. As it happened, the authorities took advantage of the new arrangement to finance wartime expenditures. As J. R. Butchart notes (1918, 29), monopolization of the Australian currency

> opened the door for the Commonwealth Treasurers to create vast deposits by simply printing notes and paying them into the counter at the Commonwealth Bank. These notes created deposits in the books of the Commonwealth Bank. Against the deposits the Government drew its checks [which were] transferred from the Commonwealth Bank all over Australia.

The result was a dramatic rise in Australian prices that continued throughout the course of the war, and for some time thereafter.

4

Monetary Equilibrium

Having seen the limits to expansion by free banks when the demand for money is constant, it is logical to ask what happens to these banks when the demand for money changes. In preparation for this we must define concepts like the demand for money and monetary equilibrium. Not to do so would invite unnecessary misunderstanding, since those concepts have various meanings in different contexts. The particular definitions provided in this chapter, though hardly original, are the ones most useful for studying the implications of free banking. The chapter also draws attention to some consequences of monetary disequilibrium, showing that a banking system's ability or inability to preserve monetary equilibrium is extremely important.

The Demand for Money

"The demand for money" is a very slippery expression. Financial writers, and sometimes economists as well, have a habit of using this expression as a synonym for the demand for bank credit or loanable funds. Consequently they refer to particular interest rates as "the price of money" and call the short-term credit market "the money market." This use of terms is highly misleading. Bank borrowers generally acquire money balances only to spend them immediately on goods and services. The demand for money, properly understood, refers to the desire to *hold* money as part of a financial portfolio. A bank borrower contributes no more to the demand for money than a ticket agent contributes to the demand for plays and concerts; only holders of money or actual occupants of concert seats contribute to demand.

Thus to be useful the expression *demand for money* must refer to peoples' desire to *hold* money balances and not just to the fact that they agree to *receive* money in exchange for other goods and services, including later-dated claims to money.[1] It is only when people who receive money income elect to hold it rather than spend it on other assets or consumer goods that they may properly be said to have a demand for money. Edwin Cannan (1921) made this point forcefully years ago:

> We must think of the demand for [money] as being furnished, not by the number or amount of *transactions*, but by the ability and willingness of persons to *hold* money, in the same way as we think of the demand for houses as coming not from persons who buy and re-sell houses or lease and sub-lease houses, but from persons who *occupy* houses. Mere activity in the housing market—mere buying and selling of houses—may in a sense be said to involve 'increase of demand' for houses, but in a corresponding sense it may be said to involve an equal 'increase of supply'; the two things cancel. . . . In the same way, more transactions for money—more purchases and sales of commodities and services—may in a sense be said to involve increase of demand for money, but in the corresponding sense it may be said to involve an equal increase of supply of money; the two things cancel. The demand which is important for our purposes is the demand for money, not to pay away again immediately, but to hold.

Following a suggestion by Alex McLeod (1984, 68), it should also be noted that, although transactions balances are less obviously "held" than are speculative and precautionary balances, they are still, strictly speaking, part of the demand for money-to-hold. The demand for them is distinct from demand for money-to-spend insofar as the latter kind of demand, if accommodated by an increase in the nominal quantity of money, would lead to an increase in total spending and nominal income. It follows that, although all money in existence is at every moment held by someone, this does not mean that the demand for it is necessarily equal to the existing stock given the existing purchasing power of the money unit. When an excess supply of money exists, people will spend their surplus holdings. Money payments will increase, and so will the flow of money income. If the nominal supply of money and the extent of real output do not independently change, the increased spending will cause prices to rise in the long run. This will reduce the real value of the existing money stock, bringing it in line with the real demand for money balances. If the nominal supply of money is deficient the opposite adjustments occur. Therefore, although long-run changes in the value of money equate the demand for money with its supply, when considering the short run it is entirely valid to speak of an excess demand for or an excess supply of money. Moreover, since changes in the value of money fully eliminate excess supply or demand *only* in the long run (because it takes time for changes in spending to influence prices in a general way), short-run corrections in the real money supply require changes in the nominal quantity of money.

A demand may exist for either of two kinds of money: "base" or commodity money—the ultimate money of redemption—and inside money (bank notes and demand deposits) redeemable in base money. In a mature free banking system, commodity money does not circulate, its place being taken entirely by inside money. Such being the case, the unqualified expression "demand for money" used in this study will henceforth mean demand for inside money. For example, an increase in the public's demand for money means an increase in the aggregate demand to hold bank liabilities. Unless otherwise stated, a change in demand will refer to an autonomous change in both real and nominal demand, meaning a change not itself induced by any exogenous change in aggregate nominal income.[2]

The Market for Inside Money and the Market for Loanable Funds

As used here "monetary equilibrium" will mean the state of affairs that prevails when there is neither an excess demand for money nor an excess supply of it at the existing level of prices. When a change in the (nominal) supply of money is demand accommodating—that is, when it corrects what would otherwise be a short-run excess demand or excess supply—the change will be called "warranted" because it maintains monetary equilibrium.

This view of monetary equilibrium is appropriate so long as matters are considered from the perspective of the market for money balances. But it is also possible to define monetary equilibrium in terms of conditions in the market for bank credit or loanable funds. Though these two views of monetary equilibrium differ, they do not conflict. One defines equilibrium in terms of a stock, the other in terms of the flow from which the stock is derived. When a change in the demand for (inside) money warrants a change in its supply (in order to prevent excess demand or excess supply in the short run), the adjustment must occur by means of a change in the amount of funds lent by the banking system.

An important question, one particularly controversial among monetary economists in the middle of this century, arises at this point. Are adjustments in the supply of loanable funds, meant to preserve monetary equilibrium, also consistent with the equality of voluntary savings.and investment? The answer is yes, they are. The aggregate demand to hold balances of inside money is a reflection of the public's willingness to supply loanable funds through the banks whose liabilities are held. To hold inside money is to engage in voluntary saving.

As George Clayton notes, whoever elects to hold bank liabilities received in exchange for goods or services "is abstaining from the consumption of goods and services to which he is entitled. Such saving by holding money embraces not merely the hoarding of money for fairly long periods by particular individuals but also the collective effect of the holding of money for quite short periods by a succession of individuals."[3]

Whenever a bank expands its liabilities in the process of making new loans and investments, it is the holders of the liabilities who are the ultimate lenders of credit, and what they lend are the real resources they could acquire if, instead of holding money, they spent it.[4] When the expansion or contraction of bank liabilities proceeds in such a way as to be at all times in agreement with changing demands for inside money, the quantity of real capital funds supplied to borrowers by the banks is equal to the quantity voluntarily offered to the banks by the public. Under these conditions, banks are simply intermediaries of loanable funds.

Thus a direct connection exists between the conditions for equilibrium in the market for balances of inside money and those for equilibrium in the market for loanable funds. An increase in the demand for money warrants an increase in bank loans and investments. A decrease in the demand for money warrants a reduction in bank loans and investments. To put the matter in Wicksell's terms, changes in the supply of loanable funds that accord with changes in the demand for inside money also ensure that the money rate of interest is kept equal to the "natural rate."

Any departure from monetary equilibrium has disruptive consequences. Consider what happens when the supply of money fails to increase in response to an increase in demand for money on the part of wage earners. The wage earners attempt to increase their money balances by reducing their purchases of consumer products, but there is no offsetting increase in demand for products due to increased, bank-financed expenditures. Therefore, the reduction in demand leads to an accumulation of goods inventories. Businesses' nominal revenues become deficient relative to outlays for factors of production—the difference representing money that wage earners have withdrawn from circulation. Since each entrepreneur notices a deficiency of his own revenues only, without perceiving it as a mere prelude to a general fall in prices *including factor prices*, he views the falling off of demand for his product as symbolizing (at least in part) a lasting decline in the profitability of his particular line of business. If all entrepreneurs reduce their output, the result is a general downturn, which ends only once a general fall in prices raises the real supply of money to its desired level.[5]

As was said previously, such a crisis can occur only if banks fail to respond adequately to a general increase in the demand for inside money. The crisis involves a deflationary Wicksellian process during which bank rates of interest are temporarily above their natural level. This is opposite the inflationary Wicksellian process, with bank rates below the equilibrium or natural rate of interest, that economists of the Austrian school traditionally emphasize.[6] Nevertheless deflation (resulting from unaccommodated excess demand for inside money) has been an important factor in historical business cycles, and a banking system that promotes deflation disrupts economic activity just as surely as one that promotes inflation, although the exact nature of the disruption differs in each case.

Opinions of Other Writers

The view of monetary equilibrium presented here should not be controversial, and has been upheld by many economists. To cite but a few examples, it has been put forth by J. G. Koopmans (1933), Gottfried Haberler (1931), Fritz Machlup (1940), Jacques Reuff (1953), W. Zawadski (1937), and (in a qualified way) Friedrich A. Hayek (1935, [1933] 1975b and 1939b, 164ff), among continental European theorists. Most of these writers link the concept of monetary equilibrium to that of "neutral" money.[7] According to Koopmans (1933, 257), who has developed this approach most thoroughly, monetary policy should have the goal of "compensating for any deflation, due to hoarding, by creating a corresponding amount of new money, or of compensating for any inflation, due to dishoarding, by destroying money in like measure." When this goal is achieved "the *money outlay stream* should remain constant." In other words, money is neutral as long as Say's Law remains valid (that is, as long as excess demand for money is zero). Conversely, monetary disequilibrium occurs and money is non-neutral whenever Say's Law is violated:

> Hoarding and money destruction cause a leakage in the circular flow of income; dishoarding and money creation make, so to speak, new purchasing power spring from nowhere. In the first case, that of pure supply [of non-money goods], the situation is deflationary, in the second, where pure demand occurs, it is inflationary; in neither case does Say's Law apply. If net pure demand is nil, monetary equilibrium prevails . . . the monetary equilibrium situation corresponds to Say's Law [De Jong 1973, 24].

Machlup has the same view in mind when he writes (1940, 291 and 184–89) that "credit inflation is 'healthy' if it compensates for deflation through current net hoarding, or for an increase in the number of cash balances or in the number of 'stopping stations' in the money flow" and that credit contraction is healthy if it compensates for dishoarding ("a decrease in idle balances").

Hayek is more equivocal in his suggestions concerning an ideal monetary policy. At one point in *Prices and Production* he recommends that the money supply be kept *constant*.[8] Yet he follows this with a statement acknowledging the need to make adjustments in the money supply in response to changes in the "co-efficient of money transactions." In still another passage he mentions the need to accommodate changes in the "average velocity of circulation" of money, noting that "any change in the velocity of circulation would have to be compensated by a reciprocal change in the amount of money in circulation if money is to remain neutral towards prices."[9] Finally, in his most explicit statement concerning the importance of adjusting the nominal supply of money, he says (1939b, 165) that banks must "create additional credits for investment purposes to the same extent that holders of deposits have ceased to use them for current expenditure." This serves to avoid the "undesirable deflationary consequences" of unaccommodated saving.

Hayek's equivocation is due, on one hand, to his view that desirable adjustments in the money supply cannot be formulated into a "language of practice" (1935, 108) which, of course, does not argue for rejecting them as a theoretical ideal, and on the other to his notion that equilibrium in the market for "real capital" can be preserved only if banks do not issue unbacked (fiduciary) media (Hayek 1935, 23). The latter view contradicts our claim in the previous section: it ignores the fact that changes in the desire to hold inside money reflect the public's willingness to lend "real capital" to and through the banking system. More will be said in defense of this criticism later on.

Allowing for the ambivalent views of Hayek, all of the continental writers cited have notions of monetary equilibrium similar to the one adopted in the present work. The same may be said concerning views on monetary equilibrium entertained by many well-known British theorists, including Dennis Robertson (1926, and [1957] 1964, chap. 5, sect. 4), E. F. M. Durbin (1933), J. E. Meade (1933), A. G. B. Fisher (1935), Ralph Hawtrey (1951), and A. C. Pigou (1933). Typically these writers express the notion in question in the form of the rule that the supply of money multiplied by its income velocity of circulation should remain constant. According to Durbin (1933, 187) such a policy would "avoid income deflation on the one hand and a profit inflation on the other."[10]

J. E. Meade (1933, 8) argues along the same lines that the total increase in the supply of money in a given period of time should equal the net increase in the demand for money during the same period, with bank investments adjusted correspondingly. Besides preventing changes in final (nominal) income this policy would assure an equilibrium interest rate.

Robertson, in *Banking Policy and the Price Level*, states his views on the requirements for monetary equilibrium in very idiosyncratic language.[11] Nevertheless he also believes that an increased general desire to hoard should be offset through additional bank lending:

> Considered alone, the action of the bank imposes Automatic Stinting: considered in conjunction with the New Hoarding, it nips in the bud the Automatic Splashing which would otherwise occur as a by-product of the New Hoarding. The bank, therefore, while imposing Automatic Stinting is not imposing Automatic Lacking, but is in effect transforming Spontaneous New Hoarding into Applied Lacking very much as a "cloak-room" bank does when it accepts cash from the public and lends it out to entrepreneurs.[12]

Most of these authors explicitly distinguish the goal of accommodating changes in the demand for money through changes in nominal supply from that of stabilizing an index of prices. The two goals differ because general price movements may be caused by changes in productive efficiency, and not just by changes in the demand for money balances relative to nominal income. Offsetting price changes due to changes in productive efficiency would not preserve monetary equilibrium.[13] The reasons for this will be discussed in chapter 7. For the time being it is only necessary to note that the procedures for maintaining monetary equilibrium discussed here should not be viewed as leading to price-level stabilization.

Many past and present American monetarists would probably agree with the theoretical views of the European writers discussed above. Their preference for other policies—for price-level stabilization or a fixed money growth rate rule—stems, not from any theoretical disagreement, but from their view that these policies provide the best achievable approximation to the ideal of a truly demand-elastic money supply.[14] Other American writers have explicitly defended the monetary equilibrium ideal, calling for the adjustment of nominal money supply to avoid monetary disequilibrium. The most important of these theorists was Clark Warburton (1981), who noted the popularity of what he termed the "monetary disequilibrium" approach in American writings of the early decades of the 20th century. In the 1960s the same approach was "rediscovered" by Robert Clower (1965, 1967) and Axel Leijonhufvud (1968), who also interpreted Keynes as a monetary disequilibrium theorist. Lately Leland Yeager, who has been heavily influenced by Warburton, has defended the monetary equilibrium-disequilibrium approach against the "equilibrium always" theorizing of the new-classical school (Yeager 1986).

Finally, some remarks should be made about Keynes and Keynesian theory. It is well known that consumers' propensity to hoard and "liquidity preference," in conjunction with downward inflexibility of money wages, play a crucial role in Keynesian explanations of depression and unemployment. In general, Keynes believed, an elastic supply of inside money should prevent hoarding and liquidity preference from having any negative influence on aggregate demand: increased investment (financed by the banking system) should follow every net increase in aggregate money demand.[15] This view is quite consistent with the other views on monetary equilibrium cited here. Keynesian analysis, however, came to attach great importance to the possibility of a liquidity trap, a possibility which Keynes himself treated as an extreme, limiting case. The presence of a liquidity trap (which involves an infinitely interest-elastic demand for money balances) renders monetary expansion through conventional banking channels impotent as a spur to investment. It therefore necessitates resort to increased government spending in order to augment aggregate demand. Also, some Keynesians (and Keynes himself may be included here) suggest that employment should not be considered "full" so long as it can be increased by an expansionary policy, even if the policy leads to an *increase* in money wages.[16] This view seems to attach overriding importance to short-run reductions in unemployment without acknowledging the undesirable consequences, both in the long and in the short run, of monetary disequilibrium.[17]

Despite these important differences between Keynesian analysis and the views of other monetary-equilibrium theorists, many Keynesians might accept the prescription for monetary equilibrium offered in this chapter. Those who do not regard the liquidity trap as an important factual possibility would probably accept it as entirely adequate. Some might wish to supplement it with government spending programs, of course. Those who accept the possibility of a permanent or semi-permanent inflation-unemployment trade off, or otherwise think that the benefits of inflation generally exceed the costs, will likely reject it in favor of outright inflation.

These views of other writers are not cited as evidence of the correctness of any theory. Their purpose is merely to show that the concept of monetary equilibrium adopted in this study is neither new nor controversial. The concept is applied here to the appraisal of free banking. Any originality lies in this appraisal, rather than in the criteria on which it is based.

Transfer Credit, Created Credit, and Forced Savings

The difference between warranted and unwarranted additions to the stock of inside money is usefully illuminated by a distinction between "transfer credit" and "created credit."[18] Transfer credit is credit granted by banks in recognition of people's desire to abstain from spending by holding balances of inside money.[19] In contrast, created credit is granted independently of any voluntary abstinence from spending by holders of money balances.[20] When the demand for money falls, its nominal supply must also be reduced or else some transfer credit becomes created credit.

Obviously, created credit can exist only in the short run: a spurt of credit creation prompts an adjustment of prices which eventually restores monetary equilibrium, causing all outstanding credit to conform to the aggregate demand for money. In equilibrium all credit is transfer credit because, by our definition of monetary equilibrium, nobody holds inside money balances in excess of the balances he desires to hold. Thus any reference to created credit or to credit creation means a *temporary* excess supply of money due to excessive bank lending or investment.

Credit creation, Fritz Machlup notes (1940, 183), "places money at the disposal of the market . . . without any corresponding release of productive factors . . . due to voluntary refraining from consumption." Unlike operations involving credit transfer it "makes it possible for investment to take place in the absence of voluntary savings." Such investment "gives rise to the development of disproportionalities in the production process."

Whereas voluntary savings support transfer credit, real resources invested by means of credit creation represent "forced savings." The notion of forced savings, which Hayek (1939a, 183–97) traces back to Bentham, refers to the reduction of real income suffered by earners of fixed money incomes when goods they normally purchase are bid away by recipients of new income having its source in credit creation.[21] Malthus's discussion of this phenomenon, which appeared in an 1811 issue of the *Edinburgh Review*, assumes a case where credit is created exclusively in the form of bank notes:

> The new notes go into the market as so much additional capital, to purchase what is necessary for the conduct of the concern. But, before the produce of the country has been increased, it is impossible for one person to have more of it, without diminishing the shares of some others. This dimunition is affected by the rise of prices occasioned by the competition of the new notes.[22]

This artificial diversion of resources to new industries does not continue once prices adjust to eliminate the excess supply of money:

The banking system's power to change [via forced savings] the distribution of real resources in favor of capital formation is purely transitory. The initial extension of credit may give borrowers more control over real resources, but it will eventually raise prices proportionately so that whilst larger bank balances will be held in terms of money, they will not represent increased real purchasing power. As loans come up for renewal, borrowers will demand increased sums in money terms; and the final allocation of real resources will not be significantly changed.[23]

What begins, in other words, as both a nominal and a real increase in loanable funds becomes, after a general adjustment of prices, a nominal increase only, which cannot support the needs of capital maintenance and project completion for both new (post-expansion) and old (pre-expansion) employers of credit. Marginal borrowers will be excluded from the market for loanable funds, and their investments may have to be liquidated, resulting in a slump.

The point of this discussion is to show how forced savings and its consequences are bound up with created credit. They arise whenever the granting of credit gives rise to bank liabilities in excess of the demand for balances of inside money. They do not arise insofar as credit offered by banks consists solely of transfer credit, i.e., of credit the granting of which gives rise to liabilities in amounts consistent with the demand for inside money. The distinction between created credit and transfer credit will be employed later in examining the response of a free banking system to changes in the demand for money.

A contrasting view of bank credit appears in the writings of several of the Austrian economists, especially Ludwig von Mises, who give the phenomenon of forced savings a prominent place in their elaborations of the monetary theory of the business cycle.[24] According to these writers *any* credit expansion or increase in the supply of fiduciary media—inside money not backed 100 percent by reserves of commodity or base money—is unwarranted. "The notion of 'normal' credit expansion," according to Mises, "is absurd":

Issuance of fiduciary media, no matter what its quantity may be, always sets in motion those changes in the price structure the description of which is the task of the theory of the trade cycle. Of course, if the additional amount issued is not large, neither are the inevitable effects of the expansion.[25]

In other words, all net expansion of fiduciary credit is a cause of loan-market disequilibrium. It causes bank rates of interest to fall below their "natural" levels, leading to forced savings and other trade-cycle phenomena. This contrasts with the view defended here, which holds that no ill consequences result from the issue of fiduciary media in response to a greater demand for balances of inside money. According to the latter view it is perfectly possible that fiduciary media may arise from loans or investments involving transfer credit only. The expansion of bank liabilities may represent a response to greater abstinence by money holders and, hence, to a fall in the "natural" rate of interest. In this case the fiduciary issue conforms with the "golden rule" referred to by Mises ([1953] 1980, 295). According to this rule, "the credit that [a] bank grants must correspond . . . to the credit that it takes up."

If some issue of fiduciary media does not involve credit creation, then Mises's "commodity credit," which is supposed to be credit not based on fiduciary media (and hence, in Mises's view, not having trade-cycle consequences), must be a mere fraction of what we are calling transfer credit. In fact precisely what Mises means by commodity credit is not clear. If the phrase refers to bank issues backed 100 percent by reserves of commodity money (which would make it the complement of what Mises calls "fiduciary" or "circulation" credit) then it does not refer to a form of credit at all. A bank holding 100 percent reserves against all of its liabilities is not a credit-granting institution, but a warehouse.

Alternatively, it may be that by commodity credit Mises means credit granted by banks on the basis of *time* liabilities, as opposed to liabilities redeemable on demand but not backed by 100 percent reserves. But in this case Mises confuses a difference of degree with one of substance. Holders of demand liabilities are granters of credit just as are holders of time liabilities. The only difference is that in the former case the duration of individual loans is unspecified; they are "call loans" that may mature at any time. Bankers must rely upon their entrepreneurial judgment to avoid violating the "golden rule" of not lending more than what is offered to them.[26]

However one interprets it, Mises's view that commodity credit is the only sort of credit consistent with loan market equilibrium causes him to be critical of fractional reserve banking.[27] This puts him in a league with such writers as P. J. Geyer (1867) and J. L. Tellkampf (1867), who called for the abolition of fiduciary media in Germany, and with Henri Cernuschi (1865) and P. Modeste (1866), who lobbied for its suppression in France.[28] Indeed, Mises's support for free banking is based in part on his agreement with Cernuschi, who (along with Modeste) believed that freedom of note issue would automatically lead to 100 percent reserve banking.[29]

This difference of opinion has implications for the appraisal of free banking's consistency with monetary and loan-market equilibrium. If the view defended in this chapter is correct, then it is desirable, not that free banks should prevent *all* issues of fiduciary media, but rather that they should only prevent issues that are inconsistent with changing demands for money balances. If free banks function this way they are merely transferring credit, not creating it.

Chapter 3 showed why individual free banks cannot create credit as long as the demand for money is constant. But it did not show that they preserve monetary equilibrium when the demand for money is increasing or decreasing. Nor did it show whether credit creation is possible under either static or changing conditions for free banks acting in unison. How free banks respond to changes in demand, and whether there are any adequate restraints on their collective behavior, will be the subjects of the next two chapters.

5

Changes in the Demand for Inside Money

EXCEPT IN CHAPTER 2, where account was taken of the effects from a lowering of the exchange value of commodity money in response to fiduciary substitution, this study has assumed a demand for money balances fixed in both real and nominal terms. We must now consider how a free banking system responds to *changes* in the demand for money. Would a free banking system accommodate an increase in the demand for money? Would it automatically reduce the supply of money in response to a fall in the demand for it? Would it, in short, continue to maintain monetary equilibrium?

A change in the demand for money—meaning real demand to hold inside money—can be due to a change in the number of bank liability holders, a change in the holdings of the same individuals, or a combination of both. It does not necessarily involve any redistribution of existing demands among various banks. References to an increasing or decreasing demand in this chapter will mean changes in aggregate or total demand. Thus when the demand to hold the liabilities of one bank increases, it is assumed, unless otherwise stated, that there is no change in the demand to hold liabilities of other banks.

Increased Money Demand

Suppose then that there is a growth in the total demand for inside money that takes the form of a growth in demand for the liabilities (notes and deposit balances) of one bank. How can this increased demand be satisfied? We have seen that, in a mature system where there is no more outside money in circulation to be deposited, all fresh sums of inside money make their first appearance through new loans and investments. In general such newly issued liabilities do not at first come into the hands of those persons who happen to desire to hold more of them. There is an exception to this, though, which also provides the simplest example of how a bank may profitably expand its liabilities (with a fixed supply of reserves) in response to the increased money demands of its clients. This exception involves so-called compensating balances. These are balances held by bank borrower-customers as part of their loan agreement. A person or firm that holds compensating balances is simultaneously a borrower and a lender of the sum in question: in accepting a loan the person or firm becomes a debtor to the bank, but to the extent that borrowed funds are willingly held (rather than spent) the borrower is also a creditor. The bank has issued claims to commodity money, but these claims are not going to be redeemed by anyone. Some of the commodity money that has been "borrowed" is, in effect, never taken from the bank. Hence the bank can lend it to someone else.

When a bank borrower explicitly agrees to keep a compensating balance, the banker knows in advance that the balance will be held rather than spent and that it will therefore not become a source of adverse clearings like other loan-created deposits. A bank's compensating-balance liabilities are one of its most reliable sources of credit.

The holders of compensating balances, in turn, also benefit by holding them so long as their borrowed holdings do not exceed their ordinary demands for money balances. The benefit is due to the fact that loan rates are generally lower for loans involving compensating balance agreements, which reflects the banker's preference for having his liabilities outstanding in a form not likely to contribute to unanticipated clearing losses.[1]

That banks can accommodate the fluctuating money demands of their borrower customers by means of changes in compensating balances is obvious enough. But how might they satisfy the increased demands of would-be note and deposit holders who are not among their borrower customers? Recall that every day a certain number of a bank's notes and checks enter the clearing apparatus and become a source of debits against it. If the bank is in equilibrium vis-à-vis its rivals, it will on average have clearing credits equal to its clearing debits, and so it can maintain its outstanding liabilities, replacing its earning assets as they mature. Now suppose that some of the bank's depositor customers write fewer checks on their balances (without increasing the average size of their checks), or that more individuals who come into possession of the bank's notes hold on to them instead of spending them. The result will be a reduced flow of the bank's liabilities into the clearing mechanism—a reduction in adverse clearings against it—much like the reduction that would occur if borrower customers elected to increase the portion of their borrowings represented by compensating balances.

A metaphorical description of the process of demand expansion may be helpful. The outstanding supply of inside money may be thought of as flowing through the economy in a stream of money income and expenditures. Along this stream are pockets or "reservoirs" representing individuals' and firms' holdings of inside-money balances. When the demand for money increases, either the number of reservoirs increases (as when the number of firms or people that want to hold money increases), or existing reservoirs deepen (as when demands of existing money holders become more intense). Either case results in a withdrawal of funds from the income stream. When the increased demand is for the liabilities of one particular bank, then that bank's liabilities are removed from the flow of spending and income. Instead of being cancelled by the clearing mechanism, they become lodged in the reservoirs of demand.

The withdrawn liabilities thus cease to contribute to their bank's reserve demand: the reserves held by their issuer—formerly just adequate to sustain its liabilities—become excessive as positive net clearings accumulate. To maximize its profits, the bank whose liabilities are in greater demand expands credit. This newly expanded credit is transfer credit, because it is issued in response to the desire of certain people to hold more of the liabilities of the bank that grants it. Hence it does not lead to any forced savings or upward pressure on prices. It allows the bank to recover its equilibrium vis-à-vis other banks in the system.

It should be noted that, as far as the maintenance of monetary equilibrium is concerned, the specific point of the injection of new liabilities is not crucial: the bank can be expected to make new credits available to borrowers in a way that satisfies the principle of equimarginal returns.[2] All that matters is that the bank recognizes the decision to save made by holders of inside money.

Now consider the consequences of an increased *general* demand for inside money, one that confronts all banks at once. No bank in this case witnesses any improvement in its circumstance relative to other banks, that is, any positive net average clearings. Nevertheless each bank will have fewer gross clearings than before, insofar as the banks considered as a group do not respond to the increased demand, and this will reduce each bank's need for (precautionary) reserves relative to its actual reserve supply. Thus the banks will find it profitable to expand until their total gross clearings are such as to again raise the demand for reserves to the level of available supply. A more complete explanation of this requires a discussion of the economic determinants of reserve demand, which is deferred until the next chapter.

To summarize, a general increase in the demand for inside money is equivalent to a general decline in the rate of turnover of inside money. Bank notes change hands less frequently, and holders of demand deposits write fewer (or perhaps smaller) checks. As a result, bank liabilities pass less frequently into the hands of persons or rival issuers who return them to their points of origin for redemption. The reduction in turnover of liabilities leads directly to a fall in the volume of bank clearings. When this happens banks find they have excess reserves relative to the existing level of their liabilities, and so they are able to increase their holdings of interest-earning assets, which they do by expanding the supply of inside money in a manner that accommodates the growth in demand for it. In standard textbook terminology, there is an increase in the reserve multiplier. Liability expansion continues so long as there are unfilled reservoirs of demand. Any issues in excess of demand, however, will lead to additions to the stream of payments, causing an increase in bank clearings and reserve requirements.

Yet another way to put the argument is to speak in terms of velocity rather than turnover. Then free banks can be said to accommodate a fall in the velocity of inside money with an increase in its supply. Regardless of how one phrases it, the actions of the banks are precisely the ones required for the maintenance of monetary equilibrium. For reasons that will be made clear later on, this cannot generally be the case for central-banking systems or for otherwise unregulated systems lacking freedom of note issue.

An issue arises at this point concerning the relative maturity structures of bank assets and liabilities. Individual money-holders' offerings of credit to their banks are, generally speaking, of much shorter (as well as more uncertain) duration than the banks' resulting offerings to their borrower customers. Hence the bankers must be able to transform short-term credits of unknown duration into longer-term loans and investments. They do so by taking advantage of the law of large numbers in the same way as goldsmith bankers took advantage of it in making the first loans based on fiduciary media (see above, chapter 2). The actions of large numbers of independently motivated users of inside money will largely offset one another in the day to day course of things. One person spends his deposit balance previously held at Bank A, thereby ceasing to be one of its creditors. Another simultaneously adds to his deposit account at Bank A. The same kind of largely offsetting transactions occur at all other banks. As a result, the sum of short-lived, individual demands for inside money can be treated by the banks as a fund suitable for investing in a portfolio of earning assets the average maturity of which significantly exceeds the average turnover period of individual notes or deposit credits. The maturity structure and quantity of a bank's loans and investments therefore depends on the expected behavior of the *aggregate* demand for its liabilities, and not on changes in the composition of individual demands from which the aggregate is derived.

Decreased Money Demand

Now consider what happens when the demand for inside money falls. Supposing once more that the fall affects the liabilities of one bank only, it means the shrinking or disappearance of reservoirs in which that bank's liabilities were formerly lodged. The liabilities return to the stream of money income, where they pass into the clearing mechanism and become debits to their issuer. To adjust its position vis-à-vis its competitors the bank, experiencing reduced demand for its liabilities, calls back some of its loans and liquidates some investments or at least ceases to renew some existing loans as they mature. Thus, just as the supply of inside money is increased through the expansion of credit, it may be reduced through the absorption of credit, that is, by the retirement of loans and investments.[3]

It is even possible for unwanted liabilities to be directly returned to their points of origin by way of the repayment of loans. Suppose, for example, that the surplus liabilities no longer wanted in money balances are paid over to someone who happens to be indebted to their issuer, and that the individual in question uses them to repay his loan. What is the overall result of this transaction? The bank suffers no clearing loss and no change in the volume of clearings against it.[4] Yet the sum of its outstanding liabilities has fallen, assuming that the bank does not make any new loans or investments. If, on the other hand, the bank attempts to restore its assets and liabilities to their previous level by new extensions of credit it will suffer adverse clearings approximately equal to the new issues. Presumably the bank had no excess reserves to begin with (i.e., before the demand for its liabilities fell and before one of its loans was repaid). Since nothing has happened since to supply it with excess reserves, the bank cannot sustain further adverse clearings, and so it must ultimately accept a reduction in its business.

Similar consequences follow if the liabilities of one bank, the demand for which has fallen, are used to repay loans at another bank. What happens here is best understood as a two-step process. First imagine that Y, who is indebted to Bank B, receives inside money from X, who in making the payment in question permanently reduces his holdings at Bank A. Suppose furthermore that Y at first deposits the sum received from X at Bank B. Then Bank A will, other things being equal, suffer an adverse clearing equal to the amount of the payment made by X to Y. In response to this loss Bank A has to contract its liabilities. On the other hand, Bank B has become a recipient of new, excess reserves, and so it can expand its liabilities. The overall result so far is a zero net change in the supply of inside money, since Y's increased holdings precisely offset the reduction of demand on the part of X.

Now, however, we must consider the second step of the loan repayment process, in which Y withdraws his new deposit by writing a check to his bank in repayment of a loan that was previously granted to him. This is identical to what happens when unwanted liabilities are used directly to repay loans from their original issuer. It leads to the extinction of the liabilities, with no possibility for offsetting expansion by the bank to which they are repaid. Thus when unwanted liabilities from Bank A are used to repay loans from Bank B, the overall result is an extinction of Bank A's liabilities to the extent of the fall in demand with no offsetting increase (of any significant duration) in the supply of liabilities from Bank B or from any other bank.

The processes described here can once again be generalized for the case of an all-around reduction in the demand for inside money. In this case there is an increase in the rate of turnover (or velocity) of bank liabilities, which means that bank clearing assets have to "turn over" more rapidly as well. In other words, the liquidity needs of the banking system increase, and an existing volume of reserves can no longer support the same amount of inside money. Therefore assets and liabilities must contract, and the reserve multiplier falls. Once again the explanation of reserve demands involved in this generalization must wait until the next chapter.

Thus the capacity of free banks to maintain equilibrium applies also to conditions where the demand for inside money is changing. This result is just an extension of the static rule of excess reserves since it rests on the demonstration, to be completed in the next chapter, that the overall availability of excess reserves (or conversely the overall excess demand for reserves) is a function of the aggregate demand for inside money. It does *not* apply to systems with monopolized currency issue: adjustments in the money supply in such systems have to be achieved, assuming they can be achieved at all, by deliberate policy. The possibilities for controlling the money supply by means of central banking will be critically examined in chapters 7 and 8. Prior to this, though, it is necessary to examine certain common ideas concerning reserve requirements that might cast doubt upon the conclusions just arrived at.

6

Economic Reserve Requirements

THE FINDING THAT free banks will maintain monetary equilibrium even as the demand for money changes rests upon the claim that the reserve multiplier alters in sympathy with changes in the demand for inside money. Many conventional discussions contradict this claim. Some treat the reserve multiplier as an institutionally given constant, rather than as a variable that adjusts in response to changes in the public's behavior and in response to bankers' reactions to changes in the public's behavior. Others go to the opposite extreme and hold the reserve multiplier to be, in some situations at least, indeterminate. The purpose of this chapter is to show that both of these alternative views are, for a free banking system, incorrect.

The Conservation Theory

The view that the reserve multiplier is a constant may be dubbed the "conservation theory" of bank money.[1] It concurs that an *individual* bank may expand or contract credit as a result of persons holding greater or lesser amounts of its liabilities. But it denies that *system-wide* expansions or contractions of the money supply can happen in response to changes in aggregate demand: individual banks may gain or lose business relative to one another, but gains by some banks are always compensated by losses of other banks.[2] As long as the reserve base is unchanged, the system as a whole will support only a certain amount of inside money—no more, no less.[3]

The conservation theory looks upon the volume of liabilities in a banking system as if it were like the volume of water in a waterbed. A little pressure on one part of the waterbed reduces the amount of water there but causes an equal increase in its amount somewhere else. Likewise, a fall in the demand for one bank's liabilities is supposed to cause that bank to contract, but only with the accompanying effect of an offsetting shift of reserves and lending power to other banks. In contrast, an increase in supply of one bank's liabilities is held to be possible only if its rivals contract.

In money and banking literature the conservation theory is generally expressed in terms of bank deposits only, since competitive note issue is rarely discussed. John Philip Wernette's argument (1933, 32) that "an effective thrift campaign cannot increase the total deposits of an entire banking system" is typical:

> If A is persuaded to reduce his expenditures on consumers' goods below his cash income, and to build up a bank deposit with the difference, A's Hoarding is matched by an equivalent amount of Dis-hoarding on the part of other persons. Their bank balances decrease as A's increases; the total deposits are not changed by A's action. A's bank, by its thrift campaign, may thus succeed in increasing its deposits; but only by drawing on the deposits of other banks.

Another example is George Clayton. Although he concedes that banks may respond positively to growing demands for inside money in the early stages of their development, Clayton denies that this is possible in the "developed stage" of banking. He states that the "immobilization" of part of a bank's liabilities as the result of deposits "left inactive at the bank . . . does not put the bank in a position to lend or invest any more money than before."[4] Thus deflation, according to Clayton (1955, 98), "can only be overcome by a deliberate policy of credit expansion under the direction of the central bank, which would have to provide the extra cash reserves necessary to maintain the [reserve] ratio." Other theorists have made similar statements denying the possibility of a general *contraction* of inside money given a fixed amount of bank reserves.

The problem with the conservation theory is that it miscomprehends the forces that determine banks' need for reserves. It assumes that this need depends only on the amount of banks' outstanding liabilities and not on the demand for these liabilities relative to income as it affects their turnover.[5] This error may stem from conservation theorists' identification of economic reserve requirements with *statutory* reserve requirements. These are legally prescribed, minimum ratios of reserves to total liabilities. Obviously statutory reserve requirements are institutionally "given," and they set an upward limit to the reserve multiplier. But statutory reserve requirements do not exist in all central banking systems, and are absent from a free banking system. Under free banking, reserve requirements are determined by the optimizing decisions of bankers. They are *economic*, rather than statutory, requirements. Granting this, the critical questions become, what factors determine a free bank's economic reserve demand?[6] and will this reserve demand necessarily be a constant fraction of a bank's total outstanding liabilities?

Determinants of Reserve Demand

A free bank's economic reserve demand for any planning period can be thought of as having two components. These are, first, a component equal to what the bank, because of the structure of its assets and liabilities, anticipates will be the difference between its total clearing debits and its total clearing credits for the period—its "average net reserve demand"—and, second, a component to cover the bank against any adverse clearings it may face during the planning period that (singly or cumulatively) exceed its average net reserve demand. The latter component is the bank's "precautionary reserve demand."[7] It protects the bank, not from such adverse clearings as might be predicted given a determinate structure of the demand for the bank's liabilities, but from temporary, random fluctuations in these adverse clearings above their expected value. A bank that fails to hold precautionary reserves might, on average, have credit clearings equal to its debit clearings, so that its average net reserve demand would be zero. Yet the bank would stand a great risk (one chance in two in fact) of being unable to redeem all its debits at the clearinghouse during any particular clearing session if it held zero reserves. It follows that banks have to hold positive precautionary reserves so long as the exact incidence of clearing debits is unknowable or uncertain,[8] and even though they may have no reason to doubt that their clearing debits and credits will be equal in the long run.[9]

Both of these components of a free bank's reserve demand are related to the total clearing debits it faces, and not necessarily to the total of its outstanding liabilities. Moreover, the quantity of a bank's liabilities returned to it through the clearing mechanism depends just as much on their average turnover as on the quantity of them outstanding. Thus, to take the limiting case, additional liabilities with zero turnover would not add to an expanding bank's reserve demand, and contraction of zero turnover liabilities by a bank would not add to its excess reserves. On the other hand, a bank's reserve demand may increase even though it has not expanded its liabilities, because turnover of its liabilities has increased. Finally, a bank's reserve needs may fall although its liabilities are unchanged because the average period the public holds its liabilities has increased.

In long-run equilibrium the average net reserve demand for every bank in a system with a fixed supply of reserve media has to be zero. A bank cannot continue to suffer a positive average net reserve demand without eventually disappearing, and it cannot have a continuously negative average net reserve demand unless it fails to exploit fully the demand to hold its liabilities and hence its lending power. Profit-maximizing banks will strive to adjust their outstanding liabilities to compensate for demand-induced changes in their net clearing debits so as to keep their average net reserve demand equal to zero: a bank that expects to acquire more reserves than it expects to lose during a planning period (because the demand to hold its liabilities has increased) will expand its loans and investments to make up the difference; one that expects to lose more than it gains (because the demand to hold its liabilities has fallen) will contract. A bank that does not adjust its issues when faced with changes in the demand for them is in no less unprofitable a position in relation to its rivals than one that overexpands or underexpands relative to its rivals when faced with an unchanged demand for inside money.

Does extending this conclusion to the banking *system* and hence to adjustments in aggregate liabilities involve a fallacy of composition? It does not, because expansion by any one bank in response to reduced clearing debits against it does not, in the case of an increased demand for (reduced turnover of) its liabilities, involve any reduction of the reserves or lending power of rival banks. Indeed, such expansion actually *prevents* the redistribution of reserves that would occur if the supply of inside money were not adjusted in response to demand. The same holds for credit contractions by individual banks when these contractions serve to maintain an equilibrium of supply and demand for their liabilities.

Uniform Changes in Money Demand

What has just been said refers only to actions brought about by banks' desire to maintain zero long-run net average reserve demand, that is, by their need to remain in equilibrium in relation to one another. It leaves a very crucial issue unaddressed—an issue that is sometimes raised in connection with the conservation theory. Granted that particular banks may contract or expand the aggregate sum of bank liabilities to stay in line with other banks in the face of changing demands for their liabilities only, what incentive can there be for system-wide expansion or contraction when all banks are confronted by equal and simultaneous changes in the demand for their issues? For example, if there is a general fall in the demand for inside money that uniformly raises the gross clearings of all banks no single bank will suffer a deficiency of average net reserves. Each will have its debit and credit clearings increase in equal amounts, with no change in adverse clearings. Similarly, if all banks witness equal increases in the demand for their issues, none will feel a need to expand in so far as the only motivation to do so is to prevent excess reserves (due to positive clearings) from accumulating.

Obviously banks have no incentive to contract or to expand under such circumstances if their only motivation for doing so is to keep in step with one another; they are already in step, and a uniform increase in inside-money demand will not put any of them out of it. Does it follow, therefore, that under such conditions the banks do nothing, so that the conservation theory is correct?

The answer is an emphatic "no." Forces operate in a free banking system to make the supply of inside money adjust to changes in demand even when such changes fall upon the banks simultaneously and uniformly. The reason for this has to do with the precautionary demand for reserves. Unlike the average net demand for reserves, the precautionary demand *is* affected by unaccommodated, uniform changes in the demand for inside money. The reasons for this are discussed in detail in the literature on precautionary reserve demand, beginning with Edgeworth's pioneering article.[10] The essential conclusion of this literature, based on the law of large numbers, is that the precautionary demand for reserves rises or falls along with changes in the total volume of gross bank clearings, though not necessarily in strict proportion to the change in gross clearings. Specifically, a uniform increase in the total volume of clearing debits due to an increase in the frequency of payments (such as would occur if there were an across-the-board fall in the demand for inside money with income constant) requires that precautionary reserves increase by a factor at least equal to the square root of the factor by which clearings have increased. A fall in the total volume of clearings will likewise lead to a fall in the demand for precautionary reserves.[11]

This result can be represented by a set of simple diagrams (Fig. 6.1) showing the frequency distribution of clearing debits at a representative bank before and after a doubling of the total volume of clearings. The smoothness of the diagrams implies a fairly long planning period with many clearing sessions; one might also interpret them as showing the statistical likelihood of particular net clearings based on a large number of trials. The doubling of gross clearings doubles the scale of the horizontal axis of the frequency-distribution diagram. Because of the law of large numbers, however, the distribution becomes more concentrated at its center and the variance increases, but by less than the increase in the scale of clearings.

The intuition behind the square-root result is fairly simple. As the volume of gross clearings increases, so do random fluctuations in

Figure 6.1

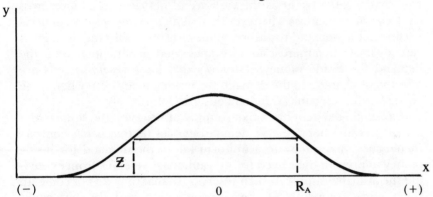

1. Total Gross Clearings = A

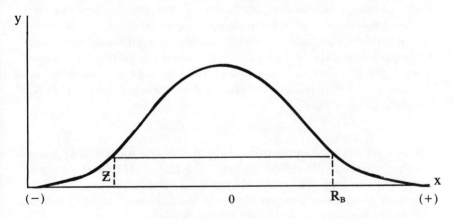

2. Total Gross Clearings = B = 2 × A

x = Clearing Balance ($)

y = Total Clearings ($) associated with
particular values of x

$\mathbb{Z}$ = Maximum Tolerable Default Risk

$R_{A,B}$ = Reserve Demand ($)

their distribution among the banks—the source of variance of net clearings faced by individual banks—only less than in proportion. This comes directly from the laws of probability. Since precautionary reserves are held against deviations of average net demand from its mean or expected value, it follows that precautionary reserve demand rises by the same factor as the variance of net clearings. Since gross bank clearings increase whenever there is an uncompensated, general decline in the demand for inside money (income constant), and gross clearings fall when there is an uncompensated, general increase in the demand for inside money, it follows that bank reserve needs are affected by changes in the demand for inside money even when these changes affect all banks simultaneously and uniformly.

If a banking system has a fixed supply of reserves, the square-root law of precautionary reserve demand implies (a) that banks contract their issues in response to a uniform fall in the demand for inside money to prevent their need for precautionary reserves from exceeding the available supply of such reserves (so that they do not come up short more frequently at the clearinghouse); and (b) that banks expand their issues in response to a uniform increase in the demand for inside money so that the aggregate demand for precautionary reserves does not fall short of the available supply.[12]

Algebraically, $R^d = f(\sigma_G^2) = f[h(G)]$ with f' and $h' > 0$, where R^d is the optimum (minimum) precautionary reserve demand for the banking system, and σ_G^2 is a measure of the variance of net clearings for a representative bank around their mean of zero for some level of gross bank clearings, G. In a state of monetary equilibrium, for some given price level, income and gross bank clearings are still positive. Let this monetary-equilibrium value of gross clearings be equal to N. Then, more generally,

$$G = N + \lambda (IM^s - IM^d)$$

where $\lambda > 0$,[13] IM^s is the nominal supply of inside money, IM^d is the nominal demand for inside money, and $IM^s - IM^d$ is the excess supply of (or negative excess demand for) inside money. Thus G increases when there is excess supply of inside money, and falls when there is excess demand for inside money. Since

$$R^d = f\left\{h\left[N + \lambda(IM^s - IM^d)\right]\right\}$$

it follows that R^d also increases whenever there is excess supply of inside money, and that R^d falls whenever there is excess demand for inside money. If available reserves, R^s, are fixed, then any change in R^d causing it to differ for R^s must be offset by an appropriate adjustment of IM^s (assuming IM^d is exogenous).

The square-root law of precautionary reserve demand assumes that bank clearings rise or fall due to changes in the *frequency* of payments. The total volume of clearings may also rise or fall because of an increase or decrease in the average *size* of individual payments where the frequency of payments is constant. This results in an increase in precautionary reserve demand proportional to the increase in bank clearings.[14] Though this possibility gives further strength to most of the conclusions just arrived at, it also points to a potential cause of monetary disequilibrium under free banking. Consider a situation where the volume of gross bank clearings per week is $1 million, consisting of 100,000 checks with an average value of ten dollars. Now suppose that bank customers alter their spending habits by writing only 50,000 checks per week with an average value of twenty dollars. The weekly volume of gross bank clearings is still $1 million, but the smaller number of larger, "lumpier" payments leads to an increased precautionary demand for bank reserves. The tendency (given a fixed volume of reserves) is, therefore, for the supply of inside money to fall. Yet the change in the public's spending habits reflects, not a smaller, but a greater demand for money balances. So the money supply, rather than adjusting in the same direction as the demand for money (as it does when average payment size is unchanging and the volume of clearings moves inversely with the demand for money) adjusts in the opposite direction.

That this is a potential defect of free banking cannot be denied. But it is unlikely to be of great practical importance. This becomes apparent if one considers that changes in the average size of payments are usually accompanied by changes in frequency in the same direction, in which case their effect is to *reinforce* demand-accommodating changes in money supply. The exceptional case, where the frequency and average size of payments move in opposite directions, is only likely to occur in response to a change in the general level of prices which is not itself a consequence of monetary disequilibrium. In this case a real balance effect might lead to a change in frequency of payments opposite the change in average payment size. The scope for this kind of price-level change under free banking is rather limited. Suppose though, for the sake of argument, that such a price-level change *did* occur, causing a disequilibrating change in the supply of inside money. The disequilibrium would be short lived, because its effect would be to reverse the movement in prices that set it in motion to begin with.

Thus the potential damage from disequilibrium money-supply changes under free banking is likely to be very slight. To the extent that such changes could occur, their effect would be to counter somewhat the already limited potential for changes in the general price structure under free banking (such as when there is a general change in productive efficiency per capita). This should be kept in mind in later chapters where the special possibility considered here is ignored and it is assumed that the structure of prices adjusts fully under free banking to reflect changes in productive efficiency.

Variability of the Reserve Multiplier

The variability of reserve demand implies that, under free banking, the reserve ratio (the ratio of reserves to demand liabilities) would vary considerably from bank to bank and also within individual banks viewed at different points of time. Other things being equal, a bank would operate with a lower reserve ratio when the demand for its liabilities is greater and vice versa. For the banking system, in turn, the reserve multiplier (the number of units of inside money supported, in the aggregate, by a unit of outside money) would increase with increases in aggregate demand for inside money balances, and would decrease when aggregate demand for inside money balances decreases (holding the number of banks and their market shares constant).

These results show the conservation theory to be invalid for a free banking system. Moreover, they suggest that it is invalid even for a system with monopolized currency supply (which is less able to accommodate changes in demand) and even where statutory reserve requirements exist. Empirical research supports this. In the United States figures for excess reserves held by banks constantly change, and some economists have even recommended that statutory requirements be modified to reflect the diverse and continually changing turnover rates of liabilities of various banks—with higher requirements for banks with greater deposit turnover. Thus Neil Jacoby (1963, 218–19) recommends that "the legal reserve requirement of an individual bank should be proportional to the contribution of its depositors to the aggregate demand for the total national product." In this way "banks whose deposits turned over rapidly would be required to carry a higher reserve per dollar of deposit balances than banks with a low deposit turnover."[15] The effect of such proposals, not acknowledged by their authors, would be to have statutory reserve requirements mimic their economic or voluntary counterparts in an unregulated system. Examples of this already exist in the United States. Lower statutory reserve requirements are imposed on certain classes of time deposits than on demand deposits, presumably because time liabilities turn over less rapidly. This arrangement approximates the actual liquidity needs for different kinds of deposits, which implies that, in a deregulated system, it would be at best superfluous.

In a comparative survey of 12 nations Joachim Ahrensdorf and S. Kanesthasan also observed money multipliers that varied substantially over time and from country to country.[16] They claim that variations in money multipliers were responses to changes in the behavior of the public, and not simply to changes in the demand for currency relative to total money demand which (under systems with monopolized currency supply) would alter the supply of bank reserves.[17]

Despite all this there is some justification for accepting the conservation theory as an approximate, though flawed, description of conditions under monopolized currency issue, even in systems without statutory reserve requirements. The reason is that, with a limited supply of high-powered money available to them, the deposit banks are limited in their ability to accommodate increases in the demand for money that involve increases in the demand for currency. The reserve multiplier in a monopolized system, given a constant supply of base money, has an imposed upper limit. Accommodative credit expansion depends on additions to the supply of base money to meet increased needs for currency in circulation. It cannot be accomplished by deposit banks acting alone except when increases in the demand for deposit balances are unassociated with any increase in currency demand.[18]

For these and other reasons traditional banking studies devote very little attention to the possibility of demand-induced changes in the supply of inside money. Most ignore this possibility entirely.[19] Their focus is on supply-side driven changes in the quantity of inside money: changes caused by the injection or withdrawal of sums of high-powered money to and from deposit bank reserves. The chain of causation they consider runs from (a) expansion or contraction of the issues of the monopoly bank to (b) multiple expansion or contraction of deposit bank liabilities (via an institutionally fixed reserve multiplier) to (c) increased or decreased nominal income and prices to (d) increased or decreased nominal demand for inside money and, finally, to (e) monetary equilibrium with nominal variables scaled up or down in the same proportion as the quantity of high-powered money.

However appropriate this approach may be for describing monopolized or central banking, it is unsuitable for describing credit expansion under free banking. Here demand-responsive changes in the supply of inside money are the rule rather than the exception. The relevant chain of causation generally runs from (a) changes in demand for inside money to (b) expansion or contraction to (c) a de facto change in the reserve multiplier and to (d) monetary equilibrium with *no* change in nominal prices or income. For example, consider a hypothetical free banking system with commodity-money reserves of $1000. The supply of inside money is $50,000 and this is, initially, the amount desired by the public. The reserve multiplier has a value of 50. Now imagine that the demand for inside money falls $10,000 to $40,000. As a result, bank demand liabilities contract $10,000, and the reserve multiplier falls to 40; that is, the final, aggregate ratio of reserves to demand liabilities rises from 2 to 2.5 percent.[20]

Of course there may also be supply-side driven changes in the quantity of inside money under free banking stemming, for example, from increases in the quantity of outside (commodity) money. The historical significance of such outside-money supply changes will be discussed later in chapter 9. For now it will suffice to note that commodity-money supply shocks have been of only minor historical significance as compared with shocks due to fluctuations in supplies of base monies caused by central banks.

Credit Expansion "in Concert"

The arguments used here to criticize the theory that the reserve multiplier is rigidly fixed also refute the view that the reserve multiplier is, under certain circumstances, indeterminate. That view is implicit in the argument that, with a fixed reserve supply, if banks expand in concert none suffer negative effects even if the expansion is not warranted by any increase in the demand for money.

Eugene A. Agger provides a very clear statement of the indeterminate-multiplier idea:

> In [the] case of a general expansion there is no check as far as the individual community is concerned. The expansion of a given bank results, it is true, in a larger volume of debit items at the clearing house, but, if the expansion is general, a particular bank will in all probability receive as deposits a larger volume of checks on the other clearing house banks, and these checks act as an offset to its own debits. While expansion for a single bank tends to increase debits at the clearinghouse, *general* expansion increases credits as well. Under general expansion the balance may remain practically undisturbed and the net result may be simply an enlarged business on a smaller volume of reserve.[21]

Thus the system as a whole is supposedly able to expand, on the basis of a fixed supply of reserves, not merely in response to a general increase in the demand for inside money (as was argued in the previous section) but also if demand does *not* increase.

Keynes takes a similar position in his *Treatise on Money*:

> Every movement forward by an individual bank weakens it but every such movement by one of its neighbors strengthens it; so that if all move

forward together no one is weakened on balance . . . Each bank chairman sitting in his parlour may regard himself as the passive instrument of outside forces over which he has no control; yet the 'outside forces' may be nothing but himself and his fellow chairmen, and certainly not his depositors.[22]

Two more examples of this view are especially interesting since they refer specifically to free-banking arrangements. The first concerns the note-clearing system supervised by the Suffolk Bank. The author writes that arrangements of this sort "keep the various banks more or less in step with one another in their emission of notes, but would not [prevent] them from preceding too fast (or too slowly) as a whole":

> Any given bank would tend to restrict its operations in order that the amount of its notes and other obligations presented at the clearinghouse would not be larger than the obligations of other banks it could present. But if all the banks [were] continually expanding loans and continually emitting fresh notes [then] any single bank would have larger quantities of notes of other banks coming into its possession and could well afford to have larger amounts of its own notes presented for redemption [Anderson 1926, 48–49].

The second example is taken from Lawrence H. White's analysis of the Scottish free banking system: "Supposing [a] group of banks expand by a common factor, no consequent adverse clearings will arise among members of the group. Adverse clearings will not arise among a group of banks in consequence of whatever degree of expansion is common to all."[23] If the group comprises a closed system, White continues (1984d, 18), then only an internal drain of reserves to meet the public's desired commodity-money holdings acts as a check on expansion. Later in his book White notes that "no important theorist of the Free Banking School" explicitly denied the theoretical possibility of in-concert overexpansion by banks in an unregulated system.[24] Nevertheless most of them "found the scenario of coordinated expansion implausible as a description of actual events."[25]

Even if one grants, following members of the Free Banking School, that in-concert overexpansion is improbable, one might still question whether the supply of inside money under free banking adjusts properly to changes in demand for it. The previous section showed why banks as a group tend to respond positively to a uniform change in demand—refuting the fixed-multiplier view. But we must also confront the possibility that in such a situation the banks can not only respond but can respond to any extent they desire, so long as they act in common. What is to prevent them, furthermore, from "responding" when there is no change in demand at all?

Once again the difficulty is resolved by considering the determinants of precautionary reserve demand. Under in-concert expansion no member of a system of banks expanding in unison (and in the face of an unchanged demand for money) will experience any increase in its *average* net reserve demand; the change in expected value of its clearing credits will be exactly equal to the change in expected value of its clearing debits. But the growth in total clearings will bring about a growth (though perhaps less than proportionate) in the *variance* of clearing debits and credits, which increases the precautionary reserve needs of every bank. Thus, given the quantity of reserve media, the demand for and turnover of inside money, and the desire of banks to protect themselves against all but a very small risk of default at the clearinghouse at any clearing session, there will be a unique equilibrium supply of inside money at any moment. It follows that spontaneous in-concert expansions will be self-correcting even without any "internal drain" of commodity money from bank reserves.

Banks as Pure Intermediaries

This and the preceding chapter have attempted to show that, even in the face of changes in the demand for inside money, free banks help to maintain monetary equilibrium. They passively adjust the supply of inside money to changes in the demand for it. They are credit transferers or intermediaries, and not credit creators.

In light of this, and granting appropriate assumptions (namely, a fixed stock of commodity money, with no demand for its use in balances of the public), what can be said about banks in a system with monopolized note issue? A monopoly bank of issue is clearly *not* a pure intermediary, since the principle of adverse clearings does not apply to it. The position of deposit banks in a system where the supply of currency is monopolized is more complicated. They can respond by a multiplicative expansion to any issues by the monopoly bank that exceed the public's pre-existing demand for currency. Since such expansion is a response to the exogenous actions of the monopoly bank and not to any change in the money-holding behavior of the public, it involves "created" credit and is disequilibrating. Similarly, if the monopoly bank of issue contracts its issue in excess of any fall in the public's demand for currency, a multiplicative, disequilibrating reduction in the supply of deposit money will result.

But what role do deposit banks play in the absence of any expansion or contraction by the monopoly bank of issue? In this context deposit banks are more like free banks and other "pure intermediaries": they cannot, generally speaking, engage in disequilibrating expansion or contraction of the money supply. There are two exceptions to this: First, insofar as the public wish to save in part by holding greater balances of currency, deposit banks are, beyond a certain point, powerless to accommodate their wants without assistance from the monopoly bank. They can issue currency from the monopoly bank held in their reserves only by sacrificing liquidity. Second, changes in the public's relative demand for currency (i.e., shifts from deposit holding to currency holding and vice-versa) are disequilibrating: they alter the supply of high-powered money available in deposit-bank reserves, and so affect lending power and the total supply of deposit money even though the overall demand for inside money (though not its division between notes and deposits) is unchanged.

Chapter 8 will discuss problems caused by changes in the demand for currency under monopolized issue in some detail. But first, given the conclusions just reached, let us compare our view—that deposit banks are intermediaries of credit—with views of other writers on this subject. J. Carl Poindexter (1946) and James Tobin (1963) have held similar beliefs, as did Edwin Cannan in his much-derided "cloak-room" theory (1921). Cannan denied that bankers are any more capable of lending more than is offered to them than cloakroom clerks are capable of "creating" hats and umbrellas. "The banker," he wrote, "is able to lend X, Y, and Z more than his own capital because A, B, and C are allowing him the temporary use of some of theirs on condition that he will let them have what they want when they ask for it" (ibid., 32).

Cannan seemed unaware, however, that *monopoly* banks of issue *can* create credit by creating new reserves, which throw deposit banks out of equilibrium in their holdings of monopoly-bank liabilities. Tobin, in contrast, recognizes a difference between possibilities for overexpansion of "bank-created" money and those for overexpansion of "government" money. "The community," he writes (1963, 415), "cannot get rid of" an excess supply of the latter. Therefore "the 'hot-potato' analogy truly applies." On the other hand, "for bank-created money . . . there is an economic mechanism of extinction as well as creation, contraction as well as expansion. . . . The burden of adaptation is not placed entirely on the rest of the community." Furthermore, for deposit banks acting alone the possibility of credit expansion "depends on whether somewhere in the chain of transactions initiated by the borrowers' outlays are found depositors who wish to hold new deposits equal in amount to the new loan" (ibid., 413). This is very close to our own view, allowing for the two provisos with regard to currency supply, except that Tobin's category of "government" money should really include all money issued by any bank with a monopoly in currency supply, whether the bank is officially a government bank or nominally a private one.

Poindexter's analysis of the role of deposit banks, although less well known than those of Cannan and Tobin, is in some ways superior. Unlike Cannan, Poindexter is fully aware of the credit-creating powers of central banks of issue. But regarding deposit banks he writes (1946, 142): "It is merely the fact that they are at the institutional center of the credit-creating and credit-destroying process of the community that gives their role the apparently unique character which is commonly imputed to them." In fact, Poindexter argues, deposit banks, like other private competitive financial institutions, cannot lend beyond what their depositors desire unless the central bank that operates alongside them alters the "data" of the system, to which they respond (ibid., 143–44). Otherwise deposit banks are merely "the institutional media through which the public determines the volume of bank deposit currency which will be created at any given moment" (ibid., 142).

Controversy has surrounded the views of J.G. Gurley and E. S. Shaw, who first argued, in a series of articles,[26] that banks always function as pure intermediaries—responding through profit signals to the wants of the public—and who later modified their position and claimed that banks and non-bank financial firms alike are equally capable of active credit creation.[27]

The error of these authors' earlier writings lay in their use of an *ex post* definition of savings. This approach failed to distinguish properly individuals' voluntary abstinence from purchasing from their involuntary abstinence due to forced saving. "Pure intermediation" should refer to credit operations based on voluntary savings only.[28]

The early Gurley and Shaw view does not really differ from Cannan's "cloakroom" approach, which also failed to recognize that *certain kinds* of banks, namely those having a monopoly or quasi-monopoly in the issue of currency, can indeed create credit, and that deposit banks also could contribute to this credit creation by responding to changes in their holdings of high-powered money having its source in unwarranted issues by a privileged bank.

In their later work, on *Banking in a Theory of Finance*, Gurley and Shaw commit the even more serious error of claiming that *all* financial institutions are equally capable of actively creating credit. Because of its failure to recognize the role of monopoly banks of issue as the ultimate source of created credit this view has served as a rationale for maintaining legal restrictions on credit expansion by deposit banks and for imposing similar restrictions on savings institutions and other non-bank financial intermediaries.[29] Such restrictions not only interfere with efficient intermediation, but reinforce the erroneous notion that competitive financial firms are independent sources of inflation, which the central bank has to "control."

Students of banking theory often get the impression that central banks are uniquely capable of preventing monetary disequilibrium: they are not inclined to think of them as throwing a wrench in the works. Yet, in contrast to deposit banks and to banks in a free banking system, central banks (or any bank with a monopoly or quasi-monopoly in currency supply) have a unique capacity for *generating* monetary disturbances. The question that has to be asked, therefore, is whether the disturbances central banks perhaps prevent outweigh the disturbances they cause that would otherwise not occur.

PART THREE

Free Banking
versus
Central Banking

7

The Dilemma of Central Banking

IF FREE BANKING did not promote a well-behaved money supply, there would be little to gain from harping on the defects of central banking. Few deny that central banks do a less than satisfactory job in controlling the money supply. But this fact, and the fact that some of the shortcomings of central banking are inherent in the institution itself, is only worth investigating if some potentially superior alternative to central banking exists.

The possibility of free banking justifies a critical appraisal of central banking. This chapter presents such an appraisal. It begins with a brief, general comparison of markets and centralized planning as means for directing the use of scarce resources. Emphasis is placed on the importance to proper resource administration of knowledge of conditions of supply and demand that is limited, dispersed, and unarticulated. The results of this discussion of the "knowledge problem" are then related to the issue of the choice between free and central banking. The chapter ends by criticizing particular central banking policies, which are attempts to overcome the knowledge problem as it confronts central bankers.

The Knowledge Problem

The goal of economic action is to employ scarce consumption goods and means of production in a way that minimizes foregone opportunities. Consumers have wants, some of which are more pressing than others, and not all of which can be satisfied by means of the limited resources available. Consumers' wants also change frequently, as do the conditions of factor supply and the technological possibilities for combining factors of production to make consumer and

89

capital goods. The economical administration of resources depends on agents being aware of changing priorities, endowments, and techniques of production.

The problem of resource administration is complicated by the fact that the knowledge relevant to its solution is divided among numerous individuals. No single person or bureau can hope to accumulate any significant part of it. This is especially true of consumers' knowledge of their own preferences, which is mainly confidential and unarticulated. But knowledge of the state of technology and natural resources is also atomistic; it remains, in the words of F. A. Hayek (1948b, 80), "knowledge of the particular circumstances of time and place," existing only as "dispersed bits" (ibid., 77). Thus, harnessing knowledge for the economic administration of resources, the "knowledge problem," is challenging, not only because of the extent of relevant knowledge, but also because of the form in which it is held. As Thomas Sowell notes (1980, 217–18),

> It is not merely the enormous amount of data that exceeds the capacity of the human mind. Conceivably, this data might be stored in a computer with sufficient capacity. The real problem is that the knowledge needed is a knowledge of *subjective patterns of trade-off that are nowhere articulated*, not even to the individual himself. I might *think* that, if faced with the stark prospect of bankruptcy, I would rather sell my automobile than my furniture, or sacrifice the refrigerator rather than the stove, but unless and until such a moment comes, I will never *know* even my own trade-offs, much less anybody else's. There is no way for such information to be fed into a computer, when no one has such information in the first place.

That conditions of supply and demand continually change is an essential aspect of the problem of resource administration, since it means that, even if the relevant knowledge were accessible, it would have to be acquired rapidly before it ceased to be relevant.

In noncentralized economies the economic administration of resources is achieved by and large through the interaction of persons in competitive markets. Entrepreneurs, referring to price and profit signals established through rivalrous buying and selling of goods and services, are led to administer supplies as if they had direct knowledge of the state of consumer preferences. Yet even the totality of entrepreneurs engaged in production and exchange in any particular market do not possess the knowledge that would be needed by a central planning agency put in place of them and in place of that market:

> Prices convey the experience and subjective feelings of some as *effective* knowledge to others; it is implicit knowledge in the form of an explicit

inducement. Price fluctuations convey knowledge of changing trade-offs among changing options as people weigh costs and benefits differently over time, with changes in tastes or technology. The totality of knowledge conveyed by the innumerable prices and their widely varying rates of change vastly exceeds what any individual can know or needs to know for his own purposes [ibid., 167].

The price system assists entrepreneurship in two ways. First, it provides information directly. This is the *ex ante* function of market prices: their contribution towards entrepreneurs' recognition of the existing state of market conditions. This *ex ante* function of market prices is emphasized by F. A. Hayek in his essay on "The Use of Knowledge in Society." Hayek considers the tin market as a case in point:

> Assume that somewhere in the world a new opportunity for the use of [tin] has arisen, or that one of the sources of supply of tin has been eliminated. It does not matter for our purpose—and it is significant that it does not matter—which of these two causes has made tin more scarce. All that the users of tin need to know is that some of the tin they used to consume is now more profitably employed elsewhere and that, in consequence, they must economize tin. There is no need for the great majority of them even to know where the more urgent need has arisen, or in favor of what other needs they ought to husband the supply [1948b, 85–86].

Available tin will, at a higher price, continue to be used only where the need for it is considered most urgent by its users. Less urgent uses will employ tin substitutes, which in turn will cause an increase in production of these substitutes. The existence of a market price for tin "brings about the solution which . . . might have been arrived at by one single mind possessing all the information which is in fact dispersed among all the people involved in the process" (ibid.). What Hayek stresses here is the ability of prices, or rather price movements, to convey knowledge of changes in *existing* conditions so that entrepreneurs will direct their actions accordingly.

The problem of economic resource administration is not, however, merely one of disseminating knowledge of existing conditions. Nor is the solution of this part of the problem the sole contribution of market prices. Economic administration of resources ultimately depends upon correct anticipation of conditions (for example, consumer preferences) of the *future*. Information describing present conditions is only partially adequate for this task. When conditions are continually changing, and when the future is unpredictable, decision makers must speculate, and their speculations may be incorrect even though they are based on the most complete information conceivable. In other words, decisions may be inadequately informed.

This need not be due to any incorrect (as opposed to insufficient) information, from price signals or from other sources; it is a necessary consequence of the inherent uncertainty of future conditions combined with the fact that action takes time. For this reason no administrative or entrepreneurial decision can be regarded as perfectly informed *ex ante*. It follows that decision makers must also be informed *ex post* of the appropriateness of their actions, and that they should be informed as quickly as possible.

Fortunately, the same price signals that inform decision makers in competitive markets of changing conditions of supply and demand also help them evaluate their actions *ex post*. Market prices, including prices reflecting entrepreneurs' *incorrect* speculations, ultimately determine the profitability of entrepreneurial ventures. (In contrast, in their *ex ante* role, prices are used to inform profitability *estimates* for projects not yet undertaken.) Suppose the problem is to supply the market for neckties. Will consumers buy wide or narrow ties? Where are their preferences headed? No available information can give a certain answer. The only knowledge to be communicated, by prices or otherwise, is knowledge of the preferences of the present or, more accurately, of the immediate past. The entrepreneur has to speculate about the future state of the necktie market. Market prices afterwards will assist him in determining whether his speculations were correct. If he misjudges the wants of consumers, that is, if he employs factors of production in a manner inconsistent with the priorities of consumers, his error will lead to an accounting loss. If, on the other hand, he correctly anticipates consumer wants, he will be awarded by profits. The incidence of profit and loss will, in the words of Israel Kirzner (1984, 200), "systematically bring about improved sets of market conditions." In helping to "stimulate the revision of initially uncoordinated decisions in the direction of greater mutual coordinatedness" (ibid., 201), profit and loss calculations based on market prices function as *ex post* guides to speculative decision making.

To summarize, prices communicate changing knowledge of market conditions and thus inform speculation; but when they enter into entrepreneurs' calculations of profit and loss, they also reveal whether or not earlier speculations were correct, and so they guide action even where knowledge relevant to its success, knowledge of *future* market conditions, is in principle unavailable to anyone before the fact.

The price system can be likened to a tapestry in which holes are always appearing but which continually patches itself. The tapestry represents the (dispersed and inarticulate) knowledge concerning conditions of supply and demand translated into price signals through processes of exchange. The holes represent the uncertainty inherent in decision making. The tapestry is self-patching because a current set of prices, while indicating actual changes in economic conditions, also generates profits and losses that signify a need to modify entrepreneurial plans informed by a previous set of prices.[1] Price and profit signals are not just "communicators" of knowledge, but knowledge "surrogates." The significance of knowledge surrogates lies not just in the use they make of data that exist somewhere, but also in their ability to compensate for data that (when first needed) do not exist at all.

Advocates of centralized resource administration commonly fail to appreciate the dynamic, speculative nature of economic action and the corresponding need for *ex post* guidance of allocative decisions. The central planner is also a speculator: he cannot escape the uncertainty of the future no matter how much data he collects concerning existing conditions, which are constantly changing. What he needs is not merely present data but also some basis for assessing rapidly the correctness of his imperfectly informed decisions.

The principal *ex post* device available to central planners anxious to identify and correct their mistakes is not profit and loss accounting, which depends on market prices, but the observation of various disequilibrium consequences of misguided decisons. Typically, shortages or surpluses of commodities are taken as signals justifying a revision of plans, but the concepts of shortage and surplus, divorced from any reference to cost and profit calculations based on freely adjusting market prices, are arbitrary. Supermarket queues and overflowing inventories give some account of how production and consumer preferences are mismatched, but not as reliable, timely, or systematic an account as is conveyed to entrepreneurs by price and profit signals.[2] The central planner is not driven to produce goods at minimum cost, that is, with a minimum of foregone opportunities, which is what systematic avoidance of shortages and surpluses implies, because the knowledge available to him does not adequately indicate the subjective desires of consumers that give the concept of cost its meaning. The planner is not, generally speaking, bound to discover the presence of error in carrying out his plans except in the most obvious and egregious cases.[3]

Even when shortages and surpluses are correctly identified in a centralized economy, their usefulness in a trial and error approach, directly or via changes in a set of centrally administered prices, is limited by the fact that conditions of supply and demand are likely to change significantly even during the course of a single "trial," before any obvious shortage or surplus becomes apparent.[4] The holes or gaps in a system of centrally administered prices, rather than being frequently patched through entrepreneurial reactions to profit and loss signals, tend instead to widen and multiply. In contrast, profit and loss signals in a market system tend systematically to reveal to agents the appropriateness or inappropriateness of their decisions well before more visible signs of discoordination become evident and therefore before conditions of supply and demand can change significantly.

The Problem of Money Supply

How is the problem of money supply the same as other problems of economic resource administration? How does it differ?

In essence, the problem of administering the supply of money is like other problems of resource administration. Consumers and businessmen have definite wants for money balances—for deposits and currency—and a banking system should satisfy these wants without diverting resources from more highly valued uses. Like other consumer demands, the demand for money balances cannot be known in advance by any individual or agency; it requires speculation. If real factor costs and banking technology are unchanging, the problem of administering the money supply boils down to one of maintaining monetary equilibrium in the short run.[5]

What makes the problem of administering the money supply unique is, first, that it is only a short-run problem. In the long run, assuming the demand for money does not change continually and by great leaps, general price adjustments will alter the value of money, causing supply (whether considered in real or nominal terms) to conform with demand. This will be the case regardless of what the nominal supply of money is. The challenge of administering the money supply is therefore one of avoiding short-term disequilibrium by having short run *nominal supply* adjustments take the place of more disruptive and costly long run price-structure adjustments that would otherwise be needed to restore equilibrium.[6]

Second, a correct supply of inside money cannot necessarily be guided by cost accounting in the usual sense—where costs are taken to mean expenditures on physical inputs involved in the "production" of bank notes and checking accounts. These "physical" costs of production—the cost of machinery, paper, ink, and labor expended in the production and issue of notes and deposit credits—are mainly fixed costs. They are not marginally increasing. Were note and deposit creation to proceed until the marginal revenue from their issue (which is approximately equal to their purchasing power) equaled the marginal cost of production, it would necessitate a significant fall in the former magnitude. That could only occur (in a stationary or progressing economy) if the nominal supply of money surpassed the demand for it.[7] Although this would still be profitable to the banks of issue, some part of the resulting output of inside money would be unnecessary and, indeed, destructive from consumers' point of view. It follows that something other than the cost of machinery, paper, ink, and administration that go into the issue of inside money must act as a guide to desired issues and as a restraint against overissue.

This brings to bear a third important difference between the economic administration of money and that of other resources. In general, centralized administration of any single market does not confront planners with any great calculational challenge, since they can rely on the existence of competitive market prices for other resources that serve as inputs for the production of the good for which they are responsible. For example, suppose shoe production is assigned to a central planning bureau, but that leather, tacks, tanning materials, and labor, are all supplied and priced in competitive markets. The shoe bureau cannot be certain it is producing at minimum cost, because it does not have to compete with other firms rivalrously experimenting with other techniques. Nevertheless it is, like any single-industry monopolist, still able to calculate costs and to produce shoes in amounts reasonably consistent with the scarcity of inputs. If markets did not exist for the means of shoe production, as they would not in a completely socialist system, then there would be no basis for making profit and loss calculations.

In contrast, the existence of competitive markets for all relevant factors used to produce inside money does not significantly lessen the knowledge problem faced by a central bank. Therefore, the risk of incorrect management of the money supply is not limited by its being the only resource in the economy subject to centralized administration. Furthermore, an improperly managed money supply leads to much greater economic discoordination than an incorrect supply of any other good or service. Excess demand or excess supply of money affects spending in numerous other markets, and hence affects the entire system of market price and profit signals. One can think of the market as being like a wheel, with money as the hub, prices as the spokes, and other goods as the rim. A change in the relation of one good to the rest is like a tightening or loosening of a single spoke: it has a great effect on one small part of the wheel, but much less effect on the rest of the wheel. A change in the relation of money to other goods is like moving the hub: it has a great effect on all parts of the wheel, because it moves all the spokes at once. Adjust a spoke—a particular price—improperly, and you make one small part of the wheel wobble; adjust the hub—money—improperly, and you bend the whole wheel out of shape.

The far-reaching consequences of monetary disequilibrium are a matter of grave concern precisely because market prices have a coordinating role to perform. Incorrect adjustments in the money supply promote *general* calculational chaos. They undermine the normal, beneficial operation of the price system in guiding entrepreneurial action. If the money industry does not function well, then the rest of the economic system cannot function well.

If reference to input costs cannot assist the managers of a centralized supply of inside money, how are the decentralized producers of inside money better off? How can profit and loss signals guide the issue of inside money if, of necessity, the costs of inputs associated with its manufacture have to be, even at the margin of production, less than its exchange value? Is the money industry the Achilles heel of market economies? Is the price system, which is supposed to be superior to central planning as a means for administering resources, itself dependent upon the centralized administration of money?

The theory of free banking suggests that it is not. In the money industry as elsewhere, the free interplay of market forces leads to effective resource administration. The key to the market solution in this case is the guidance provided by the clearing mechanism. That mechanism is the source of debit and credit signals that rapidly (and timing is critical) follow free banks' over- and underissue of inside money. By responding to these signals free bank managers are led to adjust their liabilities to conform with the public's demand for inside money balances as if they had direct knowledge of, and were concerned with satisfying, consumer wants. It is not just the costs connected with the *issue* of inside money which regulate its supply under free banking; rather, it is these costs plus the costs associated with the return of notes and checks to their issuers for redemption in base money, that is, *liquidity* costs.

When the currency supply is monopolized, as it is under central banking, the clearing mechanism ceases to be an effective guide to changing the money supply in accordance with consumer preferences. Creation of excessive currency and deposit credits by a central bank will not cause a short-run increase in its liquidity costs. This means that other knowledge surrogates (including both means for informing money-supply decisions and means for their timely *ex post* evaluation) must be found to replace surrogate knowledge naturally present under free banking. That is why there is need for "monetary policy" and money-supply "guidelines" under centralized issue. The question is, are such guidelines superior to free banking?

Defects of Monetary Guidelines

In reviewing various guidelines for central banking we shall adopt as a starting point the assumption that the monetary authorities desire to maintain monetary equilibrium, that is, that their only goal is to avoid as far as possible any difference between the nominal supply of money—of commercial bank deposits plus central bank currency in circulation—and the nominal demand for it at a given level of nominal income.[8] Furthermore, we are only concerned with whether the monetary authority can know when there is *need* for monetary expansion or contraction. Chapter 8 will consider, in the context of a particular sort of change in consumer preferences, whether a central bank can actually achieve some desired adjustment.

Some of the more popular alternatives for central bank monetary policy are:

1. money supply changes aimed at stabilizing some index of prices;
2. money supply changes aimed at pegging some interest or discount rate;
3. money supply changes aimed at achieving "full employment"; and
4. money supply changes aimed at achieving a fixed percent rate of growth of the monetary base or of some monetary aggregate.

Each of these alternatives involves a knowledge surrogate or policy guideline which substitutes for knowledge surrogates present under free banking.

To simplify discussion, let us assume that the central bank is not restricted by factors such as convertibility of its issues in some commodity money. This does not mean that the conclusions reached are inapplicable to, say, a central bank tied to a gold standard. Rather, given the assumption of a "world" central bank, with no demand for gold in circulation and with a sufficiently inelastic industrial demand for gold, gold-standard convertibility requirements would still allow a central issuer substantial leeway to pursue any policy it wanted.

Price-level stabilization had many proponents during the 1920s and 1930s and continues to have advocates today.[9] Its appeal is based on the reasoning that, since an excessive or deficient supply of money results in a rising or falling general structure of prices (other things being equal), stabilization of the price structure or of some index representing it will preserve monetary equilibrium.[10] There is a serious theoretical flaw in this argument, but before examining it we should consider briefly some practical difficulties that frustrate construction of a reliable price index.

Before a price index can be constructed, three problems must be solved. The first and most obvious is that of choosing goods and services to include in the index. The second concerns choosing a measure of central tendency to collapse the chosen set of prices into a single value. The last is assigning to each price a weight or measure of relative importance.[11] For example, should a change in the price of a bale of cotton influence the index to the same or to a greater or lesser extent than a proportional change in the price of an ounce of gold? Furthermore, assuming that a value can be chosen for each "coefficient of importance," will it have to be modified regularly according to changes in the relative prominence of particular goods? Would the coefficient of importance of slide rules be the same today as it might have been twenty years ago?

Such practical issues might be of minor importance were it not for the fact that each of the countless ways of resolving them (there is no obvious, right solution) leads to a different index which would, in turn, suggest a different schedule of money supply adjustments. Presumably, if any one schedule is correct for maintaining monetary equilibrium, the others cannot be. Chances are that the correct schedule would not be the one actually adopted.[12]

Yet the problem is even more complicated than this because, contrary to the reasoning of advocates of price-level stabilization, the value of a consumer-goods price index, no matter how carefully constructed, may actually have to rise or fall for monetary equilibrium to be preserved. This will be the case whenever there is a significant change in the efficiency of production of one or more goods included in the price index. When there are changes in the volume of real output, a rise or fall in prices of the affected goods reflecting the change in their average cost of production is the only means for avoiding unwarranted profit and loss signals[13] while also allowing the goods market to clear. A price index does not itself reveal whether its movements reflect changes in the conditions of real output or are symptoms of monetary disequilibrium.

The effect that a change in productivity should have on prices and on the nominal supply of inside money depends on the influence that increased real output has on the demand for real money balances. There are two possibilities: One is that the real demand for money balances is constant; the other is that the real demand for money balances *relative to real income* ("k" in the Cambridge equation of exchange) is constant. In the second case an increase in real per-capita output brings about a proportional increase in real money demand.

When k is constant, a fall in prices following an increased volume of output ensures market clearing (at a constant level of nominal income) while simultaneously increasing the value of money in agreement with the increased demand for it. Any effort to offset such price reductions by increasing the nominal money supply would only interfere with monetary and goods-market equilibrium. For example, suppose that technical innovations lead to an increase in per-capita output of several consumer goods, with a proportional increase in the real demand for inside money balances. In this case the prices of the more abundant goods should be allowed to fall in sympathy with the fall in their per-unit cost of production, allowing for differences in price-elasticities of demand. The fall in prices itself provides the desired increase in the real supply of money balances. Also, with the total nominal outlay of producers unchanged, and an unchanged nominal demand for money balances, the aggregate nominal demand for goods remains the same as before the expansion in per-capita output, and this demand will be just adequate to purchase the increased total output *only* if the per-unit selling price of goods now supplied in greater quantities is lower than it was before the increase in output. Therefore, when the per-unit real cost of a good falls, its selling price should fall as well to preserve monetary equilibrium.[14]

To see that a fall in prices in response to reduced per-unit costs is, not only consistent with, but essential to the maintenance of equilibrium, consider what would happen if the money supply were increased so that a greater output of goods could be purchased without any fall in the general price structure. Then producers would, following the injection of new money, have nominal revenues exceeding their nominal outlays: illusory profit signals would be generated, spurring additional investment. As Haberler notes, "the *entrepreneurs* would be led on by the double inducement of (1) reduced costs [without reduced revenues] and (2) interest rates falsified by the increase in the volume of money to undertake capital improvements on too large a scale" (1931, 21):

> Suppose, in a particular branch of industry, production is increased as the result of a technical improvement, aggregate costs remaining stationary, by 10 per cent (equivalent to a reduction of average costs of 10 per cent). If the demand increases by exactly the same figure [i.e., is unit elastic with respect to nominal price, holding other prices constant] the price of the product will fall by 10 per cent, and the economic position will otherwise be unchanged. If, however, the effect of this reduction of price on the price-level is compensated by increasing the volume of money . . . new purchasing power will be created which will clearly produce exactly the same results as . . . inflation.

The illusion ends once the excessive money supply has its effects on wage rates and on the prices of other factors of production: an injection of money has the same discoordinating consequences whether it results in absolute inflation (rising prices) or only in relative inflation which, instead of causing prices to rise, merely prevents them from falling in accordance with increased productivity. Relative inflation does not reveal itself in a rising consumer price index, although it does result in an upward movement in the prices of factors of production.[15]

E. F. M. Durbin, in comparing the consequences of expanding the money supply to offset increased productive efficiency with those from expanding it to meet an increased demand for money balances relative to income, says (1933, 186–87) that the latter "will exert no effect on relative price levels. . . . It will merely maintain the level of money incomes and allow prices to decline in proportion to costs." The former, on the other hand, will add to the aggregate stream of money payments, thereby interfering with those adjustments that would otherwise guide relative prices to their proper levels.

What if there is a *decline* in productive efficiency, that is, what if the per-unit cost of production of a number of consumer goods increases? Stabilization of a consumer-goods price index would then cause a *reduction* of consumers' aggregate nominal income and expenditure. This would in turn lead to a deficiency of producer revenues relative to outlays, to the disappointment of entrepreneurs' "expectations of normal profit,"[16] and to further curtailment of production. The lull in productive activity continues until factor prices, including wages, fall to a level consistent with the restoration of producer profits.

R. G. Hawtrey provides a quantitative illustration (1951, 143–44):

> Suppose . . . that a consumer's outlay of £100,000,000 has been applied to 100,000,000 units of goods, and that producers who have hitherto received £20,000,000 for 20,000,000 units find their output reduced to 10,000,000 units, but the price of their product doubled. They still receive £20,000,000 and the other producers can continue to receive £80,000,000 for 80,000,000 units.
>
> But as £100,000,000 is now spent on 90,000,000 units the price level has risen by one-ninth. In order to counteract that rise, the consumers' outlay must be reduced from £100,000,000 to £90,000,000. Every group of producers will find the total proceeds of its sales reduced by 10 percent. Wages, profits and prices will be thrown out of proportion, and every industry will have to face the adverse effects of flagging demand. . . . The producers whose prices have been raised by scarcity will be no exception. Their total receipts are reduced in the same proportion, and they must reduce wages like their neighbors.

Nor, Hawtrey continues (ibid., 147) does this depend on the assumption that goods have a unitary price-elasticity of demand:

> If the shortage is in a product of which the elasticity is greater than unity, the adverse effect on the producers of that product is greater and on other producers less. If elasticity is less than unity the adverse effect on the former is less and may be more than counteracted, but what they gain their neighbors loose. Whatever the circumstances, the stabilization of the community price level in the face of [increased] scarcity will always tend to cause depressions.

It is somewhat less obvious that maintenance of monetary equilibrium may require a price-index change even when the *absolute* level of demand for real balances is constant. Suppose there is a general increase in productive efficiency which leads to a general reduction in goods prices. The fall initially seems necessary (given a constant nominal money supply) to clear the goods markets while also keeping selling prices in line with average per unit costs of production. But a general fall in prices will also increase the real value of existing nominal money balances. If the demand for real balances is unchanged, the nominal supply of money will become excessive. It is tempting to think in light of this that the increase in productive efficiency independent of any increase in the real demand for money should leave the price level unchanged after all, because the spending of excess balances would, other things being equal, cause prices to return more or less to their original levels.[17] Therefore, it might be argued, changes in productivity are not after all an independent cause of the price-level changes that should be of concern to a monetary authority.

Nevertheless the argument is mistaken. The return of prices due to the real-balance effect occurs only after some delay, during which a monetary authority following a price-level stabilization policy might be tempted to increase the nominal supply of money. Yet what is really needed to maintain monetary equilibrium in the face of a real-balance effect following an increase in productivity is, not an *expansion* of the nominal money supply, but a *contraction*. Otherwise the spending-off of surplus nominal balances will increase nominal income, generating false profit signals. The sequence of adjustment should be: increased output, reduced prices, real-balance effect, and contraction of the nominal money supply. The procedure that best maintains monetary equilibrium—one that accounts for the fact that the real-balance effect does not take place instantaneously—is therefore one that allows lasting changes in an index of prices *even when the real demand for money has not changed*.

Thus a "neutral" monetary policy, one that maintains monetary equilibrium, is not likely to keep any price index stable. What is needed is a policy that prevents price changes due to changes in the demand for money relative to income without preventing price changes due to changes in productive efficiency.

As our earlier discussion made clear, a free banking system tends to accommodate changes in the demand for inside money with equal changes in its supply. An increase in the demand for inside money balances results in banks' discovering that their formerly optimal reserve holdings have become superoptimal—the banks are encouraged to expand their issues of inside money. Conversely, a fall in the demand for inside money exposes banks to a greater risk of default at the clearinghouse, prompting balance-sheet contraction. In both cases the system avoids unjustified fluctuations in aggregate nominal income and prices.

On the other hand, insofar as prices tend to fluctuate under free banking on account of changes in the conditions of real output (e.g., technological improvements leading to increased per-capita output, or a negative supply shock due to bad weather),[18] no countervailing adjustments in the supply of inside money will occur; instead, the nominal supply of inside money will adjust only in response to any change in spending associated with some real-balance effect. This sustains rather than prevents the movement of prices.[19] Such price movements are automatic and "painless" in the sense that they come in response to changes in per-unit costs and therefore maintain constant (elasticity of demand considerations aside) the nominal revenues of producers. In short, free banks prevent only those potentially disruptive changes in prices and in the value of money that would otherwise result from uncompensated changes in the public's demand for money balances relative to income.

This result of free banking accords perfectly with the ideal of monetary equilibrium discussed in chapter 4. Free banks maintain constant the supply of inside money multiplied by its income velocity of circulation. They are credit intermediaries only, and cause no true inflation, deflation, or forced savings.

But if this is true of the results of free banking it cannot be true of any monetary policy that prevents price changes having their source in changes in the conditions of production. The fundamental theoretical shortcoming of price-level stabilization is that it calls for changes in the money supply where none are needed to preserve equilibrium.

Yet even this does not exhaust the defects of price-level stabilization, for even if a price index could be constructed that would change only in response to monetary disequilibrium, the index would still be a defective policy guide: any corrections made by the monetary authority would come too late. They would come too late, not just because there is a lag between the actions of the central bank and adjustment of commercial bank deposits and currency in circulation, but, more fundamentally, because price changes recorded in an "ideal" price index are themselves *equilibrating* adjustments to previous money-supply errors. To the extent that general price adjustments occur in response to monetary disequilibrium, the gap between the nominal demand for money and its nominal supply is reduced. Once such price adjustments are revealed in an altered price index, the excess demand or excess supply of money has already been at least partly eliminated by changes in the purchasing power of money.

Changing the quantity of money at this point would simply cause a new disequilibrium change opposite the original disturbance. In other words, changing the money supply to return an "ideal" price index to some target level may actually make matters worse—like backing over someone to compensate for running him over in the first place.

Such compounding of error is especially likely in the face of what Milton Friedman (1959, 87–88) calls the "long and variable lag" separating changes in the money supply from their observed effects on general prices.[20] Even before the authorities realize that there has been a discrepancy between the nominal demand for money and its nominal supply at the target price level, the nominal demand for money may already have altered significantly, not only because general price-level changes have altered the real value of money balances, but also because of entirely independent changes in the demand for *real* balances. The result might be, to use Keynes's analogy in his *Treatise on Money* (1930, 2: 223–24), that the money doctors prescribe castor oil for diarrhea and bismuth for constipation!

Price-level stabilization therefore suffers from the same flaw as in the trial and error approach to overall central planning. It recognizes the need for some *ex post* guidance of money-supply decisions, but it relies upon a "knowledge surrogate"—the general level of prices—which does not signal disequilibrium fast enough. In contrast, the knowledge surrogates provided by clearing operations in a free banking system work relatively quickly: they sponsor modifications in the money supply well before money supply errors can have observable, macroeconomic consequences.

The preceding arguments also apply, with appropriate modifications, to a policy of foreign-exchange rate stabilization, discussion of which requires us to relax the assumption of a closed economy or "world" central bank. Exchange-rate movements are inappropriate as indicators of monetary disequilibrium because rates vary in the short run for reasons other than changes in the purchasing power of domestic and foreign monies, such as a change in preferences for foreign produced goods, or fear of political instability. But even if this were not true—even if the pure purchasing-power parity theory of exchange rates were valid for the very short run—exchange rates would still possess all the defects (and then some) of price indeces as guides to monetary policy: they would merely reflect perceived changes in the domestic price level relative to the foreign price level. Assuming the latter to be constant, a "pure purchasing power" exchange rate would be nothing other than another price index, made up of prices of goods involved in foreign trade. As such it would be no better than any other price index as a guide to credit expansion.

Another popular central banking policy is interest rate pegging or targeting (pegging within a specified range).[21] This policy draws attention to what may sometimes be an early symptom of monetary disequilibrium—namely, interest rate changes. It might sometimes allow money supply errors to be corrected before they could substantially influence economic activity. Indeed, this approach invokes a knowledge surrogate that would in some instances be theoretically *superior* to the surrogates involved in free banking, since credit creation or destruction involves an immediate dislocation of interest rates from their equilibrium levels.

Regrettably, this theoretical advantage has no practical counterpart. Wicksell's theory—that monetary disequilibrium arises whenever there is a difference between the market rate of interest and the natural or equilibrium rate—is consistent with pegging the market rate only if the natural rate is unchanging, and only if the market rate happens to be equal to the natural rate when the policy takes effect. Then and only then would further changes in market rates be evidence of inadequately accommodated changes in the demand for money.

In practice, as Robert Greenfield and Leland Yeager point out (1986), to regard all market interest rate movements as evidence of shifting money demand, necessitating accommodative changes in money supply, confuses the demand for money balances with the demand for credit or loanable funds. While changes in the interest rate *may* represent a departure of the market rate from an unchanging natural or equilibrium rate due to a disequilibrium money supply, they may also represent changes in the natural or equilibrium rate of interest itself. Whether observed changes in the interest rate are equilibrium changes or not depends on what is happening to the public's relative preference for present commodities, bonds, and money. The natural or equilibrium rate of interest may rise, even though the demand for money hasn't changed, because of a shift in demand away from bonds and into commodities. If the monetary authority tried to prevent this kind of increase in the interest rate through monetary expansion (as if a rise in the interest rate always meant an increase in the market rate above the equilibrium rate, due to insufficient growth of the money supply), the result would be an excess supply of money. Likewise, if the interest rate fell due to a shift in preferences from present commodities to bonds (again with no change in the demand for money), any effort to keep the rate from falling by contracting the money supply would be deflationary. Furthermore there may be times when, although the demand for money *is* changing, an accommodative change in the supply of money will not be the same as a change aimed at pegging the rate of interest.

For example, if the demand for money increases primarily at the expense of the demand for present commodities, the equilibrium rate of interest falls. Finally, if the demand for money increases primarily at the expense of the demand for bonds, there may be no change in the equilibrium rate of interest. The latter case is the *only* one consistent with a policy of pegging the rate of interest in the face of a changed demand for money.

In short, so long as market rates move in a manner consistent with changes in the (voluntary) supply of and demand for loanable funds, their movement is no indication of excessive or deficient money supply. The achievement of monetary equilibrium by interest rate pegging (or targeting) could only be an incredible, and short lived, stroke of luck.[22]

A third major guideline of monetary policy in recent years has been full employment. Like the other guidelines considered so far, its reliability as a sign of monetary equilibrium is quite limited. Obviously changes in the rate of employment may be due to the failure of the monetary authorities to preserve monetary equilibrium. An excess demand for money may lead to a rise in unemployment, especially if monopolistic elements in the labor market or other causes interfere with downward adjustments in wage rates. Likewise an excess supply of money may sometimes manifest itself in a fall in unemployment, due to delayed upward adjustment of labor-supply schedules (caused perhaps by a temporary bout of "money illusion"). But to assign to monetary policy the goal of guaranteeing "full" employment, when this means fixing a target rate of unemployment (such as in the Employment Act of 1946 and the Humphrey-Hawkins Act of 1978), is to assume that *all* fluctuations of unemployment around the targeted rate are due to maladjustments of the money supply which could be avoided by proper adjustment of the money supply. This is not so. Rather than being caused by deficient monetary expansion in the past, much of the unemployment observed today must be attributed to imperfect competition in the labor market. Unemployment caused by minimum wage laws is only the most flagrant example of this. The existence of stagflation—the simultaneous occurrence of high unemployment and rising prices—is, in a growing economy, almost certain proof that the unemployment is not due to any deficiency of aggregate demand. Attempts to combat such unemployment by further monetary expansion can only serve to augment an already satisfactory or excessive money supply, furthering the tendency of prices to rise. This in turn will provoke a new round of monopolistic wage developments, so that any temporary improvement in employment must be short lived.

A final set of monetary guidelines consists of rules prescribing a fixed rate of growth for the monetary base or for some monetary aggregate.[23] At first glance it might seem that the very crudeness of such rules makes them inferior to the other procedures just discussed: a fixed growth rate rule obviously ignores the fact that the demand for money fluctuates on a day-to-day (or at least month-to-month) basis. It would produce the stability in nominal income that its advocates desire only if the demand for money grew steadily at the prescribed money growth rate.[24]

But the rationale of monetary rules lies precisely in the fact that information is lacking for implementing more sophisticated techniques. Thus Milton Friedman, undoubtedly the best known advocate of a fixed growth-rate rule, says (1959, 98) that, although "there are persuasive theoretical grounds for desiring to vary the rate of growth [of money] to offset other factors . . . in practice, we do not know when to do so and how much." A central bank is not capable of making accurate provision for short-term fluctuations in the demand for money, and its attempts to do so using the imprecise guidelines available to it are likely to introduce more instability and disequilibrium than they eliminate. It follows that a simple growth-rate rule, although crude, may be the best attainable.

That a central monetary authority lacks the knowledge needed to execute sophisticated policies properly is not the only reason for wanting to restrict it to a fixed growth-rate rule. There are also political considerations, which weigh increasingly in the arguments of monetarists. Their claim is that a constitutionally mandated rule will prevent the monetary authorities from engaging in capricious or politically motivated manipulations of the money supply. In the words of Henry Simons, it "would be folly" to allow "temporary," discretionary departures from a rule designed for this purpose.

These arguments for having a central bank adhere to a growth-rate rule are valid and compelling. But they do not see the issue as involving a choice between central banking and free banking. They offer what is perhaps the best solution to the problem of money supply *given* that currency issue is to remain a government-controlled monopoly. Nevertheless, *central banking, even when it is based on a monetary rule, is decidedly inferior to free banking as a means for preserving monetary equilibrium.*

So far we have simplified the problem of money supply by assuming that the demand for currency is a constant or fully predictable fraction of total money demand. Suppose that we take this assumption a step further and postulate a demand for currency that is absolutely *constant* and equal to the stock of central bank currency in circulation. How does the new assumption affect the problem facing the central bank? The answer is that it makes it disappear entirely!

Once the supply of currency is assumed to be taken care of, the central bank can simply withdraw from the scene, and a policy of "free deposit banking" (without competitive note issue) is all that is needed to ensure the maintenance of monetary equilibrium. Thus the essential policy goal for a central bank—assuming that it will retain a monopoly of currency supply—is to adjust its issues to accommodate changes in the public's demand for currency without influencing the availability of excess reserves to the banking system. The reason for this is that, under the assumption of a fixed and satisfied demand for currency, the only fluctuations in money demand that could occur would be fluctuations in the demand for checkable deposits. Such fluctuations could be accommodated by unregulated commercial banks without any central bank assistance. In contrast, if the demand for currency is not stationary, commercial banks lacking the power of note issue could not independently maintain monetary equilibrium.

These conclusions should not be surprising: the issue of currency is, after all, the principal money-supply function that commercial banks are presently prohibited from undertaking themselves. To argue, in view of this, that central banks serve to "regulate" deposit creation by commercial banks by controlling the supply of currency is like arguing that a monopoly supplier of shoes for left feet would be useful for regulating the production of shoes for right feet: it overlooks that *in the absence of any monopoly* the supply of both kinds of shoes would be self regulating, and in a manner vastly superior to what could be accomplished by a centralized left-shoe supply. In the same way, the total supply of inside money would regulate itself in a desirable manner *if* part of that supply which is now monopolized—the issue of currency, were thrown open to competition.

We have already seen that central banks are not well equipped to know whether an adjustment in the supply of currency is needed. We now turn to consider a relatively simple circumstance where the total demand for money is constant. Our aim is to examine whether a central bank can respond properly to *known* changes in the *proportion* of money demand represented by demand for currency assuming that the total demand for inside money does not change.

8

The Supply of Currency

MONEY MAY BE HELD in either of two forms: deposits, from which payments can be made by check, or currency—hand-to-hand money. This chapter examines the capacity of free banks and central banks to accommodate changes in currency demand. To simplify the problem it assumes that the total demand for money is unchanging, so that the central bank can treat it as known. Then the only changes in currency demand that need to be accommodated are those arising from decisions to alter the *composition* of money holdings—their division between currency and deposits.[1]

Suppose, for example, that a shift from deposit demand to currency demand occurs in a central-banking system in which deposit banks have no excess reserves. Although the total demand for money has not changed, people want to exchange their deposit balances for currency balances. How can a central banking system provide the needed adjustment? Can it change the relative mixture of deposits and currency in circulation without disrupting monetary equilibrium? How, in this regard, will its performance compare to that of a free-banking system?

Before answering these questions we must carefully distinguish currency demand, which is simply a demand for circulating means of payment, from outside-money demand, which is demand to hold a form of money that does not involve granting credit to banks. A rise in currency demand is a routine occurrence which does not involve any loss of confidence in banks; it can in theory be satisfied by a circulating form of inside money. In contrast, a rise in outside-money demand means a demand to exchange inside money for outside money, the ultimate money of redemption. In a closed system this implies either a loss of confidence in banks issuing inside money (which contradicts the assumptions of the present part of this study) or a failure of the banking system to provide enough inside money for use as currency.[2]

108

The Relative Demand for Currency

The public's division of its demand for money between deposit demand and currency demand is not arbitrary. Particular sorts of plans call for holding currency rather than checkable deposits. Currency is more useful for making change; but more importantly the demand to hold currency reflects the degree to which sellers more readily accept currency than checks. One reason for the greater acceptability of currency is that sellers of goods and services may wish to avoid the inconvenience of depositing or cashing checks. More significantly, acceptance of a check requires a level of trust beyond what is required in the acceptance of currency of equal face value: the acceptor of a check has to have confidence not just in the bank upon which the check is drawn, which may or may not be good for the transferred sum, but also in the drawer of the check himself, who may or may not possess an adequate deposit balance.

Nor is the relative demand for currency constant. As Agger notes (1918, 85), it changes along with "basic changes in the economic life of the community" and with "changes in the disposition that is to be made of . . . borrowed funds." In the United States until the 1930s the historical trend was toward less reliance upon currency and greater use of checks and other means for direct transfer of deposit balances. This was due mainly to improvements in deposit banking, which were spurred-on in part by the suppression of competitive note issue. In the last fifty years or so the trend has changed, and the demand for currency relative to total money demand has grown substantially.[3]

Other factors have historically caused the currency-deposit mixture to alter in a less regular way. An increase in retail trade relative to wholesale trade favors greater use of currency, because the former involves smaller, anonymous exchanges where less trust is possible, whereas the latter involves larger exchanges among previously acquainted parties. In the past, when wage payments were more often made in currency, payroll requirements caused weekly and quarterly cycles in currency demand. The demand for currency also increased during the autumnal expansion of agricultural activity, and there are still seasonal peaks in demand due to holidays (such as Christmas) which involve a burst of retail trade. Besides these influences Phillip Cagan, in his study of "The Demand for Currency Relative to Total Money Supply" (1958) lists the following: (a) expected real income per capita; (b) interest rates available on demand deposits (a measure of the opportunity cost of holding currency); (c) the volume of travel; (d) the degree of urbanization; (e) the advent of war; (f) the level of taxes and incentives for tax evasion; and (g) the extent of criminal and black-market activities. Changes in the currency ratio due to these and other factors since the turn of the century are shown in figure 8.1.

A final factor already alluded to which affects the relative demand for currency is the extent of business confidence. According to Agger (1918, 86), a decline in confidence "lessons the acceptability of the check as an instrument of exchange and usually involves an increase in the demand for media of more general acceptability." Except during panics a loss of confidence extends only to individuals and not to banks so that, although it causes an increase in currency demand, it does not necessarily involve any increase in outside-money demand; that is, it does not involve a desire to remove outside money from the banking system. "Ordinarily," Agger notes, "the shifting of demand is rarely so complete [and] it is only isolated banks that suffer a complete

Figure 8.1   Ratio of Currency to Checkable Deposits since 1900. Adapted from Paul A. Meyer, *Money, Financial Institutions, and the Economy* (Homewood, Ill.: Irwin, 1986), p. 97.

loss of confidence."[4] Pressure is more likely to be exerted by depositors desiring currency, including bank notes, than by holders of notes seeking to redeem them in outside money.[5]

This variety of influencing factors makes the relative demand for currency highly variable and sometimes unpredictable.[6] In consequence, a central bank may have difficulty accommodating changes in the relative demand for currency even when the demand for inside money as a whole does not change. Yet it is essential that the public be able to acquire media of exchange in a mixture that suits its needs. Holders of inside money want to be able to switch from deposits to currency or vice versa depending upon which means of payment or combination of means suits its circumstances. If the public's wants are not satisfied significant inconvenience and reduced opportunities for making desired purchases result.

Bank borrowers also may need to receive credit in one rather than the other form (checkable deposits or currency), so that a relative deficiency of either form will cause credit-market stringency just as if the the total availability of loanable funds were reduced. As Agger puts it:

> Inability to meet an expanding demand or impediments in the way of issue of either form of bank credit may entail serious consequences. For those desiring credit in either form and unable to obtain it [for want of the desired media] the situation is alarming. The normal conduct of their business may depend upon obtaining bank accommodations of an acceptable form. Stringency in the market for such accommodation is . . . bound to be costly and a source of anxiety.[7]

The amount of credit granted in a well-working banking system should not depend on the form of payment medium wanted, so long as there is no special demand for the ultimate money of redemption. A well-working system should also permit the unrestricted interconversion of deposits and currency once either is already outstanding.

Currency Supply under Free Banking

When banks are unrestricted in their ability to issue bank notes each can meet increases in its clients' demands for currency without difficulty and without affecting its liquidity or solvency. Under such free-banking conditions the "transformation of deposits into notes will respond to demand," and banks will be able to supply credit in the form that borrowers require (Agger 1918, 154). The supply of currency is flexible under unrestricted note issue because bank note liabilities are, for a bank capable of issuing them, not significantly different from deposit liabilities.[8] "In the absence of any restriction,"

Agger writes, "it is a matter of indifference to the [note-issuing] bank which form its credit takes" (1918, 154). When the customers of a note-issuing bank—borrowers or depositors—desire currency, the bank offers them its own notes instead of a deposit balance. The issue of notes in exchange for deposit credits involves offsetting adjustments on the liability side of the bank's balance sheet, with no change on the asset side. Suppose, for example, that a deposit-holder having a balance of $500 wants to withdraw $100 in currency.[9] The bank simply hands him $100 of its notes. Then, on its balance sheet, it reduces the entry for "liabilities-deposits" $100 and increases the entry for "liabilities-circulation" $100. The composition of the bank's liabilities changes but their total amount stays the same; and this is all that ought to happen, since by hypothesis the total demand for inside money has not changed.

It is even possible, as far as currency demand is concerned, for a note-issuing bank to hold enough notes on hand (in its vault and tills) to meet currency demands of its creditors and borrowers to the full amount of its outstanding demand liabilities. The only cost involved would be the cost of the notes themselves—an investment in paper and engraving. The notes are not obligations of the bank and pose no threat to its solvency until they start circulating. On the other hand, as long as notes are in a bank's vault or tills they cannot be treated by it as a reserve asset capable of supporting its outstanding credits: unlike outside money, they are useless for settling clearing balances with other banks. A competitive bank's own notes serve one purpose only, which is to satisfy that part of its clients' demands for inside money which consists of a demand for currency. When no longer needed in circulation the notes return to the issuing bank, which may use them again the next time the demand for currency increases.[10]

In practice free banks would generally not keep on hand notes equal to 100 percent of their deposits, because the likelihood of demand for inside money shifting entirely into currency is minuscule. Even though only minor costs are involved, excessive note stockpiles would be wasteful. Banks would, instead, keep on hand as many notes as they would be likely to need to cover unusual, but not extremely freakish, demands. In the truly exceptional event of demands exceeding available note supplies relief would be no further away than the printing press.[11]

Freedom of note issue thus ensures the preservation of an equilibrium money supply as demand shifts from deposits to currency and vice versa. It assures that credit offers of persons willing to hold inside money are exploited even when the offerers want to hold bank promises in a form useful in circulation. It also assures that a growing demand for inside money that involves an *absolute* increase in currency demand is readily accommodated, instead of going unsatisfied because of a shortage of currency.[12] The ability of free banks to function smoothly as intermediaries even in the face of changing currency demand stems from their note-issuing powers.

Monopolized Currency Supply

Under monopolized currency supply the ability of non-note-issuing (deposit or commercial) banks to convert deposits into currency is restricted. Deposit banks are not able independently to fulfill currency demands. They have to draw instead on their holdings of notes or fiat currency (or deposits convertible into notes or fiat currency) of the monopoly bank of issue.[13] In doing so they reduce their reserves of high-powered money. It follows that, unless the monopoly bank of issue adjusts the amount of its credits to the deposit banks to offset their reserve losses due to currency demand,[14] their lending power decreases. The banks will have to contract their liabilities. A change in the *form* in which the public wishes to hold money balances causes a disequilibrating change in the *total supply* of money.[15]

The same conclusion holds for uncompensated reductions in the relative demand for currency, which in a system with monopolized currency issue results in a return of currency to the deposit banks, who add it to their reserve holdings and use it as a basis for credit expansion. A fall in the relative demand for currency results in monetary overexpansion even though the demand for money has not fallen and even though there is no expansion of credit by the monopoly bank of issue. If changes in the relative demand for currency are not to result in monetary disequilibrium under central banking, the central bank must engage in continual "reserve compensation." It has to adjust the supply of base or high-powered money in response to changes in the amount of base money needed in circulation.

This result, that changes in the relative demand for currency will affect total money supply under central banking unless offset by reserve compensation, is well recognized in the literature on central banking.[16] But past writers have tended to view the problem as one inherent in all fractional-reserve banking, whereas the truth is that it is inherent only to systems where the issue of currency is monopolized.[17]

The amount of reserve compensation needed under central banking to maintain a constant money supply as the demand for currency changes can be calculated using a simple formula. Let

$M_{c,f}$ = total checkable bank deposits plus currency in circulation under central banking and under free banking, respectively;

$B_{c,f}$ = the supply of base or high-powered money under central and under free banking, respectively [B_f = the supply of outside (commodity) money; B_c = the supply of commodity money plus currency and deposits of the central bank];

C_p = the public's currency holdings;

r = the ratio of reserves to monetary bank liabilities.

Then, under central banking

$$M_c = \frac{B_c - C_p(1 - r)}{r}$$

whereas, under free banking

$$M_f = \frac{B_f}{r}.^{[18]}$$

Under central banking the relation between the supply of base money and total money supply is a function of the relative demand for currency, whereas under free banking this is no longer the case. The reason for the difference is that under central banking the public's use of central bank notes as currency competes with the banks' use of them as reserves. Under free banking high-powered (outside) money is not usually used as currency.

The amount by which the supply of base money needs to be adjusted under central banking to offset a change in currency demand can be derived by assuming that M_f is equal to the demand for money. We wish, in this case, to have $M_c = M_f$. If r is the same in both systems, this requires that

$$B_c - C_p(1 - r) = B_f$$

or

$$B_c = B_f + C_p(1 - r).$$

Thus, for example, if C_p rises $1000, and $r = .10$, then the monetary base under central banking would, other things being equal, have to increase

$$(\$1000) - (\$1000) \times (.10) = \$900.$$

Put generally, the base needs to be adjusted by the amount of the increase in the relative demand for currency (the shift from deposit demand to currency demand) minus this value multipled by the reserve ratio.

Notice that this procedure is not equivalent to one of maintaining constant the level of deposit-bank reserves. This is because deposit banks only need to hold reserves against that part of the money supply that consists of deposit balances; they do not need to hold reserves against currency in circulation because it is not part of their outstanding liabilities. If, in the above example, the initial level of reserves of the deposit banks was $10,000 then, after the growth in C_p and corresponding reserve compensation, the new, equilibrium level of reserves is $10,000 - $1000 + $900 = $9,900. It follows that a central banking policy of maintaining constant the level of bank reserves, which might be desirable if the relative demand for currency were unchanging, will not preserve monetary equilibrium when the relative demand for currency flutuates.

Instruments for Reserve Compensation

Having seen the precise adjustments in the monetary base needed to compensate changes in deposit bank reserves due to changes in the relative demand for currency, we can ask how such reserve compensation might actually be undertaken by a central bank. Let us assume still that the total demand for money (currency plus deposits) is unchanging, and that only its division between currency demand and deposit demand alters. To simplify the problem even further, let us assume as well that the relative demand for currency is known to the monetary authority. We thus put aside for the moment the greater part of the knowledge problem discussed in the last chapter, which has to do with how the monetary authority could know how much currency it ought to supply, to consider whether the authority can actually make desired adjustments. Our concern is to examine the efficacy of various instruments for reserve compensation—statutory reserve requirements, open-market operations, and rediscount policy—in accommodating a known currency demand.[19]

The first instrument we have to consider, statutory reserve requirements, highlights the significant *distributional* impact of certain approaches to reserve compensation: although a correct adjustment of statutory requirements preserves monetary equilibrium on the whole, the uneven distribution of changes in liquidity brings welfare losses or gains to particular banks.[20] Since changes in the relative demand for currency do not affect all banks simultaneously or uniformly, an ideal policy would have to make continual adjustments in statutory reserve requirements, bank by bank. This poses an impossible administrative problem. It requires, moreover, that the central authority know, not just the total extent of the public's shift into (or out of) currency, but also *which banks* are affected by the shift.

Second, for adjustments in statutory reserve requirements to be adequate to accommodate substantial shifts into currency, the supply of base money held up in "free" statutory reserves would have to be large: a reduction in statutory reserve needs frees up more base money for use in circulation, but this is of no avail if the total supply that can be released is less than the increase in demand. Finally, phasing out statutory reserve requirements is obviously impossible if they are needed for reserve compensation.

The last point is important since statutory reserve requirements are themselves a barrier to automatic adjustments in the supply of deposit money. The significance of this becomes apparent when the assumption that the total demand for money is unchanging is (momentarily) relaxed. Of course the monetary authorities, if they knew the extent of changes in total money demand, could make the necessary modifications in their reserve-requirement adjustments, but this would just add another layer of complexity to an already tremendous administrative and calculational burden.[21]

A second vehicle for reserve compensation is open-market operations. The fundamental problem with this instrument is also distributive. Although it allows direct control of the total amount of base money created or withdrawn, it does not provide any means of ensuring that base money issued goes to banks that are experiencing currency withdrawals or, alternatively, that base money withdrawn is withdrawn from banks experiencing redeposits of currency. Lauchlin Currie draws attention to this in his *Supply and Control of Money in the United States* (1934, 117):

> If the reserve banks should buy bonds to the amount of the increase in cash in circulation, less the amount of the reserve formerly held against withdrawn deposits, it would appear that the composition of money has changed but not its volume. This would be true if the reserve bank funds, arising from the purchase of bonds, go to those banks . . . experiencing withdrawals.

But, Currie observes (ibid., 114), the banks receiving the new base money from open-market sales will probably be different from those stricken by currency withdrawals. Those banks receiving new base money that do not need it to offset reserve drains will employ it like any other increment of excess reserves, by increasing their loans and investments.[22]

Opposite consequences follow attempts to offset by open-market sales an inflow of currency due to a shift in demand from currency to deposits. "Here again," Currie writes, "the difficulty is that the bank gaining reserves from the deposit of cash [currency] may not be the same bank losing reserves from the selling operations of the reserve banks" (ibid.). As with adjustments in statutory reserve requirements monetary equilibrium in the gross sense will be preserved, but with substantial welfare effects.

To some extent inter-bank lending might reduce these welfare effects from reserve compensation. But this possibility is limited by the fact that banks receiving excess base money will not necessarily lend it to other banks in need of reserve compensation: this may or may not be the most profitable avenue of employment for the surplus funds. Banks suffering reserve losses from currency drains might not offer to pay a high enough interest rate to attract emergency loans, for fear that the currency withdrawals may be permanent ones, which would make it difficult to repay the loans. Or, if banks losing reserves do offer to pay higher rates, other banks may still be reluctant to lend to them because *they* fear that the rates represent increased risk that the borrowing banks are suffering, not just temporary currency withdrawals, but a permanent loss of business.

A final instrument for reserve compensation is rediscount policy. This seems to offer the advantage of automatically channeling emergency supplies of base money only to banks in need of them, without requiring the monetary authorities to make decisions on a bank-by-bank basis. Murray Polakoff, who is generally critical of rediscount policy, writes (1963, 203) that it "is particularly well suited to supply a portion of reserves for seasonal needs and reserve losses and supplying them directly and immediately to the points where they are most needed." He adds that "this is not true of open-market operations" (ibid.).[23] A defect of rediscounting, however, is that it relies on deposit banks' knowing whether currency is being withdrawn from them because of (a) an increase in their clients' demand for currency or (b) dissaving (a *fall* in the demand for inside money).[24] In general it is not possible for banks to know which of these causes is behind some withdrawal of currency by their depositors. Banks may mistakenly borrow base money from the central issuer (by rediscounting) to offset drains of the second type, forestalling the credit contraction needed in such cases to preserve monetary equilibrium. Distributing emergency base money by the rediscount mechanism does not guarantee that it goes to banks suffering from currency drains due solely to changes in the relative demand for currency.

All this assumes that banks, if they knew how, would borrow from the central issuer only the precise amount needed to compensate their losses caused by changes in the relative demand for currency. But the extent of borrowing depends on the rate of rediscount that the central bank charges. A rate below the market rate encourages borrowing, not merely for reserve compensation, but for acquiring excess reserves to relend at a profit. Furthermore, even if banks borrow from the central bank only to offset reserve losses due to currency withdrawals, the return of currency from circulation when the relative demand for it declines may not lead to offsetting repayment of borrowed reserves. If the rediscount rate is too low, the surplus base money will be re-lent instead. Winfield Riefler (1930, 161) cites an example of this in the United States just after World War I. Commercial banks had borrowed heavily from the Federal Reserve during the war to offset reserve losses due to an increased relative demand for currency. At the close of the war, when demand shifted back to deposit balances, returning Federal Reserve notes "were not used to repay member bank borrowings in any corresponding amounts." Instead, redeposited currency "went in considerable part to build up member bank reserve balances":

> Member banks as a group . . . were content to maintain their indebtedness [to the Federal Reserve banks] at about the level it had previously attained, using funds released from circulation . . . to expand their loans, for which there was an active demand at attractive rates.

The resulting expansion of the money supply undoubtedly contributed to the boom-bust cycle of 1920–1921.

An above-market rediscount rate, a "penalty" rate, also does not ensure proper borrowing for reserve compensation. A penalty charge for funds borrowed to be kept in reserve leads to a less than optimal amount of reserve compensation, since a bank that pays penalty rates for its reserves is not, at the margin, better off than one that contracts its liabilities to make do with reserves it already has. Therefore a penalty rediscount rate is likely to lead to insufficient reserve compensation at times of expanded relative demand for currency. This conclusion applies with greatest force when increases in the relative demand for currency are expected to be long lasting or permanent.[25]

All of this assumes that a penalty rate or below-market rate of interest can at least be identified. In truth the variety of interest-earning assets available to banks, all with somewhat different nominal rates of interest, makes it difficult to choose a measure for "the market rate" against which the rediscount rate may be compared. As Polakoff notes (1963, 192), the existence of a distinct market rate is a peculiarity of English banking not present in other systems:

> In Great Britain, it is the bill dealers and not the commercial banks that borrow directly from the Bank of England. Since the former specialize in a particular kind of asset—formerly commercial bills and now Treasury bills—and since the Bank rate is higher than the rate on bills, the

discount rate in that country truly can be considered to be a penalty rate when dealers are forced to seek accommodation at the central bank.

Finally, even where some reasonable rule for setting it *does* exist, the rediscount rate has to be continually adjusted to reflect changes in the market rate.[26]

Historical Illustrations

History offers many episodes of banks failing to respond to changes in the relative demand for currency. Most have been due to the failure of monopoly banks of issue to supply deposit banks with supplementary reserve media so that the deposit banks could withstand their depositors' temporary withdrawals of currency. A few examples will help to illustrate points made in the previous section.

We have already noted an episode, which occurred in the United States in 1919, where an uncompensated shift of money demand from currency to deposits resulted in an excess supply of inside money taken as a whole. More notable and frequent, however, have been cases in which the supply of inside money has been allowed to contract excessively due to insufficient issues of currency to accommodate depositor withdrawals. In London, for instance, the Bank of England has been the sole supplier of currency since it was established in 1694. Other London banks rely upon their reserves of Bank of England notes to supply depositors' currency needs. Through most of the first one and a half centuries of its existence the Bank of England felt no obligation to assist other bankers when they found themselves stripped of cash by a shift of demand from deposits to currency. Partly in consequence of this a series of financial crises occurred in 1763, 1772, 1783, 1793, 1797, 1826, 1836, and 1839. Every one was marked by a significant increase in the demand for currency for making payments in and around London: confidence in Bank of England notes was not lacking, and there were few demands to redeem these in specie. Nor was there any evidence of a rush to redeem country bank notes or to exchange them *en masse* for Bank of England notes. The problem was that country bank notes were not suitable for use in London where their issue and redemption was prohibited. A drop in the acceptability of checks and other noncurrency means of payment therefore translated entirely into greater requests for the notes of London's sole issuing bank.

Henry Thornton (1802, 113), referring to the crisis of 1797, observed that "the distress arising in London . . . was a distress for notes of the Bank of England":

So great was the demand for notes, that interest of money, for a few days before the suspension of payments of the bank, may be estimated . . . to have been about sixteen or seventeen per cent. per ann.

If other London banks had been allowed to issue notes the pressure might have been significantly reduced, since customers might simply have converted their deposits into notes which were also liabilities for the banks making the conversion. Then Bank of England notes would not have occupied a privileged position in bank portfolios; they would have been routinely returned to their issuer for redemption like other competitively issued liabilities. The public, in turn, would have had no special reason to demand Bank of England notes, since notes of other banks would probably have been just as useful for making payments around the city of London. As matters stood, however, the extraordinary demand for currency in London could only result in an extraordinary demand for Bank of England notes. The directors of the Bank of England were, however, concerned only with keeping it solvent; they did not manage its issues to protect other London banks or to prevent a general contraction of credit. Instead, observing the prevailing state of panic and confusion, and fearing that bank closings would generate a general loss of confidence which would threaten the Bank's (specie) reserves, they actually *contracted* its issues, making matters even worse. This action was perhaps not calculated even to serve the interests of the Bank of England, but then the extent of that Bank's involvement in the monetary affairs of the rest of the country was not fully appreciated. Indeed, although changes in the relative demand for currency were a frequent cause of what later became known as "internal drains" upon the resources of the London banks, Hayek observes in his introduction (p. 39) to Thornton's *Paper Credit of Great Britain* that "it took some years . . . for the Bank of England to learn that the way to meet such an internal drain was to grant credits liberally."

The Bank Act of 1844, although it restricted the ability of the Bank of England to generate excessive quantities of base money (as the Bank had, according to the Bullion committee, in the years following the suspension of 1797), also prevented it from making needed adjustments to the supply of currency in response to greater demand. Furthermore, by limiting the note issues of the country banks the Act caused them to employ Bank of England notes to meet depositors' demands where before they might have been able to rely exclusively upon their own issues.

Thus after 1844 episodes of credit stringency were as frequent as before, with interest rates fluctuating in response to the periodic ebb and flow of the relative demand for currency. Rates rose every autumn—when currency was used instead of checkbook money for agricultural transactions—and also at the close of every quarter when stock dividends were paid (often in cash). Jevons was so impressed by this pattern that he devoted a lengthy article to an analysis of it (1884, 160–93). He observed the growing tendency of the London and country banks "to use the Bank of England as a bank of support, and of last resort" (ibid., 170–71).[27] He remarked, in addition, that freedom of note issue along the lines of the Scottish banks was an inviting alternative means for English banks to accommodate their clients' demands for currency, especially since additional currency issued this way would "return spontaneously as the seasons go round" (ibid., 179).[28] In spite of his observations, however, Jevons did not recommend that England adopt free banking; on the contrary, he ended his article by defending the Bank of England's quasi-monopoly of note issue, suggesting incoherently that proponents of free banking were guilty of "confusing" free banking with freedom of trade (ibid., 181).

In many ways Jevons's opinions, except for his opposition to free banking, anticipated[29] those of Walter Bagehot who, in *Lombard Street* (1874, 235–53) drew so much attention to the "lender of last resort" function that it came to be regarded as an official responsibility of the Bank of England and as a rationale for centralizig reserves and note—issue. Because of his influence Bagehot is sometimes viewed as the first champion of scientific central banking. Yet the truth is that Bagehot preferred in principle the "natural system" of competitive note issue—the kind of system that "would have sprung up if Government had let banking alone." His formula for central banking was not a *recommendation* of monopolized note issue but an attempt to make an "anomalous," monopolized system work tolerably well. Bagehot did not want to "propose a revolution" (1874, 67ff). Nor would he have seen any need for one—or for a lender of last resort—save for the fact that monopolization of note issue prevented banks other than the Bank of England from using their own notes to fulfill depositors' demands for currency.[30]

Bagehot was aware of the true connection between monopolization of note issue and the need for a centrally directed monetary policy. Unfortunately, many of those who followed him, including later advocates of central banking, forgot it. Ralph Hawtrey wrote (1932, 285): "When a paper currency is an essential part of the monetary circulation *and one bank possesses a monopoly of note issue*, that bank can secure to itself the position of central bank. It can cut short the supply of currency and drive other banks to borrow directly or indirectly from it." Precisely. Yet Hawtrey, who more than anyone saw the lender of last resort function as the principal rationale for central banking, did not see how central banks' ability to cut short the supply of currency once they possess a monopoly of note issue creates the need for them to serve as lenders of last resort in the first place. If there is competitive note issue, the traditional argument for a lender of last resort carries much less weight.

The case of England is only the most notorious example of problems arising from a lack of currency under monopolized note issue. In Germany a law similar to the Bank Act was passed in 1875. It placed a ceiling on the note issues of the Imperial Bank, Germany's monopoly bank of issue. According to Charles Conant (1905, 128) "high discount rates became the rule . . . as soon as the business of the country grew up to the limit of the note issue." If banks other than the Imperial Bank had been free to issue notes this might have been avoided, because there would not have been any shortage of media to supply the growing demand for currency. There would not have been any great danger of inflation, either (as there was when the Imperial Bank took advantage of its monopoly privilege) because competitively-issued notes would not have served as base money. If issued in excess by any bank, notes would have been returned to their issuer for redemption. As it happened, interest rates in Germany did not return to normal until 1901, when "the limit of the 'uncovered circulation' [of Imperial Bank notes] was raised to conform to the increased needs for currency growing out of the expansion of business."[31]

Another significant financial stringency caused by an uncompensated drain of currency from bank reserves was the "great contraction" in the United States from 1930 to 1932. This involved a large-scale movement from deposits to currency, which was only partly offset by Federal Reserve note issues. The result was a drastic decline in the total money stock followed by a terrible banking collapse.[32]

According to James Boughton and Elmus Wicker (1979, 406), this particular shift from deposits to currency was triggered by the "massive decline in income and interest rates" that began in the fall of 1929.[33] That meant an increase in the relative frequency of small payments combined with a reduced opportunity cost of holding currency. Also encouraging the shift from deposits to currency were a 2 percent federal tax on checks (enacted in June 1932) and an increase from two to three cents in the postal rate for local letters (from July 1932 to June 1933), which increased the cost of paying local bills by check (ibid., 409). Finally, when state authorities began declaring bank holidays in response to insolvencies caused by currency withdrawals and loan losses, they unwittingly provoked even greater withdrawals of currency by depositors. When banks go on holiday, deposits are immobilized, and checks become practically useless in making payments. Currency can, however, still circulate while banks are temporarily closed. Therefore, any suspicion by the public that their banks will go on holiday will lead to a wholesale flight to currency as consumers rush to protect themselves against the risk of being stuck without any means for making purchases.[34] The failure of the Federal authorities to provide adequate reserve compensation during this flight to currency contributed significantly to the severity of this phase of the Great Depression. It caused interest rates, which for a decade before were probably below their "natural" level, to suddenly rise substantially above it.

The American crises under the pre-Federal Reserve National Banking System were also aggravated—and in some cases perhaps caused—by restrictions on note issue by deposit banks. Here, however, the problem was not monopolization of the currency supply, since note issue was still decentralized. Instead, the currency supply was restricted by special bond-collateral requirements on National bank note issues.[35] When eligible bond collateral was in short supply and commanded a premium, note issue became excessively costly. In consequence, banks sometimes met their depositors' requests for currency by allowing them to withdraw greenbacks, a form of currency issued by the Treasury that also functioned as a reserve medium. The consequence was a contraction of total bank liabilities equal to a multiple of the lost reserves.[36] That greenbacks were sometimes not available in desired, small denominations also added to the inconvenience suffered by the public.[37]

The problems of the pre-Federal Reserve National Banking System would have been much less severe had note issue been unrestricted, that is, had banks been able to issue notes on the same terms as they created demand deposits. Free note issue would have satisfied most customers' currency requirements while leaving banks' reserves in place. It also might have made it unnecessary to resort to an agency for reserve compensation such as finally emerged in the shape of the Federal Reserve System.[38] As Friedman and Schwartz note in their *Monetary History of the United States* (1963, 295fn), the troubles of the National Banking System "resulted much less from the absence of elasticity of the total stock of money than from the absence of interconvertibility of deposits and currency." To achieve the latter, free note issue would have been, not only adequate, but more reliable than centralized note issue.[39]

In all of these historical episodes undesirable changes in the total supply of money occurred as a result of changes—sometimes merely seasonal changes—in the relative demand for currency. Had it not been prohibited freedom of note issue would have gone far in eliminating this problem, and where note issue *was* relatively free, as it was in Scotland and Canada, the problem did not arise.[40] Reliance upon a lender of last resort, on the other hand, does *not* get to the root of the problem, since it generally involves a monopolized currency supply which is also "inelastic" and which can be managed properly only with great difficulty, if at all.

The findings of this and the previous chapter contradict the claim that central banking is superior to free banking as a means for guaranteeing monetary equilibrium and general economic stability. But before any broad conclusion can be reached concerning the relative merits of free and central banking we must consider some other, potential shortcomings of unregulated banking. In particular we must consider the possibility that free banking may be unstable due to causes not dealt with in preceeding pages, along with the possibility that it may be inefficient. These issues are taken up in chapter 9.

Appendix: Reserve-Compensation Formulae

A. CENTRAL BANKING

$$M_c = S_p + N_p^{cb} + D_p$$

where M_c = total checkable deposits plus currency held by the public under central banking;

S_p = specie held by the public (assumed = 0);

N_p^{cb} = central bank currency (notes) held by the public; and

D_p = deposits held by the public.

The reserve ratio is defined as:

$$r = \frac{S_b + N_b^{cb} + D_b^{cb}}{D_b} = \frac{\text{commercial bank reserves}}{\text{commercial bank liabilities}}$$

where S_b = specie held by commercial banks (assumed = 0);*

N_b^{cb} = central bank currency held by commercial banks;

D_b^{cb} = central bank deposits held by commercial banks.

By definition, since $S_p = O$, $N_p^{cb} = C_p$ (currency held by the public). Also, B_c (high-powered money) = $N_b^{cb} + N_p^{cb} + D_b^{cb}$ (since S_p and S_b = 0)

---

* It is assumed that under central banking commercial banks convert all specie holdings into deposits or notes of the central bank.

Therefore, $r = \dfrac{B_c - C_p}{D_p}$ and $D_p = \dfrac{B_c - C_p}{r}$.

By substitution, $M_c = C_p + \dfrac{B_c - C_p}{r} = \dfrac{B_c - C_p(1 - r)}{r}$.

B. FREE BANKING

$$M_f = S_p + N_p^b + D_p$$

where M_f = total deposits plus currency held by the public under free banking;

S_p = specie held by the public;

N_p^b = bank notes held by the public

D_p = deposits held by the public.

The reserve ratio is:

$$r = \frac{S_b}{N_p^b + D_p}$$

Since B_f (high-powered money) $= S_p + S_b = S$ and S_p is assumed $= 0$, it follows that

$$r = \frac{B_f}{N_p^b + D_p}$$

By substitution, $M_f = N_p^b + D_p = \dfrac{B_f}{r}$.

9

Stability and Efficiency

W**E HAVE SEEN** that under free banking the supply of inside money tends to be demand elastic. Changes in the price structure due to changes in the demand for money balances are avoided. To this extent the value of the monetary unit is stabilized, and events in the money market do not disturb the normal course of production and exchange. On the other hand, banking systems with centralized currency supply are not as likely to escape monetary disequilibrium and its consequences.

There are, however, three problems related to the stability of free banking that still have to be addressed. These are: unanticipated revaluation of long-term debts due to those movements in general prices that free banking would not prevent, monetary disequilibrium caused by commodity-money supply shocks, and disturbances caused by bank runs and panics. This chapter examines briefly each of these problems. After reaching a verdict as to whether free banking is stable, it turns to consider its efficiency.

Debtor-Creditor Injustice

Chapters 5 and 6 showed how a free banking system tends to prevent changes in the general level of prices that might arise from changes in the aggregate demand for balances of inside money. Free banks, however, do *not* prevent general price movements having as their source either (a) a general advance in per-capita output or productive efficiency or (b) a general decline in per-capita output or productive efficiency. This result is desirable as far as the maintenance of monetary equilibrium is concerned. But it might also involve a revaluation of long-term debts that would be contrary to the expectations and interests of debtors or creditors. If free banking is likely to frustrate the intentions of buyers and sellers of long-term debt—if it leads to frequent debtor-creditor "injustice"—then a search for some less defective alternative would be warranted.

To address the problem of debtor-creditor injustice, one must first understand how different kinds of price changes actually affect the well-being of parties on either side of a debt contract. One also has to have a definition of injustice. For the latter we may adopt the following: parties to a long-term debt contract may be said to be victims of injustice caused by price-level changes if, when the debt matures, either (a) the debtors on average find their real burden of repayment *greater* than what they anticipated at the time of the original contract and creditors find the real value of the sums repaid to them greater on average than what they anticipated; or (b) the creditors find the real value of the sums repaid to them *smaller* on average than what they anticipated and debtors find their real burden of repayment smaller than what they anticipated at the time of the original contract. When injustice occurs the parties to the debt contract, if they had had perfect foresight, would have contracted at a nominal rate of interest different from the one actually chosen.

It is not always appreciated that *not all movements in the general level of prices involve injustice to debtors or creditors*. Unanticipated general price movements associated with changes in per-capita output, such as could occur under free banking, do not affect the fortunes of debtors and creditors in the same, unambiguous way as do unanticipated price movements associated with monetary disequilibrium. Where price movements are due to changes in per-capita output, it is not possible to conclude that unanticipated price reductions favor creditors at the expense of debtors. Nor can it be demonstrated that unanticipated price increases favor debtors at the expense of creditors. The standard argument that unanticipated price changes are a cause of injustice is only applicable to price changes caused by unwarranted changes in money supply or by unaccommodated changes in money demand.

This is so because in one of the cases being considered aggregate per-capita output is changing, whereas in the other it is stationary. In both cases a fall in prices increases the value of the monetary unit and increases the overall burden of indebtedness, whereas a rise in prices reduces the overall burden, other things being equal. In the case where per-capita output is stationary (the monetary disequilibrium case), the analysis need go no further, and it is possible to conclude that falling prices injure debtors and help creditors and vice versa. Were parties to long-term debt contracts able to perfectly anticipate price movements, they would, in anticipation of higher prices, contract at higher nominal rates of interest; in anticipation of lower prices they would contract at lower nominal rates of interest. In the first case the ordinary real rate of interest is increased by an inflation premium; in the latter, it is reduced by a deflation discount. These

adjustments of interest rates to anticipated depreciation or appreciation of the monetary unit are named the "Fisher" effect, after Irving
Fisher who discussed them in an article written just before the turn of
the century.[1]

When per-capita output is *changing*, one must take into account, in
addition to the Fisher effect, any intertemporal-substitution effect
associated with changes in anticipated availability of future real income.[2] Here (assuming no monetary disequilibrium) reduced prices
are a consequence of increased real income, and increased prices are
a consequence of reduced real income. Taking the former case,
although the real value of long-term debts increases, debtors do not
necessarily face a greater real burden of repayment since (on average)
their real income has also risen. In nominal terms they are also not
affected because, as distinct from the case of falling prices due to a
shortage of money, their nominal income is unchanged. Thus debtors
need not suffer any overall hardship: the damage done by the
unanticipated fall in prices may be compensated by the advantage
provided by the unanticipated growth of real income. If the parties to
the debt contract had in this situation actually negotiated with the
help of perfect foresight, their anticipation of reduced prices would
have caused the nominal rate of interest to be reduced by a deflation
discount—the Fisher effect. But their anticipation of increased real
income would also reduce their valuations of future income relative to
present income, raising the real component of the nominal rate of
interest—the intertemporal-substitution effect. Since the Fisher effect
and the intertemporal substitution effect work in opposite directions
it is not clear that the perfect-foresight loan agreement would have
differed from the one reached in the absence of perfect foresight—at
least, the *direction* in which it would have differed is not obvious. So
there is no reason to conclude that a monetary policy that permits
prices to fall in response to increased production would prejudice the
interests of debtors.

Similarly, to allow prices to rise in response to reduced per-capita
output would not result in any necessary injustice to creditors, even if
the price increases were not anticipated. Here the Fisher effect in a
perfect-foresight agreement would be positive, and the intertemporal
substitution effect would be negative, so it cannot be said a priori that
the perfect-foresight nominal rate of interest would differ from the
rate agreed upon in the absence of perfect foresight.

In short, as far as the avoidance of debtor-creditor injustice is
concerned, free banking is not defective despite its failure to prevent
all general price changes. Though it would tend to prevent price
changes that might lead to debtor-creditor injustice, it would also
allow price changes to occur that would *not* result in obvious injustice.

A policy of price-level stabilization, substituted for free banking, would, on the other hand, merely be a more likely source of monetary disequilibrium, without serving to reduce instances of debtor-creditor injustice.

All this implies that monetary reform proposals aimed at achieving money of constant purchasing power are superfluous. One such proposal recommends the use of inside money that is a claim to an assortment or "basket" of commodities.[3] Besides being more complicated and costly to administer, a multiple-commodity standard actually has no advantage over free banking with a single-commodity standard as a means for eliminating debtor-creditor injustice, so there is no reason for considering it.[4]

Commodity-Money Supply Shocks

This brings us to another criticism frequently leveled at single-commodity standards: that they are subject to "shocks" in the supply of the money commodity. In previous chapters it has been assumed that the supply of commodity money is constant. This would be a correct description of conditions under free banking if the only inducement to increase production of commodity money were an increase in its relative price, given that the complete substitution of inside money for outside money in persons' balances makes such an increase in the relative price of commodity money unlikely.[5] But increased production of commodity money may also occur because of a fall in its cost of production, due perhaps to some technological innovation or to a discovery of new sources (if the commodity is a natural resource) with lower marginal extraction costs than those already in use.

In the long run, automatic forces tend to limit cost-related changes in the output of commodity money. Michael Bordo (1984, 201) explains this in reference to gold:

> A rapid increase in the output of gold due to gold discoveries or technological improvements in gold mining would raise the prices of all other goods in terms of gold, making them more profitable to produce than gold and thus ultimately leading to a reduction in gold output. Moreover, the initial reduction in the purchasing power of gold would lead to a shift in the demand for gold for nonmonetary use, thus reinforcing the output effects.

The question is, how serious are short-run shocks likely to be? There are as many potential answers to this question as there are potential money commodities. Particularly intriguing is the historical performance of the gold standard, since gold would probably have continued to serve as base money if governments in previous centuries had permitted free banking. Was the gold standard as inherently unstable as critics suggest? How does its record compare, for instance, to that of the fiat dollar?

One cannot adequately answer such questions by simply noting that gold output has fluctuated widely during the so-called gold standard era, or that changes in the relative price of gold have occurred.[6] Changes in gold output may have been exogenous supply shocks or they may have come in response to shifts in the demand for gold. Only exogenous changes in output, which imply a shift in the supply schedule of gold (rather than mere movement *along* the supply schedule) support the conclusion that gold output has been unstable. As for changes in the relative price of gold—which are the proximate cause of endogenous changes in its supply—it is necessary to ask whether these are due to shifts in the demand schedule for gold such as might occur under free banking, or whether they are linked to the existence of centralization or other kinds of government interference. With these points in mind, let us look at the historical evidence.

Charts of world gold production since the 19th century, the first period for which fairly reliable statistics exist, show an obvious pattern of peaks and valleys, like a series of U's strung together, usually in ascending fashion (figure 9.1). The question is, does this pattern

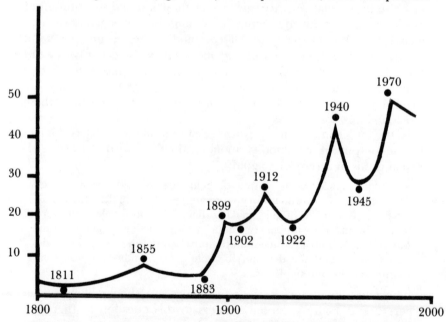

Figure 9.1 World gold production, millions of troy ounces, since 1800. Data are from the United States Gold Commission *Report*, pp. 188–89 and 195–96.

indicate a series of supply shocks (the upward strokes of the U's), or does it indicate a response to changes in demand?

Both theory and history show the pattern to be a response to existing demand. The economics of mining are such that at a fixed price for the mineral produced, the pattern of output that yields the greatest time-discounted income stream looks something like the interval between the troughs of two adjacent U's. That pattern is the product of two counteracting forces. One is the rate of interest: were mining to require no capital investment, at any rate of interest greater than zero it would pay to extract ore as quickly as technologically possible so as to receive the greatest possible present income. The other force is capital investment: were the rate of interest zero, given some initial capital investment it would pay to extend the mine's life as long as necessary to extract all the ore (assuming all of the ore to be of a uniform grade). Typically, mining does require a capital investment and the rate of interest is greater than zero, so production follows a curve that maximizes time-discounted income per unit of capital invested. It neither extracts all the ore at once nor extends the mine's life to the maximum technologically feasible.[7]

Once this is understood, the claim that gold has a "backward-rising" supply curve, which supposedly detracts from its desirability as outside money, can be shown to be incorrect.[8] It is true that when the price of gold goes up, gold production at first often decreases. This happens because certain factors of ore production, most notably the crushing and refining equipment, are fixed in the short run. When gold production becomes cheaper a lower grade of ore becomes newly profitable to mine; hence if the equipment is always working at full capacity, it will produce less gold than before. Were the lower-grade ore not mined then, it might never be, since a rise in production costs would make its extraction unprofitable. Any other mining strategy would also be uneconomical, for it would extract a lower time-discounted value of gold than is profitable. If the cost of production remained low, though, it would pay to bring new deposits into production, build new refineries, etc., thus increasing gold supply.

History supports the view that gold discoveries and improvements in extraction techniques are best understood as responses to increased demand for gold rather than as supply shocks. A recent, careful study of the great 19th-century gold discoveries concludes that only the California discovery of 1849 was accidental. The rest, those of Siberia (1814, 1829), eastern Australia (1851), western Australia (1889), and South Africa (1886), were results of more or less methodical searches encouraged by high real prices for gold. Even in the case of the California discovery most accounts suggest that gold would sooner or later have been found by methodical search, as prospecting was taking place elsewhere in the state.[9]

The major technological advance in gold mining during the 19th century was the MacArthur-Forrest process for using cyanide to leach gold from crushed ore. In some areas it increased yields as much as 50 percent. The process, first used commercially in 1889, replaced a chlorination process discovered in 1848. Both methods were developed during periods of high real prices for gold, and evidence suggests that the high real gold prices were the motivating force behind them.[10]

The record of gold production in this century is as free of supply shocks as that of the 19th century. The only major accidental discovery of gold was the Amazon River discovery of early 1980. Like the California discovery of 1848, this was a find of alluvial (riverbed) gold. Alluvial gold is much easier to mine than underground gold. The former takes the form of nuggets or particles that can be dredged and sifted with nothing more elaborate than a pan, whereas the latter occurs mixed in the rock with other minerals, and requires more complicated equipment to mine and separate. The cheapness of mining alluvial gold, and its quality of being less predictable in deposit size than underground gold, make it a likelier source of supply shocks. However, as the number of unexplored rivers diminishes, so does the chance of large new discoveries of alluvial gold. Most of the easily accessible gold seems to have been mined already. For this reason gold mining today is more institutional than it was in the past,[11] making its supply even less prone to supply shocks.[12] Recent advances in mining technology, like those of the 19th century, also seem to have been brought on by increases in the real price of gold. The carbon-in-pulp extraction process, though known in rudimentary form since the last century, was not used commercially until 1973, the year the price of gold surpassed $100 an ounce (Weston 1983, 134).

A final point to bear in mind when looking at the historical record of gold production is that during the period of the so-called classical gold standard few nations allowed completely free banking. Nor did they permit their central banks to take advantage of the true economies of fiduciary substitution. Statutory reserve requirements and prohibitions against small notes spurred much gold production that, under free banking, would never have taken place.

By far the most important source of disturbances to gold supply has been, not accidental discoveries, but political interference. The "golden avalanche" of the 1930s (as a contemporary book termed it) and the recent great increase in gold production both resulted from inflation by central banks leading to currency devaluations. In addition, the chief gold-producing nations of the 19th and 20th centuries have all taxed, regulated or subsidized the gold mining industry in ways that have systematically distorted output. Wars and revolutions, such as the Boer War of 1899–1902 in South Africa and World War II, have also affected production (ibid., 633–39).[13] Still, there is no evidence that political interference has had any worse effects on gold production than it has had on the production of other commodities, on international trade, or on labor migrations; hence a gold standard is at least no worse in this respect than any other conceivable commodity standard.

Still another kind of shock to which a commodity standard may be vulnerable is a change in the nonmonetary demand for the money commodity. As fiduciary substitution becomes more complete, the consequences of such demand shocks become more serious. The extreme case is that of a pure credit banking system of the sort mentioned in chapter 2, in which there are no reserves of commodity money. As Knut Wicksell noted (1935, 125), in such a system an increase in the nonmonetary demand for the money commodity might make it necessary for banks to contract drastically their issues, forcing prices to fall so that redemption demands are checked and further production of the money commodity is encouraged. Thus, under a commodity standard the goal of preserving monetary equilibrium may come into conflict with that of achieving maximum efficiency by minimizing resource costs. (This must be kept in mind when we appraise the efficiency of free banking in section 4 below.)

Bank Runs and Panics

The above arguments concerning the long-run stability of free banking ignore the possibility of contractions and crises due to bank runs. In its broadest sense a bank run is an incident where customers of a bank turn to it *en masse* to convert its liabilities. There are two kinds of bank runs. One is a run to convert deposits into currency, where currency includes competitively issued bank notes. This can be called a "currency run." The second is a run to convert deposits or competitively issued notes into high-powered money, meaning commodity money, redeemable notes of a monopoly bank of issue, or centrally issued fiat money. This can be called an "redemption run." Because we are still assuming the existence of a commodity standard, the case of runs for fiat money will not be considered here.

The above-noted difference between a currency run and a redemption run is subtle but crucial. Arrangements satisfactory for handling increases in currency demand may be worthless when it comes to handling increases in the demand for high-powered money. On the other hand, arrangements for the emergency supply of high-powered money, while perhaps necessary to combat redemption runs, can also bring about inflation, and are therefore not desirable if all that is needed is some way to provide depositors with media for making hand-to-hand payments.

As was shown in chapter 8, there is no reason for a currency run to be a cause of stringency in a free banking system, since banks in such a system are unrestricted in their ability to issue notes in exchange for outstanding deposits. Such note issues do not affect the liquidity or solvency of banks undertaking them.

This state of affairs differs greatly from what transpires under centralized banking or wherever note issue is artificially restricted. A currency run under these conditions can easily exhaust the resources of unprivileged banks, draining them of their reserves of high-powered money. Yet the same banks might meet demands up to the full value of their deposits if they could resort to unrestricted note issue. As was shown in chapter 8, there is considerable evidence showing that many past banking crises were consequences of currency runs in the face of restrictions upon note issue.[14]

In addition to their other differences, there is also a big difference between the causes of a currency run and those of a redemption run. A currency run may be triggered by any event that reduces the acceptability of checks relative to currency. An example mentioned in chapter 8 was a decline in business confidence leading to greater fear of persons writing bad checks, i.e., tendering spurious claims against their bank. This risk does not exist when bank notes are tendered (provided the notes are not forgeries). Tradespeople might be perfectly willing to accept bank notes from persons whose checks they would refuse.

Redemption runs involve a loss of confidence of a much higher order. Here, it is not would-be check writers, but the banks themselves, which are suspect. When loss of confidence goes this far, freedom to issue bank notes is no solution, since a suspect bank's notes, as well as its deposits, are equally distrusted. Until something happens to restore their confidence those who hold such liabilities will opt for nothing less than their redemption in high-powered money. If the bank in question is a monopoly bank of issue, then the run will be a run for commodity money exclusively.

A currency shortage, besides provoking a currency run, may cause a redemption run as well. If by virtue of some restriction a deposit holder seeking currency cannot be accommodated by a further issue of notes, his bank will have no alternative but to satisfy him by drawing on its reserves of high-powered money. Thus a currency run in the face of restrictions on note issue causes banks to suffer a loss of liquidity just as if the run had been for high-powered money in the first place. The loss of liquidity increases the risk that the bank will be unable to redeem its issues. If the precariousness of the bank's position is discovered, this can in turn cause its liability holders to lose confidence in it and to convert even its notes into high-powered money. In general, however, a redemption run can occur in response to any event that liability-holders view as a threat to their bank's net worth. Historically, war, recession, or the failure of one or more large businesses have been taken as warning signs.[15]

There is nothing unreasonable about this sort of behavior on the part of holders of bank liabilities. People want to avoid losses from having their savings improperly managed. Nor is it undesirable in principle that individual banks be allowed to fail: if a bank is poorly managed then it is in the best interest of consumers to have it yield its share of the market to more reliable firms. Relieved of the prospect of failure, firms in any industry are apt to become stagnant and inefficient. This is no less true of banks. Banks will be more adept at managing the supply of inside money if the worst of them are allowed to perish.

Such failures need not involve losses to those holding liabilities of failed banks. Responsibility for these liabilities could be assumed by other banks, as when an insolvent bank is liquidated by a merger with one of its rivals. This was how many Scottish and Canadian free banks, aided by the absence of restrictions on branch banking, wound up their affairs. Some holders of liabilities of Scottish banks were also protected by their banks' shareholders being subject to unlimited liability, making them personally responsible for all of their banks' debts. Although as many as 19 banks went out of business during the Scottish free banking era,[16] their closings cost liability holders only £32,000.[17]

Private insurance could also protect note and deposit holders against losses due to bank failures.[18] Such insurance, provided on a competitive basis, would have a distinct advantage over present government-administered insurance. Government insurance assesses individual banks using a flat-rate schedule, charging them only according to their total deposits. This procedure subsidizes high-risk banks at the expense of low-risk ones, creating a serious moral-hazard problem—itself a cause of more frequent bank failures. In contrast, profit maximizing, competing private insurers would attempt to charge every bank a premium reflecting the riskiness of its particular assets.[19] While available information would be inadequate to guarantee perfect risk-pricing *ex ante*, premiums could be continually readjusted *ex post*, with the help of frequent audits. Another possibility would be combination insurance-safety fund arrangements, perhaps administered by clearinghouse associations, in which participant banks establish escrow-type accounts by depositing assets with the insurer as a condition for being insured.[20] The safety-fund accounts could be continually "marked to market" to reflect loan losses, and they could be attached by the insurer whenever a failure resulted in losses exceeding amounts predicted in the original insurance estimate. Such an arrangement would be very close to the full-information ideal, which entirely eliminates subsidization of risk. Though some mismeasurement would still occur, it would not pose any more serious a problem than risk-measurement problems routinely dealt with in other private casualty insurance.

Still another private means for giving protection to bank-liability holders would involve banks protecting one another's liabilities through a system of cross-guarantees.[21] A failed bank with its liabilities guaranteed by a group of other banks could draw on the capital of those banks to the extent of its insolvency loss. Guarantees could be arranged so that no bank would be both a guarantor of and guaranteed by another bank. Such an arrangement would disperse losses widely, making the liabilities of each bank a contingent claim on the equity capital of numerous other banks. This would be similar in its effects on bank-customer confidence to the unlimited-liability provisions in Scottish free banking.

As was said in chapter 2, a free banking system also presents greater opportunities for the establishment of equity or mutual-fund type accounts with full checkability privileges. Such accounts might be offered by banks as well as by non-bank firms. To the extent that equity accounts take the place of conventional bank debt liabilities, the burden placed on private means for depositor-protection is correspondingly reduced. As regulatory restrictions (such as the Glass-Steagall Act) are phased-out, equity accounts would take up a growing share of the public's financial holdings, and private deposit-guarantees would become more and more feasible. Many criticisms of private deposit-guarantee arrangements, based as they are on comparisons of the current value of bank or insurance-industry capital with the *current* value of bank debt, are therefore not relevant for assessing the merits of private guarantees in a fully deregulated banking system.

If a bank that suffers a redemption run is solvent, so that its assets, liquidated in an orderly fashion, could pay its debts, then it might be unfortunate from the point of view of consumers for the bank to fail simply because it lacked sufficient base money to pay its anxious customers on the spot. Still, a bank that is run on for any reason is likely to be unable to liquidate its assets in an orderly fashion to redeem its liabilities. It may have to sell assets in a rush, and therefore realize much less than their potential value, or else close its doors. Either way, its customers will be disappointed.

Fortunately such a bank, if it alone is distressed or if it is one of a small number of threatened banks, can seek assistance from unaffected branches of its own parent banking firm or from other banking firms, directly or through a clearinghouse. Other banks can make a profit by lending emergency funds to their troubled rivals, so long as the latter offer adequate collateral. An alternative method for dealing with isolated runs, adopted for a time by the Scottish free banks, is to have an "option clause" on circulating notes.[22] Such a clause would allow notes to be paid *either* on demand *or* within six months following their original presentation for redemption, with interest paid for the length of the delay. This arrangement would permit illiquid banks to suspend payment to their customers for a period up to six months, time enough to liquidate their loans and investments, avoiding the more costly alternative of borrowing emergency funds from rivals. The option clause would resemble, and be really no more sinister than, the notice of withdrawal clauses now appended to many passbook-savings agreements. The latter are also meant to protect bankers against short-term liquidity crises.[23]

Of greater concern are runs that, instead of being restricted to one or a few particular banks, spread like a contagion to a large number of banks in a system. Such a rash of bank runs is called a panic. When a panic occurs, unthreatened banks may be too few in number to supply adequate emergency funds. When the entire system is in danger of collapsing, it would seem that only universal suspension or resort to an outside source of high-powered money, such as a central bank operating outside the limits of lost confidence, could offer any hope for rescue.

But why should panics ever occur? Why should liability holders suddenly lose confidence in all or many banks just because something has happened to cause a run on or the failure of one or several of them? According to one theory, panics happen because liability holders lack bank-specific information about changes in the banking systems' total net worth. For example, they may be aware that some event has resulted in losses to certain banking firms. Yet they may lack information regarding precisely which banks are affected, because an "information externality" prevents the price system from performing its normal function of disseminating information about the riskiness of particular liabilities. In other words, panics occur when liability holders feel a need to test the safety of their balances.[24]

If deposits are guaranteed using some of the means discussed a moment ago, depositors would have little reason to run on their banks, and panic would likewise be curtailed. But there is reason to suspect that, under free banking, panics would be unlikely even *without* deposit guarantees. As Gary Gorton has shown in several articles (Gorton 1985a, 1985c; Gorton and Mullineaux 1985), in a market where bank liabilities are competitively bought and sold there would not be any risk-information externality. Note and deposit exchange rates would reflect potentials for capital losses depending on the soundness of underlying bank loans and investments. Chapter 2 showed how note brokerage systematically eliminates note-discounting except when it is based on risk-default generally acknowledged by professional note dealers, including banks themselves. In short, note brokerage produces information on bank-specific risk. With such information available to depositors, no information externality could cause bank runs to spread indiscriminantly through a banking system. After confirming through the newspaper that there is no discount on the notes he holds, a bank customer would feel no urge to redeem them in a hurry. Gorton also points out that, even though no distinct secondary (arbitrage) market exists for the risk-pricing of deposit liabilities,[25] so long as notes and deposits of any one bank are backed by the same asset portfolio (as would be the case under free banking) the existence of a secondary note market provides depositors with all the information required to prevent them from staging a redemption run.

Thus under free banking no risk-information externality problem would arise. This may explain why failure of individual banks never precipitated general runs either in the Scottish free banking system or in Canada during the period when its banks engaged in relatively unregulated note issue.

In the United States, on the other hand, there have been banking panics, not only since 1914 (when plural note issue was eliminated), but also throughout the 19th century when many banks issued notes. Obviously the secondary market for notes in this case failed to be a useful indicator of bank-specific risk. There were at least three reasons for this, all of them connected to legislative restrictions: (a) the requirement of special asset backing for note issues, (b) the consequent non-price rationed deficiency of the note supply relative to the demand for currency, and (c) the requirement, after 1866, of mandatory par note acceptance by all nationally chartered banks, which were at the time the only banks able to issue notes. Under the bond collateral laws, beginning with the misleadingly named "free banking" laws passed in many states after 1837, deposits of special bond-collateral were required to secure bank-note issues. Since the special collateral applied to notes only (and not to deposits), risk premiums attached to notes did not always reflect the riskiness of deposits. Therefore, in the case of deposit liabilities, an information externality still existed. Holders of these liabilities could not rely on price signals from the note market as guides to the safety of portfolios backing their balances. The Panic of 1857 occurred under these circumstances, and, as might be expected, the evidence suggests that it began as a panic of deposit holders which note holders subsequently joined.[26]

The currency shortages that plagued the National Banking System caused varying premiums to be placed on notes of all kinds, interfering with the ability of note prices to indicate changes in the riskiness of underlying bank portfolios. This must also have contributed to risk-information externalities. Finally, the forced par acceptance of post-Civil War currency mandated by the government to prevent discounting of greenbacks (which were unredeemable at the time of their issue) short-circuited the secondary market for bank notes, ending any remaining possibility for efficient pricing of bank-specific risk. Market prices failed to reflect, even in rough fashion, the expected value of risky redemption promises.

These are some compelling reasons for viewing banking panics, not as phenomena likely to occur under unregulated banking, but rather as events caused by interference with the natural development of note issue and note exchange.

The Efficiency of Free Banking

Opponents of commodity standards, and of the gold standard in particular, often criticize them as being inefficient. They deplore the wastefulness of expending resources in producing commodity money, such as in gold mining, pointing out that, were there some other monetary standard (usually a fiat standard), these resources could be used to satisfy other wants. Three quotations from influential sources, one by a banker financier of the 18th century and the others by economists of this century, illustrate the persistence and respectability of this line of reasoning:

> all this part [that is, all the gold and silver in monetary use] has been withdrawn from ordinary commerce by a law for which there were reasons under the old government, but which is a disadvantage in itself. It is as if a part of the wool or silk in the kingdom were set aside to make exchange tokens: would it not be more commodious if these were given over to their natural use, and the exchange tokens made of materials which in themselves serve no useful purpose?[27]

> gold mines are of the greatest value and importance to civilization. Just as wars have been the only form of large-scale loan expenditure which statesmen have thought justifiable, so gold-mining has been the only

pretext for digging holes in the ground which has recommended itself to bankers as sound finance; and each of these activities has played its part in progress—failing something better.[28]

The fundamental defect of a commodity standard, from the point of view of society as a whole, is that it requires the use of real resources to add to the stock of money. People must work hard to dig something out of the ground in one place—to dig gold out of the ground in south Africa—in order to rebury it in Fort Knox, or some similar place.[29]

Since the hypothetical free banking system we have so far been concerned with is based on a commodity standard, do these criticisms apply to it? In answer it must be noted that, although free banking may require the existence of some base money,[30] it also promotes maximum fiduciary substitution—the replacement of base money with unbacked inside money—given the constraint that inside money must continue to be redeemable in base money. By allowing any increased demand for money balances to be met through an increased supply of inside money, free banking minimizes the devotion of resources to production of the base-money commodity.

Given this arrangement, would-be investments in commodity money—such as might take place if bank money had to be backed by 100 percent reserves—are translated into increased loanable funds. This, as was shown in chapter 2, is the principal economic advantage of fractional-reserve banking. The extent to which commodity money is economized also tends to increase as the banking system develops over time. This happens because of the economies of scale in reserve holding (especially marked in systems with branch banking) and because of improvements in clearing arrangements and practices. The latter improvements are made so long as their marginal contribution to bank revenues, through their incremental effects on the size of the loan fund, exceed their marginal costs, including costs associated with any increased risk of non-payment of clearing balances.

When these considerations are taken into account, the costs of maintaining a commodity standard under free banking are seen to be much lower than those of maintaining the same standard in a more restrictive system. This can be illustrated for the case of the gold standard. Perhaps the most widely-accepted estimate of the cost of a gold standard is Milton Friedman's estimate (1960, 104fn), which claims that the cost of a pure gold standard would be approximately 2.5 percent of net national product, based on figures from 1960. But this result assumes that banks hold gold reserves equal to 100 percent of their liabilities. Past experience suggests that the reserve ratio under free banking would be closer to 2 percent.[31] Lawrence H. White (1984d, 148–49fn), using 1982 figures together with facts relating to the Scottish free banking episode, derives an alternative estimate of the proportion of GNP which, under free banking, would be devoted to production of monetary gold. He arrives at a figure of 0.014 percent. Even this is too high, however, since it assumes that the public would keep gold coin in circulation costing about 0.010 percent of GNP to produce. If free banks are not hampered (as they were in Scotland) by prohibitions against small notes, the tendency would be for less gold to circulate. Finally, White also assumes that monetary gold production would increase along with the demand for inside money; but since complete reliance by the public on inside money makes this unnecessary, even 0.004 percent of GNP is probably too high an estimate of the resource costs of a free banking gold standard.

A well-developed free-banking system, rather than divert resources into production of commodity money, can function on whatever stock of commodity money happens to be available in bank reserves; it does not promote production of commodity money, since it is not a source of upward pressure on the relative price of the money commodity. Ideally, then, the annual resource cost of a free-banking commodity standard would be close to zero, if only the costs of acquiring additional sums of commodity money are considered. Remaining costs would be sunk costs, and these could even diminish as further fiduciary substitution permits more of the reserve base to be released for industrial uses and for export.

There is no reason to believe that a central-bank commodity standard would be more efficient than one based on free banking. Insofar as central banks are likely to be a source of monetary disequilibrium they would tend to raise resource costs unnecessarily. When a central bank underissues, it directly stimulates production of commodity money by causing the relative price of commodity money to rise. When a central bank overissues, it at first diverts industrial and other nonmonetary demands from regular sources of commodity money to its own redemption counter. But this must eventually force it to contract. Therefore any temporary savings from reduced production of commodity money are illusory, whereas the costs of monetary disequilibrium due to the ensuing disruption of economic activity are very real.

Even if opponents of a free-banking commodity standard concede that the costs from using commodity money may all be sunk costs, they can still point to the ongoing costs of storing gold in bank vaults rather than selling it for nonmonetary use. Based on this they may argue that an inconvertible fiat standard could be less costly than any commodity-money standard, including a free-banking commodity-money standard. But there are other opportunity costs besides the cost of commodity money that make the switch from a commodity standard to fiat money so unattractive that it has rarely, if ever, been made without coercion. If experience teaches anything, it teaches that there are tremendous costs to a fiat-money regime, mainly in the form of inappropriate responses to changes in the demand for inside money and the disruptions and business cycles they cause. Trying to save resources by forcing a switch from a commodity standard to a fiat standard is like trying to save resources by forcing people to take off the locks on their doors and give them to scrap-metal dealers. It is obvious that the cost of making locks is far less than the cost of losing one's property. The same is true of the cost of holding claims redeemable in commodity money. If consumers were willing to accept a fiat standard voluntarily, banks could induce them to do so by offering higher interest rates than competitors who still held commodity-money reserves, reflecting the lower operating costs of not having to hold non-interest earning assets. If this does not happen, one must conclude that consumers perceive a commodity standard as a higher-quality good than a fiat standard.[32]

A further disadvantage of a forced fiat standard is that, like a central-bank–based commodity standard, it is actually likely to *increase* the resources devoted to production of commodity money. It may do so by creating a new motive for holding commodity money that would not exist under a commodity standard—the speculative demand to hold commodity money against the possibility of a fall in the fiat currency's value.[33] That fiat money may be issued costlessly, because it is not a liability but rather a form of wealth to its issuers, does not merely present possibilities for greater economy: it also acts as a temptation to the issuers. Informed by the great inflations of history, the public is not blind to this, and it takes appropriate precautions. The experience with gold in the 1930s and in the years since 1968 amply illustrate this truth. In both periods steps were taken to limit the convertibility of inside money, and gold jumped up in price— from $20.67 to $35 an ounce in the 1930s, and from $35 to $42.50 and as high as $850 since 1968. Gold production also shot up.[34] In the most recent episode of currency devaluation, huge futures markets in gold have sprung up where none existed before, resulting in an estimated additional demand of several million ounces of gold just for clearing contracts that are rarely held for delivery. In short, recent history suggests that substantially *more* resources are being devoted to "digging for gold in order to bury it again" than in the days when persons could place their confidence in claims supposed to be redeemable in gold. In the face of such palpable evidence of the increase in resources devoted to gold production (and to the building of organized futures markets and other inflation-inspired institutions) it is ludicrous to maintain that a forced fiat standard is less costly than a gold standard.[35]

Although its arguments have been in defense of gold, this chapter is not aimed at advocating a return to the gold standard. Nor should it be interpreted as saying that *any* sort of commodity standard is desirable. Its purpose has been to show that the traditional view that commodity standards are inherently unstable and inefficient is not necessarily valid, especially as regards a free-banking commodity standard. Nevertheless, free banking does not have to be based on a reproducible commodity money. It can also be based on any generally accepted, noncommodity medium of exchange, such as fiat currency. Such an arrangement is considered in chapter 11, where a possible free banking reform is outlined. In the proposed reform there is no possibility of a base-money supply shock. Furthermore, the opportunity costs of maintaining a stock of fiat base money are zero, so it is inconceivable even in theory that replacement of inside money convertible in it with inconvertible paper could produce any savings whatsoever.

10

Miscellaneous Criticisms of Free Banking

THE PRECEDING CHAPTERS addressed the major, traditional criticisms of free banking. They showed that free banking is not
inflationary, that it does not promote monetary disequilibrium, that it
does not allow undesirable fluctuations in the value of money, that it is
not otherwise unstable or especially subject to runs and panics, and
that it does not use resources inefficiently.

But some criticisms of free banking still need to be discussed. Many
lack substance, being products of conventional wisdom. Other, more
sophisticated criticisms are that free banking encourages fraud, that it
inhibits economic growth, that it is inconsistent with full employment,
that note issue is a natural monopoly, that the production of money is
a public good, that there are externalities in the production or
consumption of money that cause its competitive supply to be deficient or excessive, and that a banking system needs a lender of last
resort. Finally, some criticisms of free banking are based on considerations of expediency; they refer, not to any theoretical shortcoming of
free banking, but to the claim that free banking is unpopular, politically unacceptable, or difficult to implement and hence impractical as
a means of reform.

Criticisms from Conventional Wisdom

The first criticism we must consider, based on conventional wisdom,
holds that free banking cannot be desirable because, were it desirable,
it would have been adopted long ago; at least there would be no such
widespread support for central banking as currently exists among
theorists and policy makers.[1] This poses a form of argument by
authority, and would not merit attention were it not the major reason

why free banking is not considered a serious alternative for monetary reform.

In response it must be said that the vast majority of economists, including monetary economists, have never given serious thought to the possibility of free banking: they take centralization for granted, not because they have compared it with free banking and found it superior, but because they are unfamiliar with free banking and because they prefer to study money and banking as they find them in economies today. Also, economists are prone to make the unwarranted assumption that legislation and institutions are generally sponsored by considerations of social welfare. The truth, as we have seen, is that many central banks are an outgrowth of monopoly banks of issue established by governments anxious to monetize their debt but not particularly interested in promoting monetary stability. Furthermore, in many places centralized banking prevailed only after a struggle, with respectable theorists participating on both sides.[2]

A related criticism holds that central banking has triumphed because free banking has historically failed to work. This claim, as chapter 1 showed, is simply false. Though episodes of free banking have been rare in history, where they occurred (as in Scotland, Sweden, China and, to a less complete extent, Canada) the evidence does not indicate that they were replaced because they were not functioning well. On the contrary, the record of these systems was quite favorable. The test they failed was political, not economic.

Banking in the United States in the first half of the 19th century is often cited as an instance of the failure of laissez faire. This, too, is incorrect: the free banks that are supposed to have performed so poorly throughout this era were not truly free at all.[3] They are more accurately called "bond deposit" banks because of the special security needed for their note issues. State laws also prohibited them from forming branch networks that would have added to their stability and efficiency. Comparing the theoretical implications of these restrictions to the actual performance of America's "free" banks shows the U.S. episode to be evidence, not of the shortcomings of free banking, but of the shortcomings of regulations.

Another common argument against free banking is that note issue is a government prerogative. Drawing a parallel with coinage, the argument claims that, because coinage has everywhere for centuries been a prerogative of government, the issue of currency should also be subject to government control. But the analogy to coinage is not persuasive. Even if governments must monopolize the production of coins it does not follow that they must monopolize currency. Otherwise one might with equal reason argue that the government should monopolize the production of checkable deposits and other financial assets, since these have as much in common with paper currency as it has with coin. Of course, very few theorists argue for nationalization of deposit banking. They see a crucial difference between deposits and bank notes. Still, it must be shown that the difference is crucial enough to warrant nationalization of one but not the other, and a mere analogy with coinage does not do this.

Even if the analogy of bank notes with coin were airtight, it would justify nationalization of currency production only if the government's coinage prerogative were itself justified. Yet no convincing argument exists to show that private coinage is inefficient. Jevons's argument for government coinage—one of the only attempts to give theoretical justification to this institution—which criticized Herbert Spencer's defense of private coinage,[4] is based on a misunderstanding of Gresham's Law. Jevons (1882, 64–65) wrote that "if coining were left free, those who sold light coins at reduced prices would drive the best trade." He failed to see that there is no more reason for sellers "of light coins at reduced prices" to be preferred to sellers of heavier coins at higher prices than there is for sellers of milk at 75¢ a quart to be preferred to those selling it at $1.50 a half-gallon. If consumers show a preference in such cases, it must be for size rather than quality. Such preferences have nothing to do with Gresham's Law that "bad money will drive out good money," to which Jevons tried to appeal. Indeed, it is only when light coins *do not* sell at reduced prices relative to heavy coins—that is, if their exchange rates are not allowed to reflect their lower metallic content—that Gresham's Law takes effect. This would not happen in a free market where exchange rates reflect consumer preferences.

Empirical evidence also disputes the argument that governments must monopolize production of coin. As we observed in chapter 2, the first coins were produced by private mints rather than governments, and there is no evidence that government issues when they appeared were superior to private ones.[5] Instead, the government prerogative in coinage required the use of force to outlaw private competitors whose issues the public preferred.

The coinage monopoly of the United States government has been challenged on several occasions. The gold coins of Templeton Reid of Georgia—which actually had a bullion value slightly above their face value—and the gold Bechtler coins of North Carolina—minted in the 1830s and still in circulation half a century later—competed successfully with coins produced by nearby Federal rivals, and the Bechtler coinage (over three million dollars worth) was for some time the favored money of the mid-Atlantic states.[6] During the California gold rush at least fifteen private mints struck coins to satisfy a demand that would otherwise have gone unfulfilled due to the absence of any government mint. Some of them produced inferior coin, but those that did so fell rapidly into disrepute and were outcompeted by other firms such as Moffat & Co., Kellogg & Co., and Wass, Molitor & Co. The latter firms enjoyed excellent reputations (in addition to tacit government approval) even though private coinage had become a misdemeanor in California law after April 1850 (Adams 1913, xii).

One of the last American private mints, Clark, Gruber & Co., operated between 1860 and 1862 and produced high-quality gold coins often superior to United States coins of like denomination. In its two years of existence, it produced approximately $3,000,000 of coin and threatened to rob the Federal mints of a substantial part of their market. To guard against this the government bought the mint out in 1863 for $25,000 (Watner 1976, 27–28). Two years later the Federal government passed a law prohibiting all private coinage.

Fraud and Counterfeiting

A more substantive argument against free banking is that it is prone to fraud. Thomas Tooke, in his *History of Prices*, endorsed the opinion of an anonymous American writer that "free trade in banking is synonymous with free trade in swindling" (Tooke 1840, 205).[7] Milton Friedman, who has since modified his views on this subject, was only slightly more charitable in *A Program for Monetary Stability*. He claimed that bank note contracts "are peculiarly difficult to enforce":

> The very performance of its central function requires money to be generally acceptable and to pass from hand to hand. As a result, individuals may be led to enter into contracts with persons far removed in space and acquaintance, and a long period may elapse between the issue of a promise and the demand for its fulfilment. In fraud as in other activities, opportunities for profit are not likely to go unexploited. A fiduciary currency is therefore likely . . . to be overissued.[8]

To support his argument, Friedman referred to the occurance of fraud during the so-called "free banking" era in the U. S. We have already seen why many inferences concerning free banking drawn from this episode are inappropriate: American "free banks" were regulated bond-deposit banks, and bond-deposit requirements, rather than anything inherent in free banking, were responsible for the worst episodes of fraud.[9]

The substance of Friedman's argument is also defective. It seems to say that because money (i.e., commodity money) must be generally acceptable, so must bank notes. It is true that banks, in order to stay in the business of note issue, must establish a fairly wide market for their notes, but no bank when it first begins business is presented with such a market as a given. Every bank must slowly construct a market for its notes by consistently honoring its promises. Some banks might establish their reliability in the businesses of lending and deposit administration, using this as a way of securing entry into the market for notes. In any event a bank is likely to have to make a considerable investment in brand-name capital before its notes can travel to persons "far removed in space and acquaintance" who will unhesitatingly accept them. The circumstances are not especially favorable to fraud. This is not to say that fraud will not take place, but only that there is no reason to believe that it will happen more regularly than in a system of deposit banks. Indeed, the danger of fraud is likely to be greatest under monopolized banking: a monopoly bank of issue can defraud its customers with impunity, especially if it is aided by a suspension of payment sanctioned by the government. History bears evidence to this time after time.

Connected to the idea that free banks will be prone to fraud is the belief that their notes, once issued, will circulate for long periods before being returned as clearings which will test the reliability of their issuer.[10] This delay between issue and reflux is supposed to invite swindlers, who can use it as an opportunity to escape to some far-off hideaway.

This argument compounds the error of assuming that bank notes of uncertain reputation are readily put into circulation by suggesting that their acceptance will be so general that few persons will discriminate against them by exchanging them for liabilities of other banks. But passive acceptance is not likely to take place where note issue is competitive, even for the notes of well-established banks: diverse consumer preferences as regards notes from various issuers will cause the average circulation period for notes of any single issuer to be fairly short. In 1873 (when, due to the influence of the Bank Act, the Scottish system was undergoing substantial consolidation) the average period of circulation for a Scottish bank note was still only 10 or 11 days (Somers 1873, 161). It may have been even shorter at the height of the free-banking era, when Scotland had twice as many note-issuing institutions. If one considers the same degree of competition combined with modern means of communication and transport it is easy to see how the delay would be still shorter. In fact, for note issues in excess of demand there is no reason to assume a delay or float period exceeding the average float period for checks written in an unregulated system. The error of authors who assume that notes would behave differently may stem from improper generalization from the behavior of currency in a centralized system. The currency of a monopoly bank of issue will be returned to its source less frequently than currencies that are not high-powered money.

That competitively issued notes would have brief circulation periods also undermines the charge that free banking would promote counterfeiting, a particular form of fraudulant note issue. The likelihood of detection of counterfeit notes is inversely related to their average period of circulation. It rises with the frequency with which the notes pass under the specially trained eyes of tellers at the legitimate bank of issue. Counterfeiting should therefore be less lucrative and less tempting under free banking than under monopolized note issue. Experience confirms this. According to Emmanuel Coppieters, during the free-banking era Scottish bank notes, which had a short period of circulation, were rarely forged or counterfeited, whereas Bank of England notes—which circulated for long average periods or even indefinitely—were forged continually.[11]

A final argument concerning fraud claims that sellers of goods or services cannot possibly scrutinize all the notes offered to them in exchange, even though they are bound to accept notes that are not really familiar to them. This is supposed to invite overissue.[12] This argument misconstrues the nature of the checks against overissue under free banking. Individuals do not need to keep informed of the reliability and solvency of all the diverse banks of issue whose notes might be offered to them. They only need to be convinced of the reliability and solvency of the bank with which they do most of their business, and to accept at par in addition to that bank's notes only those notes that it will accept (for deposit or redemption) at par.[13] Thus proximate responsibility for the testing or monitoring of note issues falls, not upon the public, but upon the rival issuers themselves. That no non-bank individual wishes to take on this task does not, therefore, mean that it is a public good which the private market would not supply.[14]

Restriction of Economic Growth and Full Employment

Another argument sometimes made against free banking is that it may restrict economic growth.[15] F. Crouzet (1972, 46fn), in disputing the claims of Rondo Cameron, has claimed that this was the case in the Scottish system.[16] But his claim has been convincingly answered by Munn in the latter's study of the provincial banking companies (1981, 229–33). Even the halfhearted American experiment in "free banking"—with all its restrictions against branch banking and note issue—does not seem to have frustrated economic growth in any discernible way.[17] New England, which for most of the first half of the 19th century had the least regulated banking system in the U.S., witnessed the greatest industrial progress. Sweden and Canada also prospered during the era when their banks were relatively unregulated and free to issue notes. Freedom of note issue seems, if anything, to *promote* economic growth.

Still, examples from history do not completely settle the issue. The real question is whether the amount of lending and investment financed by a free banking system would be greater or less than it ought to be to promote maximum sustainable economic growth. Most theorists agree that a banking system should utilize all voluntary savings made available to it, without creating credit in excess of voluntary savings which causes monetary disequilibrium.[18] The limits of a banking system's contribution to economic growth then become a function of its efficiency in attracting and investing private savings. We have already seen in the last part of chapter 4 that free note issue does not interfere with the efficiency of intermediation. We may conclude from this that free banks do not inhibit economic growth, either.[19]

Related to the issue of economic growth is that of full employment. Earlier it was shown that free banking maintains equilibrium in the market for inside money. For this to be regarded as inconsistent with full employment the latter must be supposed to require either deflation, meaning changes in the supply of inside money such as will result in sustained excess demand for it, or inflation, meaning changes in supply such as will result in sustained excess supply. No economists believe that full employment requires deflation. Some Keynesians do believe that it requires inflation. Their views have, however, been the object of mounting criticisms by economists of the Monetarist, New Classical (Rational Expectations), and Austrian schools.[20] These theorists have pointed out that the alleged inflation-unemployment tradeoff to which many Keynesians refer assumes that firms or their employees suffer from long-run money illusion. Such a dubious assumption does not constitute a strong basis for rejecting free banking.[21]

Money Supply as Natural Monopoly

Another argument against free banking holds that the issue of currency is a natural monopoly.[22] This implies that a single banking firm is more efficient in supplying the demand for currency than any combination of smaller firms. But once a firm achieves a monopoly of currency supply, its issues are not limited by adverse clearings, and it can exploit its monopoly of currency supply by overissuing. Therefore the monopoly bank has to be regulated, or a government-controlled bank has to be erected in its place.

Although a monopoly in currency supply allows the monopoly bank to escape adverse clearings in the short run, for such a monopoly to be "natural," that is, for it to represent a stable market equilibrium, it must be able to maintain its notes in circulation more efficiently than rival firms in an environment of free entry where adverse clearings result in demands for its reserves. In other words, the average costs of maintaining notes in circulation, i.e., of building a market for currency holding by the public so that adverse clearings are avoided, must be declining with scale or at least subadditive.[23] For a single bank to gain a monopoly of note issue it is not sufficient that banking involve substantial fixed costs, with relatively small marginal costs, from *issuing* additional notes. The bank must also take steps to improve the popularity of its notes relative to commodity money or relative to notes of other banks, or it must suffer the expense of redeeming them soon after their issue. If the costs to the bank of extending the market or of redemption rise rapidly enough at the margin,[24] its average costs per unit of outstanding currency will rise above the minimum level long before the point at which it would saturate the market for currency. In this case the industry cannot be considered a natural monopoly, and no single firm will be able to avoid the consequences of rivals establishing their own circulations and returning its excess notes to it for redemption.

An error sometimes committed in considering the natural monopoly question is to assume that the only marginal costs of currency issue are the cost of paper and ink, which do not rise significantly at the margin and may even fall due to economies of large-scale purchasing. This implies that banks face an inexhaustible demand for their notes, or that they will not be asked to redeem them in base money. But, where notes are convertible, this can happen only if the issuer has a monopoly of currency supply to begin with—one based, for example, on special legislation prohibiting the entry of other note-issuing banks that might redeem their rival's issues.[25] To assume the existence of a monopoly in currency supply in order to explain its "natural" occurrence obviously begs the question.

Allowing that there are costs of maintaining a note circulation (including, but not limited to, marketing and liquidity costs) which individual firms must reckon with, the possibility of natural monopoly still exists, but its plausibility is much diminished. There is no strong a priori case for the view that competition in currency supply will lead to the emergence of a single bank of issue.

What, then, does the empirical evidence suggest? Simply this: that throughout the experience of both Europe and America the tendency under unrestricted entry has always been toward a plurality of note-issuing banks.[26] The appearance of monopoly banks of issue in these areas has in every instance been due to legislation restraining rival issuers by limiting their issues, imposing special capitalization or geographical constraints upon them, setting up barriers to new entry, or overtly and directly forcing them out of the issue business altogether. Where such measures were not taken no obvious tendencies toward monopolization were seen.[27]

Even if the natural monopoly argument were valid it would not justify erecting barriers to entry in the note-issue business. If the issue of currency is indeed a natural monopoly the monopoly bank should be be able to employ its advantage in production (an advantage which it must maintain even as competitors threaten to return its issues for redemption) to discourage or outcompete any rival that might enter into competition with it.[28] In the meantime, the potential entrants encourage the monopoly issuer to operate as efficiently as possible while standing ready to supplement its output in case it should fail to fulfill entirely the needs of the public.

To support their claim that currency production is a natural monopoly, which to them constitutes a rationale for limiting entry into the business of note issue, Michael Melvin (1984, 13–14) and Benjamin Klein (1978) argue that confidence building is more costly for private issuers than it is for government. Melvin writes that "the history of money production observed over the past 2,000 years is likely due to economic efficiency and not to 2,000 years of ignorance or coercion." Despite what Melvin considers likely, the facts show that government monopolies in money production have everywhere been achieved by coercion: governments have outlawed private coinage, passed forced-tender laws, restricted private and incorporated banking, prohibited branch banking and note exchange, taxed bank notes out of existence, passed bond-deposit legislation, refused to enforce redemption contracts, and imposed exchange controls. All of these measures discouraged private, competitive production of money while encouraging production by governments. Most were undertaken to aid the monetization of government debt, which means they were undertaken precisely because confidence in governments was too *low* to allow them to obtain funds through normal channels.

Nor has confidence in government currencies been enhanced by their performance over time. The record of all has been one of eventual depreciation. Examples of government-issued currency outcompeting privately issued ones without having to outlaw or otherwise restrict them are rare.[29] Yet there have been numerous episodes in which private currencies have competed successfully with state issued ones. For instance, the American state-bank note issues of 1863–1865 competed successfully against greenbacks and against the government-bond based issues of nationally chartered banks. The government responded to this successful competition by imposing a prohibitive 10 percent tax on state bank notes. Another example is the plural note-issue episode of Sweden, in which private issues, despite barriers thrown in their way by the Swedish government, successfully challenged the note-issue monopoly of the Riksbank.[30]

If the reasoning of Klein and Melvin proves anything at all, it proves too much, because most of the costs expended by note-issuing private banks in gaining the confidence of potential customers are also expended by deposit banks: once a bank has established the reliability of its checkable deposits the additional costs of building confidence in its note-issues are not especially great. If governments are more efficient in building confidence, why restrict their prerogative to currency issue? Why not extend it to deposit banking as well? By the same token, why permit traveler's checks to be competitively supplied if the government should be able to supply them at lower cost?

Yet another point against the natural monopoly argument is that, if it is valid, another argument used historically to justify government regulation and monopolization of currency supply must necessarily be false. This is the argument that free banking leads to a proliferation of banks of issue and to a bewildering variety of note brands. If the natural monopoly argument is correct, then multiplication of bank-note brands could not be a long-run consequence of free banking.

Finally, mention should be made of the view that money production is shown to be a natural monopoly by the fact that consumers benefit from having a common medium of exchange. This confuses two issues, one being whether the market tends to adopt a single unit of account (e.g., an ounce of gold or a pound of silver) and the other being whether the production or issue of *material representatives* of this standard unit is most efficiently undertaken by one or several firms. Our review of the evolution of money in chapter 2 made clear that adoption of a single standard monetary unit does not imply that production of money is a natural monopoly. The relation between the monetary unit and actual money—its material representatives—can be likened to that of a standard unit of length, such as the yard, and its material embodiment, the yardstick. The yard is a standard unit of measurement throughout the United States; one can call this a "natural monopoly" if one likes, but such a label would be irrelevant since yards are not objects of production or exchange, and what is not produced or exchanged cannot be produced or exchanged inefficiently, by a monopoly or otherwise. The same is true of other standards—such as shoe sizes and rules of spelling. Only when it comes to material embodiments of these standards, namely, yardsticks, shoes, and dictionaries—does the question of natural monopoly arise. In the case of money, it is evident that the existence of a gold standard does not mean that gold coin, and media convertible into gold coin, cannot be competitively produced. The mere fact that the market promotes the emergence of a single monetary standard does not give any validity whatsoever to the natural monopoly argument.

Public Good and Externality Arguments

Two more criticisms of free banking are closely related to the natural monopoly argument. One holds that inside money (and currency especially) is a public good because it exhibits either non-rivalrousness or nonexcludability in consumption, which make its private production in desired quantities unprofitable and hence impossible.[31] The other holds that there are externalities in inside-money production because (a) producers do not bear all the costs of it, so that profit-maximizing competitive producers will issue more inside money than the amount that equates marginal social cost with marginal revenues; or (b) that benefits from inside-money issue are not fully reflected in bank earnings, so that competing issuers will *under*produce.[32]

Is it true that inside money exhibits nonexcludability in consumption, so that some people may act as "free riders," sharing in the benefits from money balances that others have made sacrifices to acquire? Is the use of inside money by any one person nonrivalrous, so that others beside him enjoy the yield of services accruing from his balance (but without reducing his own return)? The answer in both cases is no, because a particular sum of inside money renders its service—increased purchasing opportunities—only to those who actually possess it. Those who refuse to do without other forms of wealth or who do not abstain from consumption (by holding inside money instead of consuming a flow of services from goods) cannot take advantage of the benefits associated with inside money. Of course, the same cannot be said of the standard money unit (the unit of account). But we have already seen that this is irrelevant, since the money unit is not itself an object of production, and since, in any event, the market (rather than government) was responsible for the original emergence of widely used monetary standards.[33]

Are there, then, costs associated with the issue of inside money that are not borne by competitive suppliers and which therefore imply competitive overproduction? Some possibilities that come to mind are costs of monetary disequilibrium, price-level effects, and fallen confidence. We have already seen in chapters 3 through 9 that free banking promotes neither monetary disequilibrium nor confidence externalities. Moreover, if confidence externalities did arise under free banking they would not necessarily be Pareto-relevant: each bank has an incentive, under the circumstance, to support any solvent rival suffering a run. In this case the externality is appropriable, which means that it is not Pareto-relevant—that is, not a source of market failure—and hence not grounds for rejecting free banking.[34] Those price-level effects that free banking would allow are also not Pareto-relevant, so they do not provide a rationale for regulation either.[35]

Another possible criticism of free banking comes from Milton Friedman's "optimum quantity of money" argument.[36] This holds that the benefits from money holding are maximized when the marginal gain from money holding (the nonpecuniary service yield from an addition to money balances) is just equal to the marginal social costs of producing money balances, which are assumed to be close to zero. But the private cost of adding to money balances is equal to the interest rate on alternative assets, which typically exceeds the near-zero social costs of money production. Under such conditions the public will hold a less than optimal quantity of money. As Friedman observes, the problem can be seen as involving external effects of money holding, since individuals must forego real resources to add to their balances, but produce a windfall gain to other money holders in doing so.

To induce the public to hold an optimal quantity of money, steps have to be taken to eliminate the discrepency between the equilibrium marginal service (liquidity) yield from holding money balances (L) and the social cost of producing such balances (assumed = 0). If r_c is the rate of interest on alternative, non-money assets, the suboptimal solution is where $L = r_c > 0$. On the other hand, money holdings will be optimal only if $L = 0$. The latter result can be achieved in two ways, either of which involves supplementing the nonpecuniary service yield on money holdings with some additional pecuniary return. In the solution recommended by Friedman the additional return takes the form of a capital gain on money holdings, based on a fully anticipated, steady rate of price deflation equal to the real rate of interest on capital ($\dot{P}/P = -r_c$). In equilibrium this gives

$$L = r_c + \dot{P}/P = 0.$$

The other solution is to pay explicit interest to money holders (r_m), with the level of prices assumed unchanging, equal to the rate of interest on capital (r_c) minus any costs of administering and maintaining the money supply (here assumed = 0). In equilibrium this gives

$$L = r_c - r_m = 0.$$

In the first solution, the addition to real money balances is accomplished by "crying down prices" with a fixed nominal money supply. In the second, the increase consists of an addition to nominal money holdings, with prices unchanged.

The question is, does a free-banking system succeed in promoting optimal money holding by either of these means? The answer is that it succeeds in part, but perhaps not entirely. Only inside money is held in a mature free-banking system, and a large fraction of this money is deposit money. Free banks are driven to pay competitive rates of interest on such deposits, which prevents the deposits from being held in suboptimal quantities.[37] This leaves the possibility that bank notes will be held in suboptimal quantities. The problem here is that payment of interest on notes is likely to be impossible because of the high transaction costs involved. Free banks might resort to clever means for getting around this, which would entirely solve the suboptimality problem.[38] But suppose they cannot. Then the private cost of holding bank notes would exceed the social costs, and free banks would, in Harry Johnson's words, "tend to produce a socially nonoptimum overalloction of resources to the provision of deposit money and underallocation of resources to the provision of currency for holding."

In short, there *would* be a suboptimal quantity of bank notes, but the loss from this would be partly offset by a *supra* optimal quantity of deposits. The only *net* loss would be that stemming from any inelasticity of substitution between deposits and notes. According to Johnson (1973a, 142) this net loss "would probably be a negligible fraction of national income."

Could government intervention do better? Insofar as the desired solution is payment of interest on holdings of currency, the answer must clearly be no, for government faces the same obstacles in doing this as do private issuers of bank notes. Indeed the government, or its central bank, is less likely to attempt interest payments on currency than private note issuers, since its monopoly privilege places it under less pressure to do so. This is illustrated by the current practice of the some central banks (including the Federal Reserve) of not paying interest on reserve holdings of commercial banks, even though paying interest on reserves is relatively easy compared to paying interest on currency held by the public.

So if any improvement is to be had from the government it must come through a policy of price deflation. Here, too, the revenue or seignorage-maximizing interests of a monopoly supplier of currency run counter to the policy in question. Putting this consideration aside, what gains can be expected from a policy of price deflation aimed at promoting an optimal use of currency? One possibility is that the cost, per real unit of money balances, of increasing aggregate holdings by crying down prices is lower than the cost of doing so by increasing the nominal supply of interest-bearing money units. This would make a central-bank administered deflationary policy superior to free banking even if the latter *could* pay interest to holders of bank notes. William Gramm (1974) has shown, however, that there is no justification for such a view. Starting with the assumption of a fractional-reserve banking system, Gramm argues, in essence, that the costs associated with creation of real money balances are proportionate to the real value of bank reserves multiplied by the rate of interest. Assuming that the reserve ratio ($=$ m/M, where m is the nominal quantity of the reserve commodity and M is the nominal supply of bank money) is constant, an increase in the real supply of money requires either 1) an increase in M with a proportionate increase in m or 2) a lowering of P with both M and m held constant. In either case, the change in total (opportunity) costs associated with the production and maintenance of the additional real balances is the same. If this cost is represented by the formula rpm, where r is the rate of interest and p is the value of the reserve commodity ($=$ 1/P), then in the former case rpm rises because of an increase in m, whereas in the latter case it rises *by the same amount* because of an increase in p. Thus Gramm concludes that there is no cost advantage to be had by crying down prices instead of increasing the money supply by means of an increase in the nominal quantity of money.

In fact Gramm's assumption of a constant reserve ratio, which is crucial to his result, is itself question begging: as we have seen, an increase in the nominal supply of bank money that accommodates an increase in demand under free banking does not require a proportionate increase in the nominal quantity of bank reserves. The circumstance is one that would permit the free-banking reserve ratio to fall. Thus Gramm's analysis overstates the costs of private production of money balances under laissez faire. It must also be admitted, however, that it is equally unrealistic to assume a constant reserve ratio for the case where M is constant but P is allowed to fall: a fall in the price-level reduces the nominal volume of bank transactions while simultaneously increasing the relative value of commodity money. This would give banks an excess supply of reserves, which would be aggravated by increased production of the money commodity combined with a reduced nonmonetary demand for it. Thus, crying down prices in the face of an increased demand for money balances does not, in a commodity-standard system, really achieve equilibrium in the market for money balances, for although the public may become satisfied with its nominal holdings of bank money, the banks find themselves holding excess reserves.[39] Furthermore, there is no way, in a closed system, for these excess reserves to be eliminated *except* by an increase in bank loans and investments which leads to an increased nominal quantity of bank money and to an increase in the price level sufficient to restore the volume of bank transactions (plus the level of industrial demand for the money commodity) to where there no longer is any surplus of commodity money.

Thus we may conclude that the maximum potential advantage to be expected from a policy of deflation to promote currency holding would be no greater than the small social cost under free banking from consumers' holding too many deposits and too few bank notes. Yet even this small advantage is unlikely to be achieved in practice, since it would be more than offset by the significant external *diseconomies* involved in any deflationary process. As S. C. Tsiang notes, these diseconomies would include "impairment of the efficiency of the financial market in channeling savings toward investment" and other consequences of monetary disequilibrium.[40]

These arguments have been dealt with cursorily here, because most of them have been critically treated elsewhere,[41] and also because many of them are rather inappropriate when applied to inside money, which is after all not a commodity "produced" in the usual sense of the term but a vehicle of credit representing outside money lent to banks at call. In the case of such credit instruments the overriding consideration should be whether the supply of them agrees with the public's demand for them at a given level of nominal income. The public goods and externality arguments are significant only insofar as they imply over- or underproduction in terms of this criterion. Since, as we have seen, the amount of inside money issued by a free banking system tends to conform to the demand for inside money, to say that a free bank will not produce a desirable amount of inside money is tantamount to saying that the demand for money is too intense or too meager, implying over- or underconsumption of inside money balances. The only argument that could possibly justify such a complaint is the one just discussed concerning the alleged nonoptimality of money holding under laissez faire. As we have seen, it is not convincing when applied to a free-banking system.

Alleged Need for a "Lender of Last Resort"

A final alleged shortcoming of free banking is its lack of a "lender of last resort." Some remarks have been made about this in earlier parts of this study.[42] The present section recapitulates and expands upon some of them.

To appreciate the significance of the lender of last resort doctrine to the theory of free banking, one must understand, first, its historical origin and, second, precisely what it is that a lender of last resort is (or was originally) supposed to lend. The doctrine originated in the English banking crises of the 19th century; its principal architects were Henry Thornton and Walter Bagehot.[43] It was designed to resolve problems peculiar to a system where one note-issuing bank had (limited) monopoly privileges. The existence of such privileges, which involved restrictions on the note-issue powers of other banks, caused the Bank of England to become a supplier of high-powered money: since paper currency by the 19th century had already begun to surpass coin as a preferred medium of exchange, banks unable to issue their own notes, including all banks within a 65 mile radius from the center of London except the Bank of England, were willing to hold Bank of England notes in place of specie reserves. Thus Bank of England notes were used to settle clearings among other banks, and the Bank became the sole significant repository for the system's specie.

These circumstances allowed the Bank of England considerable leeway in its issues of inside money. Its issues, unlike those of other banks, were not limited by internal adverse clearings. The principal check against the Bank's overissues was a drain of reserves to foreign countries sponsored by the price-specie-flow mechanism. So the Bank of England was in a sensitive position: if it overissued, it lost specie abroad, which eventually necessitated either contraction or suspension of payments. If it underissued, it made the conversion of deposits to notes at other English banks impossible. The Bank Act, in attempting to thwart overissue, also made note shortages more likely. It placed absolute limits on other banks' authorized note issues, while at the same time prohibiting the Bank of England from adding to its note issues without also increasing its specie reserves by the same amount. Bagehot, in arguing that the Bank of England should function as a lender of last resort, was reacting to this. He recommended that the Bank be allowed to increase its circulation to meet "internal drains" of high-powered money from the reserves of other banks, which drains were mainly caused by depositors' desire to obtain hand-to-hand media. Like the currency drains in America under the National Banking System, they were *not* due to any desire on the part of depositors to withdraw outside money *per se*. The dependence of other banks upon the Bank of England in such drains was entirely due to their inability to issue notes of their own, which placed them at the mercy of their privileged rival. Had it not been for restrictions on their rights to issue notes, the less-privileged banks could have met their depositors' requests by simply swapping their own note liabilities for what had formerly been their deposit liabilities, leaving their reserves untouched. They would not have had any need for a "lender of last resort."

This is not to deny that the classical developers of the lender of last resort doctrine spoke mainly of the need for central banks to supply ultimate money of redemption to distressed banks whose customers had lost confidence in them. A bank threatened with a redemption run cannot satisfy its panic-stricken clients by offering them its own notes.[44] Nevertheless, there is reason for regarding currency runs as of more fundamental importance than redemption runs, as redemption runs seem often to have been set off by the failure of certain banks to meet currency runs. As Bagehot observed (1874, 265–66), panic was especially likely to result if, by its refusal of assistance during a currency run, the Bank of England caused "the failure of a first-rate joint stock bank in London." The London joint-stock banks had substantial deposit liabilities, and their power to issue notes was, even before 1844, nil. During the "autumnal drain" of currency they were especially dependent upon the resources of the Bank of England.

Crucial to the present argument is Jevons's finding that, in the course of the autumnal drain, public holdings of coin and bank notes—including notes issued by the "country" banks—moved together.[45] There was not a rush for gold or Bank of England notes as such, but rather a rush for *all* types of currency. The pressure upon the Bank of England came when banks had exhausted their own authorized note issues together with available reserves of high-powered money. The facts confirm that panics were themselves a consequence of restrictions upon free note issue. The situation was similar to the one faced by banks in the United States during the post–Civil War era, except for the difference in note-issue restrictions in the two systems.[46]

In short, monopolization of note issue is simultaneously the source of the special powers of central banks and the source of difficulties that central banks are supposed to correct. The Bank of England became a last resort source of currency for the simple reason that the first resort, competitive note issue, was outlawed.

Of course, redemption runs need not always be precipitated by prior currency shortages. So a question still remains as to whether central banks can prevent such autonomous runs.[47] Here it must be remembered that restrictions upon note issue also led to the centralization of gold reserves—the "one-reserve" system criticized by Bagehot. Gold actually became somewhat *less* accessible as a result of monopolized note issue than it might have been if banks issued notes competitively. Still, the Bank of England possessed a genuine advantage over free banking, since its issues could be used to settle clearings among other banks. This made it possible for the Bank of England to use its excess reserves to make emergency loans to other banks so that they could in turn satisfy the redemption demands of the public. Another advantage the Bank of England had was that its notes were often less susceptible to a general decline in confidence.

On the other side of the ledger we must consider the following: (a) under free banking redemption runs would be rare, so that the advantages to be had by having a central bank are not necessarily great; (b) special methods for dealing with runs could also be had in a free banking system; and (c) the welfare losses from over- and underissue are likely to outweigh the potential gains from having a central bank. Concerning (a), it was shown in chapter 9 that information externalities which might give rise to a rash of bank runs are less likely to arise under free banking than under central banking. Runs that begin at a small number of bank offices can also be contained there by assistance from other branches of the affected banks. Historically, there have been relatively few bank panics in countries with branch banking as compared with those where branching has been restricted. We have already noted the cases of Sweden, which had no bank failures at all during its era of competitive note issue, Canada, which had fewer bank runs or failures than the U.S. in the decades before 1935 (when it set up a central bank), and Scotland, which had isolated bank failures but no bank panics for the entire span of its free-banking episode.[48]

Even where branch banking is absent, a bank in need of temporary assistance can, if it is the victim of an isolated run, usually obtain it at a price. Rival banks—barring an implausible conspiracy—will lend to it so long as they are satisfied that it is solvent. It is generally agreed that central banks should employ a similar criterion.[49] Notwithstanding this there is the obvious risk that a central bank, especially if it is a public institution not restricted by considerations of profit (or an issuer of fiat money having little to lose by making bad loans), will offer to assist truly insolvent banks whose misfortunes are due to poor management. This generates a moral hazard, encouraging bankers to take unwarranted risks, which in turn increases the probability of future failures.[50]

Some writers have argued that the existence of government deposit insurance, by providing an independent source of relief to deposit holders and by reducing the likelihood of runs leading to full-scale panic, renders the lender of last resort function of central banks unnecessary.[51] If the argument is correct, it applies with even greater force to a system of private bank-liability insurance, which may also reduce the risk of moral hazard by charging insurance premiums reflecting the quality of individual bank asset portfolios.

Concerning category (b), free banks could receive last-resort aid in the form of clearinghouse certificates and loan certificates, which are a short-lived form of emergency high-powered money. They might also resort to "option clauses" of the sort employed in Scotland for a short period during the free-banking era. Such clauses would provide a safety outlet for banks in case of a liquidity crisis, reducing the likelihood of runs by allowing a contractual suspension of payment. This would give banks time to contract their balance sheets. It would also be much more equitable than any non-contractual suspensions of payment, since bank customers would need to agree to the option clause arrangement ahead of time and since it would pay them interest in proportion to the duration of any suspension.

All these considerations militate against the view that central banking is superior to free banking for minimizing the harmful effects from bank runs and failures. Along with them we must reckon the additional burdens that central banks are likely to introduce—category (c) above—which have been alluded to frequently in the present study. They are the burdens of inflation and deflation, absolute as well as relative, with their damaging effects upon economic activity. The ability of central banks to aid other banks in distress—even where the distress is not due to previous central-bank misconduct—should only count as an advantage if there is reason to believe that it will be exercised at the right time and place. That central banks do not suffer when they bail out banks that really should be allowed to fail adds another dimension to the "knowledge problem" they confront, giving further reason to suspect that they will not behave properly.

Expedience

Although opposed to the Bank of England's monopoly in principle Bagehot (1874, 69) saw no point in trying to dismantle it: for better or worse, it had become an object of veneration. To oppose it was, in his view, to invite "useless ridicule." Moreover, he observed, it would take years before a new, safer banking system could grow.

Considerations such as these are no less weighty today. Indeed, despite their poor performance, support for central banks has grown along with the belief that they combat the inherent instability of decentralized banking. Furthermore, the transitional costs of adopting free banking seem greater than ever, since modern banking systems, based on fiat monies and floating exchange rates, appear further removed from the theoretical ideal of free banking than any of their 19th-century predecessors.

The popularity of central banking today rests, however, on the public's insufficient awareness of the advantages of free banking. Far from requiring theorists to dismiss the topic as a "dead issue,"[52] the situation calls for them to perform their principal duty, which is to inform people about things that are not already obvious to them. Of course a theoretical possibility, once brought to the attention of the public, may be ignored or rejected; but it is irresponsible for theorists to write off an idea because they see little prospect of its ready acceptance. Issues do not die; they are just neglected!

That political decision makers are especially prone to ignore radical alternatives is also no reason to quell discussion of them. As an English statesman and writer once observed, that politicians are mainly concerned with "tasks of the hour" is "all the more reason why as many other people as possible should busy themselves in helping prepare opinion for the practical application of unfamiliar but weighty and promising suggestions, by constant and ready discussion of them upon their merits."[53]

The matter of transition costs cannot be so tersely dealt with. Real doubts must exist concerning whether there is any way to convert existing banking arrangements so as to make them perform in the manner described in the theory of free banking. The only way to dispel such doubts is to offer an actual plan, showing how the conversion might be achieved without difficulties or costs so great as to render the plan unacceptable. This task is undertaken in the next chapter.

11

Free Banking and Monetary Reform

Rules, Authority, or Freedom?

S O LONG AS the money supply is centrally controlled, the central authority must either actively manipulate the money supply or it must adhere to a predetermined monetary rule.[1] That these are the *only* options for monetary policy is the view that has been handed down by several generations of economists. Implicitly or explicitly theorists have rejected the alternative of free banking. This is also true of many Chicago-School economists—the best-known proponents of monetary rules and opponents of monetary discretion—who otherwise argue for a free society based upon free markets.[2] For the cause of free banking the last fact is especially significant, because it means that a large and highly respected body of theorists, who might most readily have concurred with the arguments for free banking, have instead aligned themselves with advocates of monetary centralization.

Why have Chicago economists denied the efficacy of the free market in the realm of money and banking? To begin, they have doubted the very desirability of commercial banks issuing fiduciary media. Lloyd Mints (1950, 5 and 7) saw no benefits at all in such institutions; and although Simons (1951) and Friedman (1959, 8; 1953, 216–20) may not have shared this extreme position, they at least considered fractional-reserve banking to be "inherently unstable." Such a perspective does not incline its holders toward the view that banking should be entirely unregulated, except in peculiar cases (such as Mises's) where it is believed that free banking will somehow lead to the suppression of fractionally-based inside monies.

It has already been argued (in chapter 2) that fractional reserve banking is beneficial, contrary to Mints's position. It was also argued,

164

in chapters 8 and 9, that there is no "inherent instability" in free banking. In fact, the particular sort of instability emphasized by Mints and Friedman—changes in the volume of money due to changes in the *form* in which the public wishes to hold its money—arises only in systems lacking freedom of note issue.[3] The problem is indeed inherent in systems with central banking and monopolized currency supply, but it is not inherent to all fractional-reserve banking.

Elsewhere various Chicago economists—especially Milton Friedman (1959, 4–9)—have criticized free banking on the grounds that it leads to unlimited inflation, involves excessive commodity-money resource costs, and encourages fraud. For these and other reasons they have claimed that the issue of currency is a technical monopoly which must be subject to government control. Each of these arguments has been critically examined and found wanting. The Chicago School's dismissal of free banking was, in short, premature.

We are today in a much better position than the Chicago economists once were to consider free banking as an alternative monetary policy, distinct from reliance upon either rules or authorities. The best way to appreciate the advantages of this alternative is to view it in light of arguments on both sides of the rules-versus-authorities debate. Jacob Viner (1962, 244–74) provides an excellent summary of these arguments. According to him, the Chicago pro-rules position is that rules provide "protection . . . against arbitrary, malicious, capricious, stupid, clumsy, or other manipulation . . . by an 'authority' " and that they guarantee a monetary policy that is "certain" and "predictable" (ibid., 246).[4]

The principal argument for discretion is, on the other hand, the *ipso facto* deficiency of regulatory policies that "attempt to deal by simple rules with complex phenomena" (ibid.). A monetary rule necessarily precludes "the possibility of adaptation of regulation by well-intentioned, wise and skillful exercise of discretionary authority to the relevant differences in circumstances" (ibid.). Viner lists four considerations that stand in the way of the successful use of any monetary rule. They are (a) the existence of a multiplicity of policy ends, which no simple rule can fulfill; (b) the presence of more than one monetary authority or regulatory agency (which makes it difficult to assign responsibility for enforcement of a rule); (c) the existence of several instruments of monetary control (which complicates execution and enforcement of a rule even when there is a single monetary authority); and (d) the possibility that a satisfactory rule may not exist even if policy is aimed at a single end and is implemented by a single authority using a single instrument of control.

Although all these considerations are relevant, let us abstract from (a), (b), and (c) by assuming, first, that the sole end of monetary policy is to maintain monetary equilibrium (i.e., to adjust the nominal quantity of money in response to changes in demand); second, that responsibility for control of the money supply is vested with a single authority, namely, the "well-intentioned" directors of a central bank; and third, that open-market operations are the sole means for centrally administered changes in the money supply. This limits the problem to one of finding a satisfactory monetary rule. The difficulty here is that even a clearly defined policy end may involve "a quantity of some kind which is a function of several variables, all of which are important and are in unstable relation to each other" (ibid.). When this is true "there will be no fixed rule available which will be both practicable and appropriate to its objective" (ibid.).

Suppose the desired end is the accommodation of the demand for money, which is indeed "a quantity . . . of several variables . . . in unstable relation to each other." No simple monetary rule such as stabilization of a price index or a fixed percent money growth rate can fully satisfy this end. In fact the constant growth rate rule, which is now most popular, abandons any effort to accommodate seasonal and cyclical changes: it regards only secular changes in demand as predictable enough to be the basis for a steadfast formula.

And yet, as far as the desires of some advocates of monetary rules are concerned, the fixed money growth-rate proposal—especially when it is defined in terms of some monetary aggregate—is *not strict enough*. It still permits the monetary authority actively to conduct open-market operations to meet the prescribed growth rate. A pre-set schedule of open-market bond purchases cannot always be carried out, because the relevant money multipliers (which determine the effect of a given change in the supply of base money upon the supply of broader money aggregates) are not constant or fully predictable.[5] There will, therefore, always be occasions under such a rule when some discretion will have to be tolerated so that open-market purchases do not miss their target. On the other hand, if such discretion is permitted, it can be abused, and so, to state once more the warning of Henry Simons, it would make the supposed rule "a folly."

It is apparent, then, that if we must have a central monetary authority we must choose between the dangers of an imperfect and perhaps ill-maintained rule and the dangers of discretion and its possible abuse. This choice has been made somewhat less difficult in recent years, because the authorities' abuse of their discretionary powers has been such as to overshadow the potential damage that might result from blind adherence to some pre-set formula. In the United States the loss of faith in authority has given rise to a new proposal that is the ultimate expression of Simons's anti-discretion position. The proposal is that the supply of base money should be permanently *frozen*—that is, that the Federal Reserve System should cease open-market operations entirely.[6] Here at last is a rule calculated to prevent mischief: all that needs to be done to guarantee its strict observation is to close the Fed! Milton Friedman, who for years advocated a constant M-1 growth-rate rule, is now the most prominent champion of this frozen monetary base proposal.

Thus monetary policy has reached an impasse. Under a strict monetary rule, and especially in the case of the base-freeze proposal, the really desirable end of monetary policy—achieving monetary equilibrium—has to be sacrificed to the much lower, cruder end of merely preventing the authorities from introducing *more* instability into the system than might exist in the absence of any intervention, capricious or otherwise. Is such an inflexible arrangement the best that can be hoped for? So long as one clings to the assumption of centralized control and centralized currency supply, there is reason to believe that it is. We have seen, in chapter 7, why discretion, even in its best guise, is likely to hurt more than it helps.

But centralized control need not be taken for granted. The supply of currency could instead be placed on a competitive basis. This solution, unlike solutions based on centralized control, can achieve monetary stability while simultaneously eliminating government interference. Free note issue combines all the virtues of Friedman's proposal—which completely eliminates the danger of capricious manipulation of the money supply—with those of a system capable of meeting changing demands for money. Freedom of note issue resolves the "inherent instability" that afflicts centralized systems of fractional-reserve banking. By supplying an alternative form of pocket and till money—competitively issued bank notes—to accommodate changing public demands, free banking reduces the public's reliance upon base money as currency for use in everyday payments. In this way base money is allowed to remain in bank reserves to settle clearing balances. Fiat base money can thus be made to play a role similar to the one played by commodity money in the "typical" free banking system which has been given prominence through most of this study. Base money never has to move from bank reserves to circulation or vice-versa, so that, in such a system, there is no question of any need for reserve compensation to offset the ebb and flow of currency demand.

Free banking on a fiat standard may seem far from the sort of free banking discussed in previous chapters, but the difference is not really so great. True, the preceding pages discussed mainly a commodity standard, because this is the type that would most probably have evolved had banking been free all along; but events have been otherwise. For better or worse our monetary system is at present based on a fiat-dollar standard, and the momentum behind any existing standard is an argument for its retention. Existence of a fiat standard is, however, no barrier to the adoption of free banking. As far as banks today are concerned, fiat dollars are base money, which it is their business to receive and to lend and to issue claims upon. For most of the 20th century the only claims allowed (we are as usual considering ones redeemable on demand only) have been checkable deposits. What is proposed, therefore, is that commercial banks be given the right to issue their own notes, redeemable on demand for Federal Reserve Dollars, on the same assets that presently support checkable deposit liabilities.[7] Once the public becomes accustomed to using bank notes as currency, the stock of high-powered money can be permanently frozen according to a plan such as Friedman's without negative repercussions due to changes in the relative demand for currency.

This simple proposal does not involve any interference whatsoever with the dollar as the national monetary unit. Yet, it would make it possible for Federal Reserve high-powered money to be used exclusively as bank reserves, for settling interbank clearings, while allowing bank notes to take the place of Federal Reserve Dollars in fulfilling the currency needs of the public.[8]

A Practical Proposal for Reform

How can this proposal be implemented, and how can it be combined with a plan for freezing the monetary base? A reasonable starting point would be to remove archaic and obviously unnecessary regulations such as statutory reserve requirements and restrictions on regional and nationwide branch banking. The majority of nations with developed banking industries have not suffered from their lack of such regulations, evidence that their elimination in the United States would not have grave consequences. In fact, branch banking has significant micro- and macroeconomic advantages over unit banking, and its absence is probably the most important single cause of the relatively frequent failure of U. S. banks.[9] As for statutory reserve requirements, it has already been shown (in chapter 8) that they are impractical as instruments for reserve compensation. Apart from this, they serve no purpose other than to act as a kind of tax on bank liabilities. Furthermore, their existence interferes with banks' ability to accommodate changes in the demand for inside money. If the monetary base is frozen this restrictive effect is absolute. On the other hand, elimination of statutory reserve requirements, unless it proceeds in very small steps, could open the door to a serious bout of inflation. A solution would be to sterilize existing required reserves the moment the requirements are removed. This could be done as follows: suppose the statutory reserve requirement is 20 percent. Presumably banks operate with reserves of, say, 25 percent—only the excess 5 percent are an actual source of liquidity to the banks. It could then be announced that after a certain date there will be no further rediscounts by the Federal Reserve Banks (thus encouraging banks to acquire adequate excess reserves). Then when the deadline arrives reserves held for statutory purposes could be converted to Treasury bills—a non-high-powered money obligation—and the statutory reserve requirements could at the same moment be eliminated.[10]

In addition to reserve requirements and restrictions on branch banking, restrictions on bank diversification such as the Glass-Steagall Act should also be repealed. This would allow banks to set up equity accounts, reducing their exposure to runs by depositors, and opening the way to the replacement of government deposit insurance by private alternatives.

While these deregulations are in progress, Congress can proceed to restore to every commercial bank (whether national or state chartered) the right to issue its own redeemable demand notes (which might also bear an option-clause) unrestricted by bond-deposit requirements or by any tax not applicable to demand deposits. This reform would not in any way complicate the task facing the still operating Federal Reserve Board; indeed, it would reduce the Fed's need to take account of fluctuations in the public's currency needs when adjusting the money supply. The multiplier would become more stable and predictable to the extent that bank notes were employed to satisfy temporary changes in currency demand.[11] Over time banks would establish the reliability of their issues, which need not be considered any less trustworthy by the public than traveler's checks.

For competitively issued notes to displace base money from circulation entirely the public must feel comfortable using them as currency. This might be a problem: the situation differs from the case of a metallic base money, which is obviously a less convenient currency medium for most purposes than bank notes redeemable in it. There is no obvious advantage in using paper bank notes instead of equally handy paper base dollars. Nevertheless, imaginative innovations could probably induce the public to prefer bank notes. The existing base-money medium could as a deliberate policy be replaced by paper instruments of somewhat larger physical size, fitting less easily into wallets and tills. Bank notes, on the other hand, could be made the size of present Federal Reserve notes. The appearance of base dollars could also be altered in other ways, for instance, by having them engraved in red ink. In this form they might seem even less familiar to currency users than the newly available bank notes. Finally, base dollars could be made available only in less convenient denominations. Two-dollar bills would work, since they already have an established reputation for not being wanted by the public, but larger bills would be most convenient for settling interbank clearings. Banks, of course, should be allowed to issue whatever note denominations they discovered to be most desired by their customers.[12]

Other innovations need not be a matter of public policy but can be left to the private incentive of banks. Banks could stock their automatic teller machines with their own notes, and bank tellers could be instructed to give notes to depositors who desire currency, unless base dollars were specifically requested. Banks might also conduct weekly lottery drawings and offer prize money to persons possessing notes with winning serial numbers.[13] The drawings would be like similar lotteries now held by several daily newspapers. They would make notes more appealing to the public, as they would constitute an indirect way of paying interest to note holders, just as interest is now paid on some checkable deposits.

A combination of measures such as these would almost certainly lead to near-complete displacement of base dollars from circulation. Once this stage was reached—say, once 5 percent or less of the total of checkable deposits and currency in circulation consists of base dollars[14]—a date could be chosen upon which the supply of base money would be permanently frozen. When this date arrived, outstanding Federal Reserve deposit credits would be converted into paper base dollars, and banks that held deposits with the Fed would receive their balances in cash. Banks could then exercise their option to convert some of this cash into specially created Treasury obligations (see note 12). At this point the Federal Reserve Board and Federal Open-Market Committee could be disbanded. This would end the Fed's money creating activities. The System's clearing operations could be privatized by having the twelve Federal Reserve Banks and their branches placed into the hands of their member-bank stockholders.[15] The frozen stock of base dollars could then be warehoused by the newly privatized clearinghouse associations. Dollar "certificates" or clearinghouse account entries could be used to settle interbank clearings, thereby saving the dollar supply from wear and tear. Only a small amount of base dollars would actually have to be kept on hand by individual banks to satisfy rare requests for them by customers. In the unlikely event of a redemption run, a single bank in distress could be assisted by some of its more liquid branches or by other banks acting unilaterally or through the clearinghouse associations; some banks might also have recourse to option clauses written on their notes. Finally, bank liabilities might continue to be insured (by private firms), although there might not be any demand for such insurance under the more stable and less failure-prone circumstances that free banking would foster.

The above discussion assumes that base money dollars will continue to command a saleability premium and that they will therefore continue to be used to settle clearing balances among banks absent any legal restrictions compelling their use. Such need not be the case, however. Indeed, it should be emphasized that, although the above reform is designed so that a continuation of the present paper-dollar standard is possible under it, the reform is not meant to guarantee the permanence of that standard. Some other asset might replace paper dollars as the most saleable asset in the economic system and hence as the ultimate means of settling debts. This would drive the value of paper dollars to zero (since there is no nonmonetary demand for them), rendering the dollar useless as a unit of account. In this event a new unit of account, linked to the most saleable asset in the system, would evolve, thus bringing the dollar standard to an end. As Vaubel (1986) emphasizes, one aim of a complete free-banking reform should be the elimination of any barriers standing in the way of the adoption of a new monetary standard. Fiat currencies issued by other governments or even by private firms (including composite currencies like the ECU), if they were judged more advantageous by the public, could then replace the present dollar standard. Also, the way would be opened for the restoration of some kind of commodity standard, such as a gold standard. This does not mean that a change of standard would be likely; however, *if* many people desired it, it could occur. A well-working free banking system can grow on the foundation of any sort of base money that the public is likely to select, and competition in the supply of base money is no less desirable than competition in the supply of bank liabilities, including bank notes, redeemable in base money.

Of course this reform is radical, and it is not likely to be adopted in the near future. Nevertheless, there are no great logistic or material barriers standing in the way of the adoption of free banking; the transition costs of a well-framed free banking reform are negligible—with benefits as great as the potential for undesirable fluctuations in the dollar supply if it is not undertaken. Therefore, although political reality renders such reform unlikely in the near future, it would be unfortunate if this were made the excuse for avoiding the vigorous discussion that might minimize the waiting time for its implementation. The present banking system is likely to generate a need for drastic change sooner or later, and if reform is delayed until a time of crisis, there can be no question of any smooth, costless transition to a well-working, deregulated system. On the contrary, an occasion of panic is likely to breed the sort of "temporary" makeshift measures that end in *more* regulation and centralization, leaving the banking system in an even less satisfactory state, and still further removed from the practical and theoretical ideal of perfect freedom.

Conclusion

F REE BANKING in a near-perfect form has not existed anywhere
since 1845, when the Scottish free banking era was ended by Peel's
Bank Act. Its closest approximations since that time, including the
plural note issue systems of Sweden, China, and Canada, which
survived into the 20th century, have also been replaced by more
monopolistic and restrictive systems based upon central banking.
How significant is this? How serious have the actual consequences of
governments' failure to allow free banking been?

The consequences have been very serious, for reasons that should
be evident by now. When banking is regulated and centralized, the
supply of money fails to respond automatically to changes in demand.
Excessive money creation leads to forced savings and to inflation, and
these are eventually followed by a liquidation crisis. Insufficient
money creation leads to immediate depression and deflation. History
is littered with such monetary disturbances. Besides these there have
been numerous instances, in the 19th century especially, of currency
shortages, which might have been avoided had banks been completely
free to issue notes. Currency shortages rarely occur today, but the
price for avoiding them has been central banks' all too generous
expansion of supplies of high-powered money—expansion well in
excess of what has been needed to meet demands for currency. As a
result inflation has become a chronic, worldwide disorder.

That inflation has been the overall tendency of centralized banking
should not surprise anyone, because an agency able to expand its
assets gratuitously finds it difficult to resist using this power to its
uppermost limits. With free banking no longer an issue, it was merely
necessary that convertibility requirements be dismantled for these
limits to be greatly expanded. The only thing that stands between fiat

173

money creation by central banks and limitless inflation is political pressure from those who know and fear the consequences.

But these are only the direct effects of the rejection of free banking. The indirect effects have been even more unfortunate. These stem from the interventionism dynamic, in which one ill-conceived regulation justifies a myriad of others. Bond-deposit requirements, restrictions against branch banking, and other regulations plagued the National Banking System and led to crises that provoked even more regulations and centralization, giving rise to the Federal Reserve System. When the new arrangement became involved in even greater disturbances, yet another batch of restrictions on freedom of choice was imposed. The gold standard became a scapegoat, and was gradually dismantled. There was at work a kind of regulatory ratchet-effect, and the banking system we have today is the result. There have been other consequences as well. One of them is the view that the monetary authority ought to control, not just commercial banks, but all kinds of financial institutions. Another is the idea that a *world* central bank will be the ultimate cure for monetary disorder. But most significant has been a body of opinion convinced that the free market is inherently unstable, and that only far-reaching government involvement will make it work. Failure to allow the market to function in money and banking has thus encouraged the view that the market system as a whole is unreliable and in need of further state regulation and centralization.

All this should not be taken as suggesting that problems would not arise under free banking. A free banking system is not perfect. Bankers will sometimes err in their entrepreneurial decisions; they will make bad loans and investments, and some banks will fail. Exogenous fluctuations in the output of commodity money will occur due to technological innovations which are not mere responses to changes in demand, and such fluctuations will be a cause of monetary disequilibrium.[1] The nonmonetary demand for the money commodity may be unstable. Finally, changes in the total supply of inside money will also not occur in perfect correspondence with changes in demand: there may be minor episodes of aggregate excess supply or excess demand, as bankers grope to discover their maximum, sustainable issues in an environment where consumer note preferences are not perfectly stable or predictable.

Nevertheless, the equilibrating *tendencies* of free banking, which this study has attempted to analyze, are in keeping with monetary stability. Under free banking economic forces reward bankers who make decisions consistent with the maintenance of monetary equilibrium (and minimization of costs) and punish bankers who make decisions inconsistent with these goals. Although tendencies are not equivalent to perfection, this is not a special disadvantage of free banking: there is no such thing as a perfect monetary and banking system in a world without perfect human beings capable of making perfect decisions.

It also has to be admitted that free banking is not an arrangement the consequences of which are entirely predictable. There are gaps in our knowledge of how a free banking system functions, gaps that future research (aided, perhaps, by actual practice) will hopefully fill. Some of these concern the implications of free banking for the distribution of loanable funds, the effects of competitive note issue on the relative economies of unit and branch banking, the implications of free banking for government finance, the possible international uses of base money in an open free banking system and their implications for domestic stability, and the possibilities for 100 percent fiduciary substitution (elimination of outside money from bank reserve holdings) by way of advanced clearinghouse arrangements and their implications for theory and policy. Going beyond such issues it must be realized that no actual free banking system is likely to stand still. On the contrary, any such system is likely to continue to evolve new practices and techniques which theory cannot possibly anticipate. We see this happening even at present, despite the existence of prohibitions and regulations that thwart change. Innovations in electronic banking especially are progressing far more rapidly than any theory that might account for their consequences. It is evident, however, that these consequences are generally favorable ones. The same is also likely to be true of the even more numerous innovations that would be possible if banking were entirely unregulated.

In another sense, though—that which concerns the course of the money supply—the consequences of free banking *are* predictable. The environment it produces is favorable to entrepreneurial decision-making and to the undertaking of ventures expected to yield their fruits through long periods. Nothing of the sort can be said of regulated, centralized systems of money supply. This is true, not only because those in charge of a centralized system cannot have the information necessary for stability—a fact given due attention throughout this study—but also because stability is simply not in the interest of those in charge. I have for the most part refrained from emphasizing the second point; but it would be foolish to ignore it entirely and to pretend that politicians are not self-interested persons whose interests often conflict with the goal of maximum consumer welfare.[2] Admitting this, the fact remains that a centralized banking system would work badly even if angels (but not omniscient angels) were placed in charge of it.

Notes

Chapter 1: Overview

1. See especially Jonung (1985); Rockoff (1974); Rolnick and Weber (1982, 1983, 1986); Vaubel (1984c); and L. White (1984d).

2. An example of contemporary, pro-deregulation opinion is Benston (1983).

3. For more complete historical surveys see Cameron (1972); Conant (1915); and V. Smith (1936).

4. Lawrence White's excellent and comprehensive study of the Scottish system, *Free Banking in Britain*, makes it unnecessary for us to delve into the details of that episode here.

5. See Lars G. Sandberg (1978).

6. For a detailed discussion of this episode see my "Free Banking in China, 1800–1935."

7. For evidence see " 'Circulation Notes' in Rural China" (1957). Here it is reported that Agricultural People's Cooperatives (APCs) were resorting to issues of illegal currency to compensate for the insufficient provision of small-denomination notes by branches of the People's Bank.

8. The departmental banks were local monopolies the notes of which were current only in their department of issue. The government, in cooperation with the Bank of France, refused the department banks' request for permission to accept and redeem each other's notes and also rejected their 1840 petition to organize a note exchange. Despite the existence of such obstacles to competition the departmental banks retained a solid reputation. See Rondo Cameron, "France, 1800–1870," in Cameron (1972).

9. The French free-banking school had among its members Charles Coquelin, J. G. Courcelle-Seneuil, Gustave de Molinari, J. E. Horn, and (after his conversion from Saint-Simonism), Michel Chevalier. Of their scholarly contributions the most impressive is Horn's "La liberté des banques" (1866). On the history of this school see Nataf (1983).

10. At the time, this was approximately $25 million. "All the existing provincial banks, then numbering eighteen, were ordered to liquidate their circulation and transfer it to the Bank of Spain." See Conant (1915, 313).

A railroad-bond mania during the 1860s ended in a wave of private bank failures, which ultimately contributed to the overthrow of the monarchy. It should be noted, however, that this speculative bubble was itself the result of a railway law passed in 1855. See Gabriel Tortella, "Spain 1829–1874" in Cameron (1972).

11. "During the period 1861–90 the government's budget was in deficit every year, and the public debt grew from 2.4 billion lire in 1861 to 12.1 billion lire in 1890." See Jon S. Cohen, "Italy 1861–1914," in Cameron (1972). This article gives

a good, concise account of the course of centralization of the Italian currency system.

12. According to Conant (1915, 21–22) the "unauthorized" issue involved "the guilty connivance of public officials" who were the initial recipients of most of it.

13. Two contemporary writers whose views generally correspond to those of Di Nardi are Michele Fratianni and Franco Spinelli (1984).

14. Although there are only five major Canadian banks today, there were about 40 in 1880, 20 in 1910, and 11 in 1930. Most of these had extensive branch networks.

15. Ontario and Quebec adopted New York style "free banking" laws during the 1850s and 1860s, so that their banks' note-issues were for a time restricted by bond-deposit requirements. But banks already in existence in these provinces when the laws were passed did not have to conform to them. As a result, in the words of Horace White, the unregulated banks "crowded the free banks to the wall." The free banking laws were finally repealed in 1866. See Horace White (1896, 360–61).

16. "The matter of securing an additional supply of funds was what was uppermost in the minds of most of the advocates of a central bank. Most . . . had no clear idea of what its functions should be" (Stokes 1939, 52). See also Plumptre (1938) and Bordo and Redish (1986, 18–22).

17. See Plumptre (1938).

18. Ibid., 199. Later, similar pressure was put on the British Commonwealth countries.

19. Ibid.

20. See V. Smith (1936, 36).

21. See Hammond (1957, 618–21) and Rockoff (1974, 145–46). Ironically, the wildcat banks are often used to illustrate unregulated banking and its consequences.

Wildcat banks were also less common than is frequently supposed. According to Rolnick and Weber (1982), only 7 percent of the bond-deposit banks incorporated in New York, Indiana, Wisconsin, and Minnesota closed within a year of their establishment with assets insufficient to redeem their notes.

22. According to Friedman and Schwartz (1963, 128), between 1882 and 1891 the supply of national bank notes fell from $350 million to $160 million.

23. For a more detailed discussion of events leading up to the adoption of the Federal Reserve Act see V. Smith (1936, 128–46).

24. On the Suffolk system see Whitney (1881) and Trivoli (1979).

25. This task has, however, been undertaken in Vera Smith's admirable though neglected work. See also Schwartz (1984).

Chapter 2: The Evolution of a Free Banking System

Lawrence H. White has assisted me in writing this chapter. A somewhat altered version has appeared in *Economic Inquiry*.

1. See, for example, Black (1970); Fama (1980, 1983); Greenfield and Yeager (1983); Hall (1982); Hayek (1978); Wallace (1983); L. White (1984c); Woolsey (1984); and Yeager (1983, 1985).

2. The same view appears in Carlisle (1901, 5); and Ridgeway (1892, 47). Ridgeway opines that "the doctrine of primal convention with regard to the use of any one particular article as a medium of exchange is just as false as the old belief in an original convention at the first beginning of Language and Law."

3. On some alleged, non-metallic monies of primitive peoples see Temple (1899). According to Jacques Melitz (1974, 95), one must be skeptical concerning accounts of primitive monies, including especially non-metallic monies (with the exception of cowries in China), since many of these are based on loose definitions.

For example, the Yap stones of Melanesia could hardly be described as serving as a general medium of exchange. An exceptionally sedate review of anthropological findings in this area is Quiggin (1963).

The most successful of the metallic monies—gold—appeared in many places as the "direct successor" of the cow barter-unit (see Burns 1927a, 288). According to Ridgeway (1892, 133), the earliest gold coins, found throughout the ancient world from Central Asia to the Atlantic, contain approximately 130–135 grains of gold, which was the approximate value in gold of a cow. "This uniformity of the gold unit," Ridgeway argues, "is due to the fact that in all the various countries where we have found it, it originally represented the value in gold of a cow, the universal unit of barter in the same regions." Many early gold coins also bore the image of a cow or ox. Carlisle observes (1901, 30) that "In all such cases, for the transition of meaning [from the barter-unit to a money unit of account] to take place at all, there must have been a 'bimetallic' period . . . in which the old unit and the new, as far as value was concerned, meant one and the same thing."

4. In contrast to Ridgeway, Historian J. B. Bury (1902, 116) gives credit for the invention of coinage to Gyges (687–652 B.C.)—another Lydian king who, according to A. R. Burns (1927b, 83), was responsible not for the invention of coinage, but for the establishment of a state coinage *monopoly*.

5. According to Burns (1927b, 78), "There is no evidence that, as a general rule, the officers of the royal or public treasury, by their greater honesty, made the royal or civic seal a mark more reliable than the seals of the [merchants]."

6. On Gresham's Law and its proper interpretation see Rothbard (1970, 783–84).

7. Transactions of this kind marked the earliest beginnings of banking in 12th-century Genoa and also (on a smaller scale) at medieval trade fairs in Champagne. See Usher (1943); De Roover (1974); and Lopez (1979). In time there were "transfer banks," as De Roover (1974, 184), calls them, in all the major European trading centers.

8. In England, scriveners were the earliest pioneers in the banking trade; in Stuart times they were almost entirely displaced by goldsmith-bankers. The confiscation by Charles I of gold deposited for safekeeping at the Royal Mint ended that institution's participation in the process of banking development. Nevertheless, one may conjecture that, had they existed, private mints would have been logical sites for the undertaking of banking activities.

9. The same holds for the receipts given by bill-brokers to their trader-depositors, although ownership of these may be subject to more routine transfer than occurs at first at other "warehouse banks."

10. "It is obvious that . . . the advantage of being able to place money at safe custody and at interest, while at the same time retaining it within comparatively easy reach . . . would be so palatable as to attract custom from many quarters" (Powell 1966, 56–57).

11. Quoted in Bisschop (1910, 18).

12. According to Usher (1943, 7–8) oral-transfers continued to be the norm in Europe "long after the bill of exchange was well established" whereas "the use of checks and orders of payment seems to have been incidental and sporadic before 1500."

13. The use of nonnegotiable checks, although it allows customers to avoid some visits to the bank, does not allow banks to reduce their reserve needs by extending the scope of clearing transactions. "Each check would have to become the basis of specific journal and ledger entries so that to the bookkeeper it made no difference whether the entry originated in an oral order or a written order. [Negotiable checks] made it possible to establish clearinghouses in which all transactions among a group of banks were liquidated by drawing up general debit and credit balances between each bank and the clearinghouse" (ibid., 23).

14. "There can be no true note until the law is willing to recognize the right of the bearer to sue in his own name without any supplementary proof of bona fide possession" (ibid., 177).

15. "Anyone who saves a part of his income [by hoarding] to that extent exercises a depressing influence on prices, even though it may be infinitesimal as regards each individual. Other individuals thereby obtain more for their money; in other words they divide among themselves that part of consumption which is renounced by those who save" (Wicksell 1935, 11–12).

16. Ibid. See also Marget (1926, 275–76) and (on the importance of free note issue in particular) Conant (1905, chap. 6).

An author who denies that fractional-reserve banking can be beneficial is Lloyd W. Mints, in *Monetary Policy for a Competitive Society* (1950). Mints writes (p. 5) that fractional-reserve banking institutions are "at the best unnecessary" and that (p. 7) "they constitute no positively desirable element in the economy."

17. Much of what is said here about notes applies also to checkable deposit credits. For expository convenience, and also because unrestricted note issue is a defining feature of free banking, I will sometimes refer explicitly to bank notes only.

18. To keep notes from banks of each locality dealt with on hand would probably be prohibitively costly in terms of foregone interest.

19. See Trivoli (1979).

20. See Lake (1947, 188), and also Trivoli (1979, 10–12, 17).

21. Small amounts of gold coin continued to be used in these places because of restrictions upon the issue of "token" coin and of small denomination notes. In an entirely free system such restrictions would not exist.

22. See Leslie (1950, 8–9). On note-dueling in the Suffolk system see Magee (1923, 440–44).

23. This result is contrary to Eugene Fama's suggestion (1983, 19) that note-dueling will persist indefinitely. It is an example of the "tit for tat" strategy, as discussed by Robert Axelrod (1984), proving dominant in a repeated-game setting.

24. The "$" symbol is used for expository convenience only. $1 here is some fixed amount of commodity money.

25. Even $40,000 is a savings compared to the $50,000 of reserves that would be needed if even bilateral offsetting of debts did not take place.

26. For an account of the origins of the Suffolk clearing system, which emerged under rather special circumstances, see Trivoli (1979).

27. There is an example of this in Boston banking history: in 1858 the Bank of Mutual Redemption was set up to compete with the Suffolk Bank as a note-clearing agency. The Suffolk Bank first resorted to note-dueling to quash its rival, but later became discouraged and largely gave up the business of clearing country bank notes. In response, the other Boston banks established a new organization, the New England Sorting House, to take the Suffolk's place. The Sorting House accepted the notes of Bank of Mutual Redemption members, which the Suffolk Bank had refused, and this allowed it and the Bank of Mutual Redemption to clear with each other.

28. A later edition of Cannon's book was published in 1910. This is the most comprehensive work on the subject of clearinghouses.

29. "The clearinghouse, which was begun simply as a labor-saving device, has united the banking interests in various communities in closer bands of sympathy and union and has developed into a marvelous instrumentality for the protection of the community from the evil effects of panics and of bad banking" Cannon (1910, 24).

30. See Cannon (1908, 99–112); Andrew (1908); R. H. Timberlake, Jr. (1984); and Gary Gorton (1985c).

31. This contradicts Neil Wallace's hypothesis that all currency would bear interest under laissez-faire. See L. White (1984d, 8–9 and 1987).

32. The possibility of bank runs and ways free banks might deal with them is discussed further in the 4th section of chapter 9.

33. Though it would probably be more economical for banks to hold reserve accounts with their clearinghouse, in later chapters it will sometimes be assumed that each bank holds its own commodity-money reserves. Though less realistic, this assumption offers advantages in conceptual clarity that will aid readers' understanding of free-banking money supply processes, while leading to the same conclusions as would be reached using more realistic assumptions.

34. Bart Taub (1985, 195–208) has shown that a dynamic inconsistency facing issuers in Klein's (1974) model will lead them to hyperinflate.

35. See for example Black (1970); Fama (1980); Greenfield and Yeager (1983); and Yeager (1985). To be sure, Greenfield and Yeager recognize that their system would be unlikely to emerge without deliberate action by government, especially given a government-dominated monetary system as the starting point.

36. This point is emphasized in L. White (1984b). See also O'Driscoll (1985); Kevin D. Hoover (1985); and Bennett T. McCallum (1984).

37. See their works cited in note 1, this chapter.

38. In contradiction to Goodhart (1984). On the question of natural monopoly see below, chapter 10.

39. We have seen that reserves do tend to centralize, on the other hand, in the clearinghouses. And clearinghouses may take on functions that are today associated with national central banks: holding reserves for clearing purposes, establishing and policing safety and soundness standards for member banks, and managing panics should they arise. But these functional similarities should not be taken to indicate that clearinghouses have (or would have) freely evolved into central banks. The similarities instead reflect the pre-emption of clearinghouse functions by legally privileged banks or, particularly in the founding of the Federal Reserve System, the deliberate nationalization of clearinghouse functions. Central banks have emerged from legislation contravening, not complementing, spontaneous market developments. See Gorton (1985c, 277 and 283; and 1985b, 274); and Timberlake (1984).

40. To simplify discussion, the possibility of a bank's adding to its capital or net worth is not considered.

41. A fuller discussion of conditions determining a free bank's optimal size is presented in L. White (1984d, 3–9).

Chapter 3: Credit Expansion with Constant Money Demand

1. Good statements of the rule of excess reserves are in Chester Arthur Phillips (1920, 33–34), Robert G. Rodkey (1928, 178–85), and Alex N. McLeod (1984, 201).

2. See Rodkey (1928, 42). The above argument assumes that, after the first clearing round, Bank A must reduce its loans $40,000 to restore its reserves. The simplest means by which this might be accomplished is if those persons holding the $40,000 of new money balances at Banks B through E use them to buy goods from a debtor of Bank A, who in turn pays back a $40,000 loan. The same sort of transactions can be imagined to occur after each clearing round. By this means one can most readily see that Bank A must soon contract by the full amount of its overexpansion.

3. Banks might also try to attract more depositors by offering them higher rates while earning the interest through riskier loans and investments. This of course is just a definition of bad banking: the high-risk loans reduce bank revenues in the long run, as default occurs. But the bank may grow inordinately in the short run.

Such banking has been behind many of the growing number of bank failures in recent times. It would not, however, be common in unregulated circumstances, where bank owners bear the full costs of failure. Its frequency today must be blamed on regulatory arrangements, including Federal deposit insurance, bank bailouts, and the promise of Federal Reserve support, that subsidize excessive risk-taking and artificially limit losses to bank stockholders.

4. The argument proves only that *spontaneous* in-concert *absolute* overexpansion is unlikely; it does not show why, facing a uniform fall in the demand for money, banks as a whole should contract their liabilities, or why a *planned* in-concert overexpansion would not be sustainable. A more general treatment of the problem of in-concert overexpansion appears in chapter 6.

5. If currency is used by the public some of the new reserve media may pass into circulation, lessening the potential expansion. In an open economy reserve media useful in international trade might also be lost to foreign banks. Here we assume that the public's demand for currency does not increase, and that the economy is a closed one.

6. Ludwig von Mises ([1928] 1978, 138). "Circulation credit" is Mises's term for bank liabilities not backed by commodity-money reserves. Elsewhere Mises uses the term "fiduciary credit" (see chapter 4 below).

7. It is reasonable to assume that most non-retail purchases are made using checks rather than notes.

8. According to Checkland (1975), the Scottish banks encouraged their customers (depositors and borrowers) to show note brand loyalty by paying in the notes of rival banks, while making their advances to others with their own bank's notes. Pressure to "push" a bank's notes was most effectively placed on those in debt to it.

9. Such behavior is assumed by Eugene E. Agger (1918, 103).

10. This example, as well as one to follow, assumes that new notes are initially issued in a proportional loan to *everybody*. This assumption is the strongest that can be made in favor of a "predatory overexpansion" scenario. If it is assumed, more realistically, that new issues are first made available to one person or group only, more of them will enter the clearing mechanism, *ceteris paribus*.

11. Compare L. White (1984d, 97fn), who employs somewhat different assumptions and concludes that an overexpanding bank's reserve losses will *fall* as the number of its rivals increases.

12. We have already seen why it makes little difference if some notes return directly to their issuers.

13. For statistics on the note circulation of various banks during the Scottish free banking era, see L. White (1984d) and Munn (1981). For statistics on note issues of Canadian banks in the 19th century, see the Dominion Bureau of Statistics *Canada Yearbook*. For evidence from the Swedish experience, see Jonung (1985).

14. The existence of legal-tender status for the notes of a privileged bank of issue, although it encourages their general acceptance, is not essential to their being held for reissue by deposit banks.

15. To recall, we are assuming that there is no public demand to hold coin as a proportion of total money balances. The conclusion also ignores the possible presence of industrial (nonmonetary) demands for the money commodity.

16. Except where otherwise noted the facts cited are from Copland (1920).

Chapter 4: Monetary Equilibrium

1. See Gilbert (1953, 144).

2. In terms of the Cambridge equation of exchange, this means a change in the value of "k."

3. See Clayton (1955, 96) and Brown (1910)

4. "In extending any particular individual a loan of a certain sum of money, the lending bank is in effect conferring upon the borrower a claim to a corresponding fraction of the wealth of the community whose real value is matched by the real value of goods which some anonymous depositor [or note holder] has refrained from exercising the right to consume" (Poindexter 1946, 135). Compare Hutt (1952, 237ff).

5. Gottfried Haberler (1931, 19) notes that such downturns may be reinforced by the aggravation of debt burdens as a result of the unanticipated fall in prices. This effect may for some time remain "an obstacle to recovery, unless relief is found in the shape of a crop of bankruptcies."

6. See Friedrich A. Hayek ([1933] 1975b and 1935). Also see Ludwig von Mises ([1928] 1978, 59–171). The Austrian economists' relative lack of attention to the problems of deflation is due in part to their views on the requirements for credit market equilibrium. These are discussed below in this chapter.

7. See Friedrich A. Lutz (1969).

8. Hayek (1935, 121). See also p. 91, where Hayek writes that "to be neutral . . . the supply of money should be invariable." Such statements give credence to the view that Hayek advocated a "do nothing" policy for business cycles. See for example Lawrence R. Klein (1966, 51). Of course, given monetary institutions that exist today and those that existed in the 1930s, even a constant money supply is not really the same as a do-nothing policy.

9. Hayek (1935, 107). Hayek refers in particular to the need to accommodate changes in the demand for money due to the multiplication of stages of industrial production.

10. Durbin's views were challenged by J. C. Gilbert (1934). This was followed by Durbin's reply (1935) with a "Rejoinder" from Gilbert and a final note by Durbin (ibid., 223–26).

11. The discussion in *Money* is clearer but at the same time less complete.

12. Robertson (1926, 53–54). Robertson's "Automatic Lacking" has the same meaning as the notion of "forced saving" that I discuss below in this chapter. The expression "cloak-room" banking is a reference to the views of Edwin Cannan, also discussed below.

13. Thus, for example, Allan G. B. Fisher writes (1935, 200) that "Apart from increases in population and from changes in the desire of individuals to hold money, economic development which takes the form of increased production per head . . . does not require any increase in the money supply." See also Robertson (1964, 80–82 and 111–14).

14. See for example Lloyd Mints (1950, 129–30).

15. Keynes (1936, 167fn) refers specifically to bank deposits. In some respects the arguments in Keynes *Treatise on Money* (1930) have even more in common with those of other authors cited above.

16. See for example Keynes (1936, 16, 303).

17. This aspect of Keynesian analysis provoked Jacob Viner to remark prophetically in 1936 that "In a world organized in accordance with Keynes' specifications there would be a constant race between the printing press and the business agents of the trade unions." See Viner ([1935] 1960, 49).

18. These terms are taken from Machlup (1940, 231–32). A third kind of credit discussed by Machlup (232–37) is credit granted out of "surplus cash balances." This results from reductions in the public's demand for base money in circulation. Since base money is assumed not to circulate under free banking (where bank notes supply demands for currency) this type of credit expansion is not relevant to it. On the other hand, it is relevant for the case of *central* banking if central bank notes or fiat money are used as currency. In this case it may be regarded as a special type of created credit.

184 □ *Notes pages 60–68*

19. When, on the other hand, the demand for money increases but its supply does not increase correspondingly (i.e., when there is a failure on the part of banks to issue transfer credit) the effect, in Machlup's terminology, is one of "credit destruction." The contraction of bank credit in the face of an unchanged demand for money is also an example of this.

20. This way of putting it seems preferable to Machlup's definition (171) of created credit as credit that provides "purchasing power . . . which has not been given up by anybody before hand." This might be interpreted as including in "created" credit credit granted in response to an increased demand for inside money (which is actually transfer credit), since persons who add to their balances of inside money do not necessarily sacrifice "purchasing power." What they sacrifice is actual *purchasing*, which is something different. The trouble lies with the expression "purchasing power," which sometimes refers to a *potential* to purchase, and sometimes to the *exercise of that potential*. Because of its ambiguity I try to avoid using this expression.

21. Good, brief discussions of this are Pigou (1933, 227–31), Clayton (1955, 98–101), and Robertson (1964, chap. 5 sect. 3 and 173ff). Pigou uses the expression "forced levies" instead of forced savings. Keynes (1936, 183) called the doctrine of forced savings "one of the worst muddles" of neoclassical economics. But he also associated it with Hayek's recommendation that the money supply should be kept constant. Keynes might have rejected Hayek's constant money supply bathwater without throwing out the forced-savings baby. For a critical discussion of the role of forced savings in Keynes's thought, see Victoria Chick (1983, 236–39).

22. Quoted in Hayek (1935, 20).

23. Clayton (1955, 99). Compare Machlup (1940, 171). Clayton's last statement would be accurate only if capital goods were homogeneous, and capital "sunk" as a result of credit creation were not a cause of permanent changes in the structure of production.

24. In addition to works of Hayek and Mises cited in the text see Ludwig von Mises ([1953] 1980, 359–67; 1949, 545–73; 1966, chap. 20) and Murray N. Rothbard (1970, 850–63).

25. Mises (1949, 439fn). Compare Rothbard (1970, 862), and Hayek (1935, 23).

26. Compare Mises (1980, 300–301).

27. In the writings of Rothbard (1970, 850–60 and 1962, 115ff) this tendency is complete.

28. On these authors see Vera Smith (1936, 91–93 and 110–12).

29. See Mises (1966, 443).

Chapter 5: Changes in the Demand for Inside Money

1. See Richard G. Davis and Jack M. Guttentag (1962), who describe compensating balances as a way for banks to guarantee that their borrower-customers will hold their working balances with them rather than elsewhere. They also note (123fn) that in many instances the requirements, rather than being based on "hard and fast agreements," take the form of informal understandings.

2. See Harold Barger (1935, 441). Barger, however, believes that monetary equilibrium can be maintained only if credits are restricted to producer (and not consumer) loans. His position seems to be based on the view that "non-productive" loans will not generate interest necessary for their repayment. This view overlooks the fact that consumer-borrowers can pay interest out of their future income even if this involves a reduction in wealth. Thus, banks' granting of loans to consumers, although it does not necessarily contribute to capital accumulation, is still consistent with the preservation of monetary equilibrium.

3. The process of inside-money absorption is discussed in Shotaro Kojima (1943, 17–18).

4. It is assumed that before being paid-in the liabilities were strictly "idle," so that they were not a cause of any bank clearings.

Chapter 6: Economic Reserve Requirements

1. By analogy with the "law of conservation of energy" (the first law of thermodynamics), which states that energy can be moved from one place to another but cannot be created or destroyed.

2. "That any single person can make his own balance at [a] bank rise by paying in money . . . (whether in cash or in checks) and make it fall by withdrawing cash or paying away checks, everyone who has ever had a balance to his credit knows. No one denies this, but some theorists have denied that what is true of each lender taken separately is true of the whole body of lenders taken together." Edwin Cannan, "Growth and Fluctuations of Bankers' Liabilities to Customers" (1935, 8).

3. It is generally recognized that, in systems with monopolized currency supply, changes in the demand for currency relative to deposits will alter the base-money multiplier by causing base money to shift between bank reserves and circulation. This perverse adjustment is different from the accommodative adjustments considered here, which are adjustments in the supply of inside money in response to changes in demand when the supply of bank reserves is *constant*.

4. George Clayton (1955, 97–98). The only exception Clayton allows for is the case of a transfer of funds from demand accounts to time-deposit accounts. This reflects a presumption that different statutory reserve ratios apply to these types of accounts. On the reliance of the conservation theory on the assumption that there are binding statutory reserve requirements see below.

5. The turnover of liabilities will change temporarily if the demand for them changes (with constant supply) as consumers attempt to spend off excess balances or to add to their deficient balances.

6. Following J.H.G. Olivera (1971, 1096), "reserve demand" is used here to indicate needs arising in connection with bank clearing transactions that "make it necessary for the reserve holder to transfer some amount of the reserve asset."

7. Ernst Baltensperger (1974, 205) defines precautionary reserve demand as the "excess of total holdings of the reserve asset . . . over the expected or average net demand for ('loss' of) reserves." Olivera (1971) defines it as "the part of the total reserve which is held against possible deviations of net demand above its expected value."

8. That is, so long as "reserve changes are known in probabalistic form only" (Baltensperger 1974, 205).

9. It is assumed throughout this analysis that the demand for reserves is uninfluenced by changes in interest rates on loans and investments. In defense of this assumption it may be noted that interest rates on overnight, "emergency" loans to cover reserve deficiencies will tend to rise along with other rates of interest, so that the penalty costs for insufficient reserve holding increase with the opportunity costs of keeping adequate reserves on hand. This suggests that high interest rates do not necessarily make it desirable for banks to skimp on reserves. For arguments and evidence in support of this view see Leijonhufvud (1968, 358), and Hancock (1983). Of course, if high rates are passed on to deposit holders, this might increase the quantity of money demanded and so reduce indirectly the demand for reserves.

10. F.Y. Edgeworth (1888). The best recent articles on this subject are the ones previously cited by Baltensperger and Olivera. In addition to these articles the discussion in Don Patinkin (1965, 82–88) is recommended.

11. As Baltensperger notes (1974, 205), the "square-root" law gives a *conservative* estimate of the relation between changes in gross clearings and precautionary reserve demand, in part because it assumes an increase in frequency, rather than in average size, of transactions. Edgeworth's demonstration of the square-root law

also relies on the assumption that individual clearing debits are stochastically independent and identically distributed. Olivera shows, however, that the law holds even if individual clearing debits ("the components of net average demand") are serially correlated.

12. Whether adjustments in nominal supply of bank liabilities will entirely offset changes in nominal demand depends on the extent of note-brand discrimination. An increase in demand among nondiscriminating persons results in a smaller reduction in precautionary reserve needs than an equal increase in demand (affecting all banks uniformly) of discriminating persons. When there is 100 percent (marginal) note-brand discrimination, nominal supply adjustments will be complete.

For the sake of simplicity the argument assumes that banks are in equilibrium with respect to one another, that is, it assumes that the average net demand for reserves is zero. Then precautionary demand for reserves = total demand. Olivera (1971, 1100) notes that the square-root law is relevant to "decision units taken individually" and that "its possible use as a macroeconomic relationship involves a nonlinear aggregation problem." He adds, however, that "the obvious 'aggregation condition' is that the number of reserve-holders, as well as their shares of the expected market demand, remain stationary when the latter grows." But this simply means that it is necessary to abstract from changes in average net reserve demand, which is precisely the procedure I have adopted.

13. For the banking system, every dollar's worth of excess money supply generates several dollars' worth of additional bank clearings during any extended (but finite) planning period.

14. See Patinkin (1965, 87–88 and 576–77).

15. Jacoby (1963, 220). Similar proposals were made in the 1930s, following the lead of Winfield Riefler. See George Garvey and Martin R. Blyn (1969, 56–57).

16. Joachim Ahrensdorf and S. Kanesthasan (1960). For evidence on cross-sectional and temporal variation in Scottish free banks' reserve rations, see Munn (1981).

17. See note 3 above, and also chapter 8.

18. Once again I am abstracting from problems arising due to changes in the demand for currency *relative* to total money demand. These problems are discussed at length in chapter 8.

19. See for example Albert E. Burger (1971), which is one of the more detailed, modern discussions of factors influencing the money supply. McLeod, whose analysis is also very detailed, merely hints at the possibility of a demand-elastic money supply when he notes (1984, 100) that the "credit multiplier" may rise to infinity, while the "total income multiplier" associated with a given increase in credit (bank loans and investments) may at the same time approach zero if increased lending is offset by increased holdings of inside-money balances. McLeod cites borrowings used to increase borrower's liquidity—a case similar to the one of compensating balances discussed above—as a limiting case. Our claim is a much stronger one, viz, that under free banking changes in money supply *generally* do not influence total income and spending.

20. The example assumes 100 percent marginal note discrimination.

21. Eugene E. Agger (1918, 101). Were he writing about an unregulated system Agger might also have referred to an increase in the volume of notes.

22. Keynes (1930, 1: 27). Keynes's two premises are incorrect: an individual bank may "move forward" on its own without weakening itself if the demand for its liabilities has increased, and overexpansion by one bank or set of banks generally will not inspire sympathetic overexpansion by remaining ones.

23. L. White (1984d, 17). White presumably meant to say "by the same amount" rather than "by a common factor."

24. The more important members of the Free Banking School were Sir Henry Parnell, Samuel Bailey, and James William Gilbart. (For other names see ibid., 52.)

25. L. White (1984d, 98). Not surprisingly, opponents of free banking also accepted the in-concert overexpansion argument, and were in addition more willing to view it as a description of the likely course of events under unregulated banking. They included J. R. McCulloch and Samuel Jones Loyd (cited in ibid., 98–99), and G. W. Norman, a Director of the Bank of England (cited in V. Smith, 68).

26. See especially Gurley and Shaw (1955, 1956).

27. Gurley and Shaw (1960, 202, 218).

28. Joseph Aschheim, in response to Gurley and Shaw, argues (1959, 66) that commercial banks "can make *ex post* savings exceed *ex ante* savings," i.e., can engage in credit creation that leads to forced savings. In contrast, Aschheim says, other financial institutions "can lend no more than they have received from depositors and, therefore, cannot create loanable funds." What I have tried to show, in contrast, is that deposit commercial banks are mainly passive "credit creators." The only active credit creators are those institutions having a monopoly or quasi-monopoly in the supply of currency.

29. See, for example, James M. Henderson (1960).

Chapter 7: The Dilemma of Central Banking

1. The inherent inadequacy of knowledge conveyed through the price system is, of course, only one source of entrepreneurial error. Knowledge conveyed in market prices may also be ignored or misinterpreted.

2. For one thing, inventory shortages and surpluses tell nothing about whether the entire *set* of goods being produced is the most desirable one as far as consumers are concerned. Only rivalrous competition among producers tends to provide such information.

3. See Don Lavoie (1985, 129–32).

4. See Trygve J. B. Hoff (1981, 125–27).

5. Here, and throughout the remainder of this section, I assume that decentralized markets exist for all goods and services other than money.

6. I wish to emphasize once again that there is no "nominalist" fallacy involved in this prescription; admittedly, *ceteris paribus*, a higher level of prices demands a higher nominal supply of money, and so one may be led to the conclusion that any "excess supply" of money that causes prices to rise is therefore self-justifying. This is true *once* prices have risen; but price-level adjustments do not occur instantaneously. General price adjustments are long run consequences of monetary disequilibrium. Once this is taken into account the concepts of "excess [nominal] supply" of (or "excess [nominal] demand" for) money can be viewed as potential short-run states of affairs and not just as analytical conveniences.

7. This conclusion must be modified somewhat if the issuing bank has purchased assets earning fixed nominal rates of interest. Then the bank's marginal costs include any reduction in the real yield (or market price) of its assets due to inflation. This cost does indeed rise at the margin, but it is unlikely to rise so rapidly as to encourage a non-inflationary policy.

8. To refer to our earlier discussion, this policy of having a demand-elastic supply of money is roughly equivalent to one that maintains constant the supply of money multiplied by its income velocity of circulation.

9. Most prominent among earlier proponents of price-level stabilization were members of the Stockholm school, including Knut Wicksell and Gustav Cassel; American "quantity theorists" (for want of a better label), such as Irving Fisher, Lloyd Mints, and Henry Simons; and Cambridge economist A. C. Pigou. An example of a contemporary advocate of price-level stabilization is Robert E. Hall. See his 1984, esp. 309–13, and also 1982, 111–22. Two excellent critical works on price-level stabilization are Gottfried Haberler (1931) and R. G. Hawtrey (1951).

10. Notice that I am concerned at this stage of my inquiry only with the

argument for price-level stablization that views it as a procedure for maintaining monetary equilibrium. Later on I will have occasion to discuss what, if any, advantages price-level stabilization offers as a means for protecting debtors and creditors from the consequences of changes in the value of money.

11. The last two problems are emphasized by Ludwig von Mises (1978, 87–88). See also Robertson (1964, chap. 2).

12. The experiment in price-level stabilization of the 1920s is a good example of how the use of a wrong index of prices may deceive the authorities into believing that theirs is a noninflationary credit policy. Most price indices used at that time did not include prices of stock-certificates and real estate. On this see C. A. Phillips, T. F. McManus, and R. W. Nelson (1937, passim), and also M. H. de Koch (1967, 133).

13. Apart from those that might occur because of changed *distribution* of demand caused by the fact that the price-elasticity of demand of some goods now available in greater or lesser abundance is non-unitary.

14. This is also the conclusion of the writers whose views on monetary equilibrium are cited in chapter 4. Among advocates of price-level stabilization, Mints (1950, 129–30) admits that prices may fall on account of increases in productive efficiency. He dismisses the difficulty that this poses after noting that "there is no [policy] criteria [sic] which would indicate the 'right' rate of decline in commodity prices." This is quite true as far as any central-banking policy is concerned. Still, the argument bolsters the case for free banking more than it aids the cause of price-level stabilization. For Mint's views on free banking, see ibid., 5–7.

15. The use of an index of prices of factors of production to detect such relative inflation would be a potential solution if construction of such an index were practicable. The difficulties here far exceed those of constructing a consumer-price index because of the immense number of factors of production, many of which have no readily ascertainable market price. In addition, those factor prices that can be observed may themselves be influenced by changes in the efficiency of production.

16. To use the apt phrase employed by Allen G. B. Fisher (1935, 205).

17. We are, for simplicity's sake, assuming unitary price-elasticities of demand.

18. At the moment I am not considering the possibility of changes in the supply of commodity money.

19. Obviously I am assuming in this case that the demand for inside money is constant.

20. Friedman estimates the length of this lag in the United States monetary system to be somewhere between 4 and 29 months.

21. See for example Raymond E. Lombra and Herbert Kaufman (1984); Raymond E. Lombra and Raymond G. Torto (1975); and Henry C. Wallich (1981). An example of interest-rate pegging was the policy of the Federal Reserve from 1942 to 1951, the year of the Treasury Accord.

22. The monetary authority *could* use interest-rate movements as a guide to changes in the demand for money if it could somehow tell whether movements in the market rate of interest were also movements in the natural or equilibrium rate. Unfortunately, the natural or equilibrium rate of interest is not something that can be observed or measured. For this reason it can never serve as a practical guide for monetary policy.

23. As L. White notes (1984a, 272), "the desirability of controlling [a monetary aggregate] rather than the monetary base is unclear . . . there is the uncomfortable possibility that attempting to control an aggregate containing some measure of inside monies necessarily implies inefficient restrictions on the intermediary functions of banks." See also the following note.

24. See Sherman J. Maisel (1973, 255–80). These criticisms assume that target growth rates can be successfully achieved, whereas in truth their achievement—in

the case of wider monetary aggregates—is sometimes difficult. Only the size of the monetary base is subject to direct and certain control.

Chapter 8: The Supply of Currency

1. Throughout this chapter it is assumed that the variance of bank clearings is not affected by a change in the *form* (notes or deposit-credits) of outstanding liabilities so long as the average holding time (turnover period) of the liabilities is the same. This is equivalent to assuming that precautionary reserve demand for outstanding note liabilities will be the same as for an equal amount of demand-deposit liabilities with the same average rate of turnover.

2. Under central banking with fiat money the distinction between currency demand and outside-money demand is blurred: there is no observable difference between the two, since the ultimate money of redemption is also the only currency in the system. Nevertheless it is still possible conceptually to distinguish the desire to acquire hand-to-hand media from the desire to withdraw savings from the banking system. Under central banking with a commodity standard, the former manifests itself in increased demand for the notes of the central bank, whereas the latter involves redemption of those notes for the money commodity.

3. According to Bowsher (1980, 11–17), the ratio of currency to demand deposits rose in part because of a fall in the importance of demand deposits relative to savings accounts. Nevertheless the trend is surprising in view of the development of alternatives to currency, such as credit cards, and of the substantial increase in interest rates which are a measure of the opportunity cost of holding cash. Many economists attribute this growth in demand for currency to the expansion of the "underground" economy.

4. Agger, p. 87. To consider only currency demand and not outside-money demand is not to neglect the usual consequences of a falling off in business confidence. Historically, when a general decline in confidence has led to increased outside-money demands it has been because of banks' failure to meet depositors' increased demands for currency through increased issues of inside money. For evidence of this see below. The problem of banking panics is dealt with later in this chapter.

5. Somers (1873, 204–25) writes with regard to conditions in 19th-century England that "when the situation is so bad that distrust or panic sets in it is the withdrawal of deposits [by their conversion into currency], and not the cashing in of notes, that gives the fatal blow to a tottering establishment."

6. See Cagan (1958); also Agger (1918, 78–86), and Frank Brechling, (1958, 376–393). Brechling investigates fluctuations in the relative demand for currency in twelve countries and reports both significant across-country variation and significant short-run fluctuations within individual countries. He concludes that the assumption of a constant short-run cash preference ratio, which is determined predominantly by custom and institutional factors, is not supported by the empirical evidence and should be abandoned. Another study, also involving twelve countries, which reaches similar conclusions is Joachim Ahrensdorf and S. Kanesthasan (1960, 129–132).

7. Agger (1918, 87). The surrounding general discussion (pp. 76–90) is one of the best on this whole subject.

8. See ibid. 76; and also Francis Dunbar (1917, 17–18).

9. By assumption only the composition of money demand is varying; the depositor is not seeking to reduce his average money holdings or to take his business to some other bank. For present analytical purposes—and not necessarily because it is realistic to do so—it is desirable to abstract from these other possibilities. I have already shown how a free banking system would respond to them.

10. To repeat, the notes are not useful as a basis for credit expansion, so that their return to their issuer should not provoke any addition to loans.

11. Thus the equilibrium stockpile of notes on hand depends on (1) the probability density function over levels of currency demand; (2) the difference between the price of notes ordered in normal course and that of notes ordered on a "rush job" basis; and (3) the interest cost of paying the former price sooner. The setup is identical to the choice of optimal (base money) reserves and investments. An expansion of note issue will result in clearing debits—debits that, under free banking, have to be settled in outside money—unless it is consistent with the currency needs of the public.

12. "Generally speaking, an increase in the supply of money in the form of check-currency [deposits] must normally appear as part of a composite supply, in which other types of currency are represented; . . . the absence of these other types may effectually prevent the issue of check-currency itself." See Arthur Marget (1926, 255).

13. According to Somers (1873, 207–8), "when [the unrestricted right of note issue] is stopped, and notes are only authorized from a central source, the facility a bank may enjoy in supplanting itself with currency for the uncertain demands upon it can only be in proportion to its proximity to the Issue Department."

14. The amount of "reserve compensation" needed will be less than the actual increase in currency demand.

15. Thus McLeod writes (1984, 65–66fn) that a system of competing banks of issue (where no distinction is made between note and deposit liabilities as far as reserve needs are concerned) "has certain practical advantages if, as is usually the case, there are seasonal fluctuations in the public's demand for notes relative to deposits. In [a system with monopolized currency supply] the peak seasonal demand for notes withdraws reserves from the banks and causes a seasonal credit stringency, and in a managed money system the central bank or other monetary authority must consciusly act to offset any such tendency." The same is true concerning cyclical but nonseasonal changes in the relative demand for currency.

16. See for example Cagan (1958) and Milton Friedman (1959, 66–67).

17. Friedman revealed an awareness that the problem stems from monopolization of the currency supply when he noted (1959, 69) that it might be solved by allowing competition in note-issue. At the time, however, Friedman was less sympathetic (and, one might add, less understanding) toward free banking than he is today, and he described the solution of competitive note-issue as "the economic equivalent to counterfeiting." Compare Friedman (1953, 220).

18. The formulae assume that commodity (outside) money does not circulate. Derivations appear in an appendix to this chapter.

19. By "known" I mean that the total quantity of currency demanded is known; I do not mean that the distribution of this demand—how changes in it will affect the reserve position of particular deposit banks—is known. To assume otherwise would be to grant too much in favor of the case for central banking. I have also chosen to deal only with the three more popular instruments of control. I leave it as an exercise to the reader to contemplate the practicability of other procedures not considered here.

20. Obviously these welfare changes affect not just the banks but also their borrower customers. In the event of a severe currency drain, depositors at some banks may also become victims of a restriction of payments.

21. For further comments on the shortcomings of statutory reserve requirements as instruments for monetary control see Friedman (1959, 45–50).

22. Compare Caroline Whitney (1934, 159–60).

23. For a general discussion of the *disadvantages* of rediscount policy as a means for monetary control see Joseph Aschheim (1961, 83–98).

24. This possibility does not violate the assumption of a fixed total demand for

money so long as there is an equal *increase* in money demand elsewhere in the system.

25. See Currie (1934, 113).

26. See Friedman (1959, 40ff).

27. Particularly significant is Jevons's finding that, in the course of the "autumnal drain," coin and bank notes—including notes issued by "country" banks—moved together. This confirms the view that there was no rush for gold or Bank of England notes as such, but rather a rush for all types of currency. The pressure upon the Bank of England came when the other banks had exhausted their own authorized note issues.

28. Unfortunately Jevons believed as well that emergency currency supplied by the Bank of England would also be withdrawn from the system once it was no longer needed in circulation. This was incorrect. Bank of England notes might eventually return to those banks from which they were withdrawn (assuming no change in banks' shares in the deposit business); but having come this far they went no further—they were retained as vault cash instead of being returned to the Bank of England for redemption and so their total supply would not fall to its original level. Instead, the notes were once again used as reserves to support further lending until the Bank of England made some conscious effort to contract their supply.

29. Jevons's article first appeared in the *Journal of the Statistical Society of London*, vol. 29 (June 1866), pp. 235–53.

30. See the discussion of Bagehot's views in Vera Smith (1936, 121ff) and in L. White (1984d, 145).

31. Conant (1905, 128). But compare Paul M. McGouldrick (1984, 311–49), who claims that the Reichsbank carried on a successful, countercyclical policy throughout most of the period in question.

32. For a general discussion of this episode, see Milton Friedman and Anna Jacobson Schwartz (1963, chapter 7).

33. See also James M. Boughton and Elmus R. Wicker (1984).

34. In view of this, it would have been better had state authorities declared a mere restriction of payments, prohibiting withdrawals of currency and coin, instead of outright holidays. This would have allowed checking-account transactions to continue, and would not have provoked as complete a flight to currency in neighboring states.

35. State bank note issues had ceased following a prohibitive 10 percent Federal tax on them in 1865.

36. See Friedman and Schwartz (1963, 169). Forced par collection, lack of branch facilities for convenient redemption, and the fact that bond-secured notes were perceived as being a lien on the Federal government rather than on their nominal issuers encouraged National banks to hold and reissue notes of their rivals instead of seeking actively to redeem them. Thus these notes were, unlike bank notes in an unregulated system, a kind of high-powered money. Their supply would not contract in response to any *fall* in the demand for currency, and their issue on more liberal terms (short of complete deregulation) might have led to serious inflation. This was, however, not a problem of practical concern in the latter part of the 19th century. On the downward-inelasticity of National bank notes see Charles F. Dunbar (1897, 14–22).

37. On this see Richard H. Timberlake, Jr. (1978, 124–31).

38. See Vera Smith (1936, 133–34).

39. Although many contemporary writers saw free note issue as a potential cure for the problems of the National banks, most believed that some agency was needed for supplying the system with emergency reserves. See for example Victor Morawetz (1909); Alexander Dana Noyes (1910); and John Perrin (1911). These writers, as well as O. M. W. Sprague (1910), tended to view reserve losses (and

consequent monetary contraction) as a distinct problem rather than as a consequence of restrictions on note issue.

The evidence contradicts the view that media not backed by bonds or not centrally issued would have been unacceptable for supplying depositors' demands during crises. For example, Canadian bank notes flowed readily into northern states to fill the void created by insufficient National bank note issues, even though Canadian notes were not backed by any special collateral. [See Joseph F. Johnson (1910, 118).] Also, clearinghouse certificates and loan certificates were issued in various places and were accepted even though they were of questionable legality. Finally, cashier's checks and payroll checks of well-known firms were issued in small, round denominations to serve as currency. The only shortcoming of such emergency currency was that there was not enough of it. Nonetheless what there was showed every sign of being acceptable to the public, and there is every reason to think that freely issued bank notes would also have been accepted. On emergency currencies issued during the Panic of 1907 see A. Piatt Andrew (1908). On clearinghouse note issues see Richard H. Timberlake, Jr. (1984).

40. On the supply of currency in the (pre–1935) Canadian banking system see James Holladay (1934) and L. Carroll Root (1894).

Chapter 9: Stability and Efficiency

1. See Irving Fisher (1896).

2. See Haberler (1931, 14); Tjardus Greidanus (1950, 239); and Lloyd Mints (1950, 133–34). A very early presentation of this argument is L. S. Merrian (1893).

3. The original advocates of this reform were Benjamin Graham (1937, 1944) and Frank D. Graham (1942, 94–119). See also F. A. Hayek (1948a). Critical assessments of these proposals include W.T.M. Beale, Jr., M. T. Kennedy, and W. J. Winn (1942), and Milton Friedman (1953).

4. Admittedly Hayek (1948a, 211) views the reform more as a means for avoiding short-run disequilibrium due to the lack of immediate adjustment of the supply of commodity-money (under a single-commodity standard) to changes in the demand for "highly liquid assets" (i.e., money balances), than as a means for preventing debtor-creditor injustice. Nevertheless, in this respect also the multiple-commodity standard is not superior to free banking since, in the latter, the supply of inside money tends to be elastic with respect to the demand for money balances.

5. One must also assume that there is no autonomous shift in nonmonetary demand for the money commodity.

6. As is done, for example, by Hall (1982, 113–14). Hall's reference to the recent instability of the price of gold is especially inapt, since this instability is more a reflection of the unreliability of the fiat dollar standard than anything else. Hall admits (p. 114) that the value of gold would not have fluctuated so widely had the United States remained on a gold standard. Nevertheless he states (without citing any evidence) that "large changes in the price level would certainly have occurred."

7. See Frank Walter Paish (1950, 156–63).

8. For one example of this claim, see Roy W. Jastram (1977, 186–87).

9. See Rockoff (1984, 623–26).

10. Ibid., 628–31. See also Phillip Cagan (1965, 59ff). Cagan concludes (p. 64) that gold supply in the late 1800s "was not an exogenous variable."

11. Paish (1950, 150–51), though he asserts (without citing any evidence) that 19th-century gold discoveries were largely accidental, agrees that institutional conditions in this century make present-day discoveries much likelier to be demand induced.

12. Thus the fears of some economists that a gold standard would be more prone to supply shocks today than it was in the 19th century seem unfounded. Rockoff (1984, 641) says, "It would be unwise . . . to infer from the stability and elasticity of the supply of gold in the nineteenth century that a gold standard would work similarly today." Yet why assume from such favorable experience that present-day experiences would be *un*favorable?

13. According to Cagan (1965, 59), all major changes in the gold stock during the gold-standard era "can be associated with important changes either in the value and therefore production of gold or in government policies affecting the gold stock."

14. Wicksell wrote in 1906 (1935, 122), that "nowadays we never hear of a 'run' on gold by the public, but frequently of a run by business men and bill brokers to get bills discounted at the Central Bank, in case the bank reserves or the unused portion of the statutory note issue falls [sic] unusually low and the private banks begin to restrict credit in consequence."

15. This is the view taken by Gary Gorton (1985a, 177–93). An alternative theory is offered by Douglas W. Diamond and Philip H. Dybvig (1983), who treat bank runs as randomly occurring, "bubble" phenomena. As Gorton notes, the empirical evidence contradicts the view that bank runs are random events.

16. According to Checkland (1975), tables 2, 3, 9, 11, and 16. The figure includes banks with unknown fates.

17. L. White (1984d, 41). The estimate was made in 1841. There were no losses to liability holders from 1841 to 1845.

18. The possibility of private liability insurance is examined in Eugenie D. Short and Gerald P. O'Driscoll, Jr. (1983). See also Edward J. Kane (1983).

19. On the difficulty of establishing risk-based premiums for non-competitive, government-provided deposit insurance see Kenneth Scott and Thomas Mayer (1971).

20. This is based on a suggestion by John J. Merrick and Anthony Saunders (1985, 708).

21. This has been suggested by Bert Ely (1985).

22. See L. White (1984d, 29–30), and Checkland (1975, 67–68 and 254–55). Contrary to Checkland's suggestion (p. 254), the option clause does not normally impede the equilibrating mechanism of competitive note issue. It merely forestalls a note-redemption run against any bank. However, in Scotland prior to 1785 (when the option clause was outlawed) usury laws placed a ceiling of 5 percent on interest payments on unredeemed notes. This may have been too low to discourage banks from abusing the option to suspend. Absent usury laws competition would have driven the option-clause interest rate to a punitive level.

23. The notice of withdrawal clause is also rarely taken advantage of in practice.

24. See Gary Gorton (1985a).

25. Gorton explains (1985c, 278) that "a demand deposit, unlike a bank note, is a 'double claim' since it is a claim on a specific agent's account at a specific bank. Markets for double claims would be extremely 'thin,' and it would likely be very costly for brokers to invest in information gathering on every depositor."

26. See Gary Gorton (1985b, 272), and Gibbons (1858, 394). Rolnick and Weber (1985, 209) report that in the U.S. from 1837 to 1863 bank runs were usually *not* "contagious." This is consistent with the limited role played by deposit liabilities during this period and with the fact, also reported by Rolnick and Weber (1986, 877–90), that note holders were well informed about the assets securing most bank notes.

27. John Law, third *Lettre sur le Nouveau Systeme des Finances*, 1720; cited in Charles Rist (1966, 59).

28. Keynes (1936, 130).

29. Milton Friedman (1962, 221).

30. As we observed in chapter 2, banks might even settle clearings without resort to reserves of commodity money. This limiting case—which requires a high degree of confidence on the part of both bankers and the public—limits the role of the money commodity to that of unit of account, and therefore reduces resource costs associated with its use to zero. Such complete fiduciary substitution also renders the banking system more vulnerable to instability. The use of fiat currency as base money is another way of eliminating reserve-resource (opportunity) costs in a free banking system. A practical reform based on this approach is discussed below in chapter 11.

31. See Munn (1981, 141); also Checkland (1975, 382). Checkland observes that "Because of the place of the note issue in the economy, Scotland was a country almost without gold." He cites the letter of a Scottish banker who says that the "first object" of any person who gets hold of a (gold) sovereign "is to get quit of it in exchange for a bank note." Checkland notes further that "It was difficult for the Scottish bankers facing the inquiry of 1826 to think in terms of a gold circulation or of a substantial gold reserve, for they know very little of such a system."

32. "If confidence for fiduciary [fiat] money costs as much to produce as the commodity, the social savings [from replacing commodity-money backed liabilities with fiat money] would be zero" (Benjamin Klein 1974, 435fn).

33. Rist warned of this ([1940] 1966, 330). He saw it happen in the 1930s; he would undoubtedly have experienced a certain mournful satisfaction at being vindicated had he lived to see it reoccur in the past fifteen years.

34. The price of gold as this is being written (July 1985) is approximately $350. According to Lawrence H. White (1985), after allowing for inflation, "this is equivalent to more than $110 per ounce at 1967 prices, at which time the official price of gold was $35 per ounce, and more than $51 per ounce in 1929 terms, when gold was $20.67 per ounce."

35. Another argument concerning the inefficiency of free banking, which claims that it is inefficient because it leads to suboptimal holdings of money balances, is considered below in chapter 10.

Chapter 10: Miscellaneous Criticisms of Free Banking

1. The criticisms discussed in this section are so much a part of received doctrine that it is unnecessary to cite particular occurrences of them in the literature.

2. The French case is conspicuous in this respect. It is discussed in the introduction and also in Nataf (1983). On the free vs. central banking debate in England see L. White (1984d, chapters 3–4). For debates in other nations see V. Smith (1936).

3. See the works by Rockoff and Rolnick and Weber cited in chapter 1.

4. Spencer's argument for private coinage appears in his *Social Statics* (1896, 225–28).

5. See above, chapter 2, and also George MacDonald (1916, 7).

6. In the 1920s Bechtler dollars were still being accepted at par by North Carolina banks. See Woolridge (1970, 65) and Griffen (1929). Chapter 3 of Woolridge's book is an excellent and entertaining survey of private issues of *token* (fractional) coinage in the U.S. For a good review of private coinage of fullweighted coins in the U.S. see Brian Summers (1976, 436–40).

7. It is noteworthy that in the 2nd. ed. of his *Inquiry into the Currency Principle* (1844) Tooke wrote that *de facto* convertibility into gold "together with unlimited competition as to issue" is sufficient to prevent an excessive issue of paper currency (155). He also pointed with approval to the example of Scotland (156). On the change in Tooke's views on free banking, see Arie Arnon (1984).

8. Milton Friedman (1959, 6–7). In a more recent article (Friedman and Schwartz, 1986) Friedman reconsiders this and other arguments offered in his earlier work. He and Anna J. Schwartz write that under current conditions "The possibility—and reality—of fraud . . . seems unlikely to be more serious for hand-to-hand currency than for deposits" (51). They conclude that there is "no reason currently to prohibit banks from issuing hand-to-hand currency" (52). However they regard the possibility as a "dead issue" since it has no support from "banks or other groups."

9. See the references cited in chapter 1.

10. Besides the passage from Friedman cited previously, see Robert G. King (1983, 136).

11. Emmanuel Coppieters (1955, 64–65), cited in L. White (1984d, 40). It is also relevant that the Scottish banks had a policy of accepting counterfeit money at par, in order to encourage its discovery and to assist the capture of its producers. This also eliminated any possibility of losses to note holders arising from this kind of fraud.

The average period of circulation of a Federal Reserve dollar from the time of its issue to the time of its return to a Federal Reserve bank is approximately 17 months. (See the Federal Reserve Bank of Atlanta, *Fundamental Facts About U.S. Money*.) The average period of circulation of twenty-dollar bills—which are most frequently counterfeited—is considerably longer. Approximately one-fifth of all exposed counterfeit currency is discovered at the Federal Reserve banks. (Source: Personal communication, Federal Reserve Bank of Richmond.)

12. Thus for example King (1983, 136) writes that "holders of circulating notes are unlikely to closely monitor the activities of a note issuer because notes represent a small fraction of an individual's wealth and are held only for a brief period." This, he says, will lead to banks "printing more notes than can be redeemed by securities" thereby "inflicting capital losses on noteholders if simultaneous redemption occurs." This statement has several flaws in addition to the general criticism made in the text above. First of all, the reference to "simultaneous redemption" is gratuitous, since this would obviously lead to "capital losses" even in fractional-reserve banking systems lacking competitive note issue. Also, overissue is not a matter of "printing" too many notes but rather one of putting too many into circulation by making excess loans and investments. Finally, the passage implies that notes that can be "redeemed by securities" of their issuer do not represent an overissue. This is meaningless since almost any issue of notes by a bank involves a like purchase of securities.

13. Individuals could entirely reject other notes, or they could agree to accept the notes at a discount (as they did in the U.S. in the 19th century, when merchants had "note reporters"), depending upon the extent of their distrust of them. Either practice would discourage attempts to put untrustworthy notes into circulation.

14. In contradiction to King (1983, 136).

15. See for example Allan H. Meltzer (1983, 109–10), and the reference to Crouzet below.

16. According to Cameron (1967, 94ff) the Scottish economy grew more rapidly during the century prior to 1844 than the English economy during the same period. Adam Smith, among others, argued that free banking made a significant contribution to Scotland's economic growth. See L. White (1984d, 24).

17. See Hugh Rockoff (1974, 141–67).

18. Schumpeter, however, in his *Theory of Economic Development* (1983), argues that entrepreneurial activity depends on banks' issues of "abnormal credit" giving rise to forced savings. Schumpeter was influenced by the real-bills doctrine, and so he associated abnormal credit and forced savings with bank issues not based on commodity bills. Conversely, he regarded credit based on commodity bills as

sufficient only for maintaining an economy in a stationary state. Neither proposition is correct: there is no definite limit to the amount of credit that can be granted on the basis of the supply of commodity bills, since the latter supply is itself a nominal magnitude influenced by the terms of bank lending. Thus credit based on "real bills" may finance entrepreneurial ventures away from the stationary state, including some that inflict forced saving on the public. On the other hand, credit based on assets other than commodity bills (which may also finance economic development) need not give rise to forced savings, so long as it is based on increased abstinence of holders of inside money. It follows that economic development can take place whether or not banks restrict their lending to commodity bills, and it can also take place without forced savings.

19. Returning once again to the example of Scotland, as of 1872 (after the free-banking era, but at a time when Scotland still had 10 competing banks of issue) per-capita loanable funds administered by the Scottish banks exceeded per-capita funds granted by banks in England, and this without any evidence of credit creation (Somers 1873, 86–87). This supports the argument in chapter 9 that free banking systems are *more* efficient in the administration of loanable funds than centralized banking systems.

20. See for example Milton Friedman (1975); Robert E. Lucas, Jr. and Thomas J. Sargent (1978); and F. A. Hayek (1975a, 15–29).

21. A good discussion of the proper role of monetary policy in preventing unemployment appears in Lloyd Mints (1950, 15–51).

22. The best example of this argument is Michael Melvin (1984). See also Benjamin Klein (1978, esp. 76–78). Other examples can be found in Roland Vaubel (1984a, 45ff).

23. On the distinction between subadditivity of costs and decreasing average costs see William W. Sharkey (1982, 7).

24. It is reasonable to assume, as a general rule, that the costs of market-building increase as the boundaries of the market extend further from the source of issued notes.

25. It also requires that the economy be a closed one in which there is zero demand for commodity money by the public.

26. Africa, Asia, and South America are not considered because relatively little is known about their banking history.

27. This is not to say that there were not also measures taken that had the effect of artificially limiting the extent of consolidation of banking and note issue. Most obvious of these were laws preventing branch banking, such as have long existed in the United States.

In view of this, Melvin's claim (1984, 9) that "We observe government produced money, not because of barriers to entry, but because government produced money is socially efficient" is questionable. Of course any institution that survives must be "socially efficient" in some broad sense; but the persistence of a government monopoly does not prove that it has been more effective than competition in satisfying consumer wants. The historical evidence suggests other reasons for government involvement in this area.

28. But see Sharkey for exceptions.

29. One exception is reported by Tuh-Yueh Lee (1952). Lee writes that "the currency notes issued by the Bank of China [originally established as the Chinese Government Bank in 1904 and renamed after the Revolution of 1911] begot such confidence and were held in such high esteem that even the farmers who traditionally demanded solid cash (silver dollars) came to accept [the notes] in payment for their products although they still obstinately declined the issues of any other bank."

30. See above, chapter 1.

31. Examples of the use of these arguments against free banking are given in

Vaubel (1984a, 28–45). Although most of these examples refer explicitly to outside money only, many imply that the arguments in question also apply to redeemable bank notes.

32. Analytically, the "nonrivalrousness in consumption" (public good) and "positive externality" (underproduction) arguments are not really distinct; their separation here is based on convention rather than logic.

33. See above, chapter 1.

34. See Vaubel (1984a, 32).

35. See chapter 9.

36. Milton Friedman (1969). See also Paul A. Samuelson (1969).

37. See Harry G. Johnson (1973b, 91–92).

38. One possibility is discussed below in chapter 11.

39. Recall our statement of the conditions of long-run equilibrium in a fractional-reserve banking system, given in chapter 2.

40. S. C. Tsiang (1969). See also the discussion of consequences of monetary disequilibrium above, chapter 4.

41. See Vaubel (1984a).

42. See above, chapters 8 and 9.

43. See Thomas M. Humphrey (1975); and Thomas M. Humphrey and Robert E. Keleher (1984).

44. Recall the distinction drawn in chapter 9 between a redemption run and a currency run.

45. Jevons (1884, 171 and 186, Table 6). "Country" banks included both private and joint-stock banks located outside of the 65-mile radius marking and Bank of England's region of note-issue monopoly.

46. On currency supply under the National Banking System see above, chapter 8.

47. This topic was dealt with in the third section of chapter 9.

48. There was a run for a few days in Scotland following the collapse of the Ayr Bank.

49. See for example Hawtrey (1932, 228 and 259).

50. Bailouts that reduce potential losses to bank shareholders and management also encourage a happy-go-lucky attitude in consumers of bank services.

51. See for example Friedman and Schwartz (1963, 440–41).

52. As Friedman and Schwartz (1986, 52) do.

53. John Viscount Morley (1898, 98).

Chapter 11: Free Banking and Monetary Reform

1. Some material in this chapter has appeared previously, in somewhat altered form, in G. A. Selgin, "The Case for Free Banking: Then and Now," Cato Institute *Policy Analysis* (October 21, 1985).

2. See in particular Henry C. Simons (1951); Lloyd W. Mints (1950); and Milton Friedman, (1959). Again we must note Friedman's recent reconsideration of his former views, in "Has Government Any Role in Money?" Friedman's current policy recommendations place him in fundamental agreement with reform suggestions made in this chapter. Whether other monetarists will follow him (and Anna J. Schwartz, who co-authored the above mentioned article) in this change of heart remains to be seen.

3. See above, chapter 8. It should be noted however, that Mints regarded prohibition of competitive note issue as an "unnecessary legal restriction." "I can see no reason," he wrote (1950, 187–88), "why, if fractional reserves against deposits are desirable, they are not equally desirable for notes. . . . In fact, the prevailing arrangement . . . operates to prevent a complete interconvertibility of notes and deposits" the consequence being "the preverse behavior of the volume

of bank loans." As I mentioned in chapter 8, Friedman also, in his earlier writings, recognized free note issue as a possible solution to what he nevertheless insisted on calling the "inherent instability of fractional reserve banking." Yet Friedman originally rejected this solution, in one place because it "has little support among economists, bankers, or the public" (1953, 220), and elsewhere for reasons summarized in the text above.

4. Ibid. Some rational-expectations theorists also defend a monetary rule as providing greater predictability. However, in their models rules are often only "weakly superior to" (i.e., no worse than) all possible discretionary policies.

5. An example of a variable causing changes in the money multiplier is the relative demand for currency, which was discussed at length in chapter 8.

6. See for example Milton Friedman (1984a, 1984b) and Richard H. Timberlake, Jr. (1986, 760–62).

7. Strictly speaking, issue of bank notes by commercial banks is not presently illegal; however, such issue must still meet the bond-deposit requirements established under the National Banking System or the 10 percent tax on state bank notes. Since all bonds eligible as security for circulating notes were retired before 1935 (or had the circulation privilege conferred upon them withdrawn), note issue, while not illegal, is nevertheless impossible under existing law. Restoration of commercial bank note-issuing privileges merely requires repeal of the bond deposit provisions in the original National Banking statutes and of the prohibitive tax on state bank notes.

8. Thus, in contradiction to Friedman (1984a, 47), competition in note issue need not represent an effort to replace the "national currency unit."

9. On unit banking as a source of financial instability in the United States and its role in turn-of-the-century monetary reform see Eugene Nelson White (1983).

10. Since Treasury bills bear interest, this reform would eliminate an important source of interest-free funds to the government. Since approximately $48 billion are held today to meet statutory requirements, their conversion into Treasury bills would involve a maximum gross loss to the Treasury of $2.88 billion, assuming that Treasury bills pay 6 percent interest. The net loss would be less, however, since increased bank earnings would also generate additional tax revenue.

11. Contrary to this view is the view, cited by Friedman (1984a, 49) of the "new monetary economists," who argue that prohibiting bank-note issues actually *stabilizes* the demand for high-powered money.

12. Some of these suggestions would automatically be realized if Friedman's recommendation—that the frozen stock of base dollars be converted into Treasury notes—were adopted. It would be safest, however, to have base dollars in a form capable of circulating, later allowing banks the option of converting some or all of them into special interest-earning Treasury obligations created for the purpose. The new Treasury obligations could be offset by cancelling an equivalent value of Treasury obligations held by the Federal Reserve banks.

13. This idea is suggested in J. Huston McCulloch (1986).

14. The figure is now (1985) approximately 35 percent. (Source: Federal Reserve Bank of St. Louis, *U. S. Financial Data*, March 28, 1985, 3–4.)

15. As is recommended by Richard H. Timberlake, Jr. (1986, 760). See also Joanna H. Frodin (1983). As Timberlake notes, privatization of the clearing system would probably result in an arrangement similar to what existed in the pre-Federal Reserve era.

Conclusion

1. This problem would, however, not arise in a system such as that outlined in chapter 11, in which the stock of base money consists of a permanently fixed supply of paper money.

2. The assumption that monetary authorities are self-interested (rather than altruistic) persons has fortunately been incorporated into modern monetary theory by writers in the "public-choice" tradition. See for example Richard E. Wagner (1977, 1980); W. Mark Crain and Robert B. Ekelund, Jr. (1978); Robert J. Gordon (1975); Keith Acheson and John F. Chant (1973); Mark Toma (1982); and William P. Yohe (1974).

Bibliography

Acheson, Keith, and John F. Chant. 1973. "Bureaucratic Theory and the Choice of Central Bank Goals." *Journal of Money, Credit, and Banking* 5 (May).

Adams, Edgar M. 1913. *Private Gold Coinage of California.* New York: Privately printed.

Agger, Eugene E. 1918. *Organized Banking.* New York: Henry Holt & Co.

Ahrensdorf, Joachim, and S. Kanesthasan. 1960. "Variations in the Money Multiplier and Their Implications for Central Banking." International Monetary Fund *Staff Papers* 8 (November).

Anderson, M. D. 1926. "A Note on Elasticity of the Currency." *American Economic Review* 16(1) (March).

Andrew, A. Piatt. 1908. "Substitutes for Cash in the Panic of 1907." *Quarterly Journal of Economics* 22(3) (August).

Arnon, Arie. 1984. "The Transformation in Thomas Tooke's Monetary Theory Reconsidered." *History of Political Economy* 16(2) (Summer).

Aschheim, Joseph. 1959. "Commercial Banks and Financial Intermediaries: Fallacies and Policy Implications." *Journal of Political Economy* 67(1) (February).

———. 1961. *Techniques of Monetary Control.* Baltimore: Johns Hopkins University Press.

Axelrod, Robert. 1984. *The Evolution of Cooperation.* New York: Basic Books.

Bagehot, Walter. 1874. *Lombard Street: A Description of the Money Market.* New York: Scribner, Armstrong & Co.

Baltensperger, Ernst. 1974. "The Precautionary Demand for Reserves." *American Economic Review* 64(1) (March).

———. 1980. "Alternative Approaches to the Theory of the Banking Firm." *Journal of Monetary Economics* 6 (January).

Barger, Harold. 1935. "Neutral Money and the Trade Cycle." *Economica* 2(8) (November).

Beale, W.T.M., Jr., M.T. Kennedy, and W.J. Winn. 1942. "Commodity Reserve Currency: A Critique." *Journal of Political Economy* 50 (August).

Benston, George J. 1983. "Federal Regulation of Banking: Analysis and Policy Recommendations." *Journal of Bank Research* 13(14) (Winter).

Bisschop, W. Roosegaarde. 1910. *The Rise of the London Money Market, 1640–1826.* London: P.S. King & Son.

Black, Fischer. 1970. "Banking and Interest Rates in a World Without Money: The Effects of Uncontrolled Banking." *Journal of Bank Research* 1 (Autumn).

Bordo, Michael David. 1984. "The Gold Standard: Myths and Realities." In Barry N. Siegel, ed., *Money in Crisis.* San Francisco: Pacific Institute.

Bordo, Michael D., and Angela Redish. 1986. "Why Did the Bank of Canada Emerge in 1935?" Paper prepared for the Economic History Association, September.

Boughton, James M., and Elmus R. Wicker. 1979. "The Behavior of the Currency-Deposit Ratio during the Great Depression." *Journal of Money, Credit, and Banking* 11(4) (November).

————. 1984. "A Reply" (to Trescott). *Journal of Money, Credit, and Banking* 16(3) (August).

Bowsher, Norman N. 1980. "The Demand for Currency: Is the Underground Economy Undermining Monetary Policy?" Federal Reserve Bank of St. Louis *Review* 62(1) (January).

Brechling, Frank. 1958. "The Public's Preference for Cash." *Banca Nazional del Lavoro* 11 (September).

Brown, Harry G. 1910. "Commercial Banking and the Rate of Interest." *Quarterly Journal of Economics* 24 (August).

Burger, Albert E. 1971. *The Money Supply Process*. Belmont, Calif: Wadsworth Publishing Co.

Burns, A. R. 1927a. "Early Stages in the Development of Money and Coins." In T.E. Gregory and Hugh Dalton, eds., *London Essays in Economics in Honour of Edwin Cannan* London: George Routledge & Sons.

————. 1927b. *Money and Monetary Policy in Early Times*. New York: Alfred E. Knopf.

Bury, J. B. 1902. *History of Greece*, vol. 1. London: Macmillan.

Butchart, J. R. 1918. *Money and Its Purchasing Power*. Melbourne. (n.p.)

Cagan, Phillip. 1958. "The Demand for Currency Relative to Total Money Supply." National Bureau of Economic Research *Occasional Paper* No. 62. Reprinted from the *Journal of Political Economy* (August).

————. 1965. *Determinants and Effects of Changes in the Money Stock, 1875–1960.* New York: National Bureau of Economic Research.

————. 1982. "The Choice among Monetary Aggregates as Targets and Guides for Monetary Policy." *Journal of Money Credit, and Banking* 14(4) (November).

Cameron, Rondo. 1967. *Banking in the Early Stages of Industrialization*. New York: Oxford University Press.

————. ed. 1972. *Banking and Economic Development: Some Lessons of History*. New York: Oxford University Press.

Cannan, Edwin. 1921. "The Meaning of Bank Deposits." *Economica* 1(1) (January).

————. 1935. "Growth and Fluctuations of Bankers' Liabilities to Customers." *The Manchester School* 6(1).

Cannon, James G. 1900. *Clearing Houses: Their History, Methods, and Administration.* New York: D. Appleton & Co. 2nd. ed. Washington: Government Printing Office, 1910.

————. 1908. "Clearing Houses and the Currency." In E.R.A. Seligman, ed., *The Currency Problem and the Present Financial Situation*. New York: Columbia University Press.

Carlisle, William Warran. 1901. *The Evolution of Modern Money*. London: Macmillan.

Cernuschi, Henri. 1865. "Contre le billet de banque." Paris: A. Lacroix.

Checkland, S. G. 1975. *Scottish Banking: A History, 1695–1973*. Glasgow: Collins Press.

Chick, Victoria. 1983. *Macroeconomics after Keynes*. Cambridge: MIT Press.

" 'Circulation Notes' in Rural China." 1957. *Far Eastern Economic Review* April 11.

Clayton, George. 1955. "A Note on the Banking System's Power to Lend." *Metroeconomica* 7(2) (August).

Clower, Robert W. 1965. "The Keynesian Counter Revolution: A Theoretical Appraisal." In F. H. Hahn and F. P. R. Brechling, eds., *The Theory of Interest Rates*. London: Macmillan.

————. 1967. "A Reconsideration of the Microfoundations of Monetary Theory." *Western Economic Journal* 6 (December).

Conant, Charles A. 1897. "Banking upon Business Assets." *Sound Currency* 4(23) (December).
———. 1905. *The Principles of Money and Banking*, vol. 2. New York: Harper & Brothers.
———. 1915. *A History of Modern Banks of Issue*, 5th ed. New York: G. P. Putnam's Sons.
Copland, D. B. 1920. "Currency Inflation and Price Movements in Australia." *Economic Journal* 30(120) (December).
Coppieters, Emmanuel. 1955. *English Bank Note Circulation, 1694–1954*. The Hague: Martinus Nijhoff.
Crain, W. Mark, and Robert B. Ekelund, Jr. 1978. "Deficits and Democracy." *Southern Economic Journal* 44 (April).
Crouzet, Francois. 1972. *Capital Formation in the Industrial Revolution*. London: Methuen.
Culbertson, J. M. 1958. "Intermediaries and Monetary Theory: A Criticism of the Gurley-Shaw Theory." *American Economic Review* 48 (March).
Currie, Lauchlin. 1934. *The Supply and Control of Money in the United States*. Cambridge: Harvard University Press.
Davis, Richard G., and Jack M. Guttentag. 1962. "Are Compensating Balance Requirements Irrational?" *Journal of Finance* 17(1) (March).
De Jong, Frits J. 1973. "J. G. Koopmans' Concept of Monetary Equilibrium." *Developments of Monetary Theory in the Netherlands*. Rotterdam: Rotterdam University Press.
De Koch, M. H. 1967. *Central Banking*, 3rd ed. London: Staples Press.
De Roover, Raymond. 1974. "New Interpretations of the History of Banking." In Julius Kirshner, ed., *Business, Banking and Economic Thought in Late Medieval and Early Modern Europe*. Chicago: University of Chicago Press.
Diamond, Douglas W., and Philip H. Dybvig. 1983. "Bank Runs, Deposit Insurance and Liquidity." *Journal of Political Economy* 91(3) (June).
DiNardi, Giuseppe. 1953. *Le Banche di Emissione in Italia nel Secolo XIX*. Turin: Unione Tipografico-Editore Torinese.
Dominion Bureau of Statistics (Canada). 1905–. *The Canada Year Book*. Ottawa.
Dunbar, Charles Francis. 1897. "The National Banking System." *Quarterly Journal of Economics* 12 (October).
———. 1917. *The Theory and History of Banking*, 3rd. ed. New York: G. P. Putnam's Sons.
Durbin, E. F. M. 1933. *Purchasing Power and Trade Depression*. London: Jonathan Cape, 1933.
———. 1935. "Mr. Gilbert's Defense of a Constant Circulation." *Economica* 2(6) (May).
Edgeworth, F. Y. 1888. "The Mathematical Theory of Banking." *Journal of the Royal Statistical Association* 51(1) (March).
Ely, Bert. 1985. "Yes—Private Sector Depositor Protection is a Viable Alternative to Federal Deposit Insurance!" Paper presented to the Conference on Bank Structure and Competition, Federal Reserve Bank of Chicago, May 2.
Fama, Eugene. 1980. "Banking in the Theory of Finance." *Journal of Monetary Economics* 6 (January).
———. 1983. "Financial Intermediation and Price Level Control." *Journal of Monetary Economics* (July).
Federal Reserve Bank of Atlanta (n.d.) *Fundamental Facts About U.S Money*.
Ferrara, Francesco. 1866. "El Corso Forzato de Biglietti di Banco in Italia." *Nuova Antologia* (March and June).
———. 1933. "La Questione de Banchi in Italia." In Guiseppe Bottai and Celestino Azeno, eds., *Nuova Collana di Economisti*, vol. 2: *Economisti Italiani del Risorgimento*. Turin: Unione Tipografico-Editore Torinese.

Fisher, Allan G. B. 1935. "Does an Increase in Volume of Production Call for a Corresponding Increase in Volume of Money?" *American Economic Review* 25(2) (June).

Fisher, Irving. 1896. "Appreciation and Interest." *Proceedings of the American Economic Association* 6(4) (August).

Fratianni, Michele, and Franco Spinelli. 1984. "Italy in the Gold Standard Period, 1861–1914." In Michael D. Bordo and Anna J. Schwartz, eds., *A Retrospective on the Classical Gold Standard*. Chicago: University of Chicago Press.

Friedman, Milton. 1951. "A Monetary and Fiscal Framework for Economic Stability." In American Economic Association *Readings in Monetary Theory*. Homewood, Ill.: Richard D. Irwin.

———. 1953. "Commodity Reserve Currency." In *Essays in Positive Economics*. Chicago: University of Chicago Press.

———. 1959. *A Program for Monetary Stability*. New York: Fordham University Press.

———. 1962. "Should There Be an Independent Monetary Authority?" In Leland B. Yeager, ed., *In Search of a Monetary Constitution*. Cambridge: Harvard University Press.

———. 1969. *The Optimum Quantity of Money and Other Essays*. Chicago: Aldine Pub. Co.

———. 1975. "Unemployment versus Inflation? An Evaluation of the Phillips Curve." Institute of Economic Affairs *Occasional Paper* no. 44. London: Institute of Economic Affairs.

———. 1984a. "Monetary Policy for the 1980s." In John H. Moore, ed., *To Promote Prosperity: U.S. Domestic Policy in the Mid–1980s*. Stanford, Calif.: The Hoover Institution.

———. 1984b. "Monetary Policy Structures." In *Candid Conversations on Monetary Policy*. Washington: House Republican Research Committee.

Friedman, Milton, and Anna Jacobson Schwartz. 1963. *A Monetary History of the United States, 1867–1960*. Princeton: Princeton University Press.

———. 1986. "Has Government Any Role in Money?" *Journal of Monetary Economics* 17 (January).

Frodin, JoAnna H. 1983. "The Effects of Federal Pricing on Private Clearing Arrangements for Checks." Paper presented at the meeting of the Banking and Financial Structure Committee, Federal Reserve Bank of San Francisco, July.

Garvey, George, and Martin R. Blyn. 1969. *The Velocity of Money*. New York: Federal Reserve Bank of New York.

Geyer, P. J. 1867. *Theorie und Praxis des Zettelbankwesens*. Munich: E. A. Fleischmann.

Gibbons, J. S. 1858. *The Banks of New York, Their Dealers, the Clearing House and the Panic of 1857*. New York: D. Appleton & Co.

Gilbert, J. C. 1934. "A Note on Banking Policy and the Income Velocity of Circulation of Money." *Economica* 3 (May).

———. 1953. "The Demand for Money: The Development of an Economic Concept." *Journal of Political Economy* 61(4) (August).

Goodhart, C. A. E. 1984. "The Evolution of Central Banks: A Natural Development?" Bank of England.

Gordon, Robert J. 1975. "The Demand for and Supply of Inflation." *Journal of Law and Economics* 18 (December).

Gorton, Gary. 1984. "Banking Panics and Business Cycles." University of Pennsylvania (mimeo).

———. 1985a. "Bank Suspension of Convertibility." *Journal of Monetary Economics* 15 (March).

———. 1985b. "Banking Theory and Free Banking History." *Journal of Monetary Economics* 16(2) (September).

——. 1985c. "Clearinghouses and the Origin of Central Banking in the U.S." *Journal of Economic History* 45(2) (June).

Gorton, Gary, and Donald J. Mullineaux. 1985. "The Joint Production of Confidence: Commercial Bank Clearinghouses and the Theory of Hierarchy" (unpublished).

Graham, Benjamin. 1937. *Storage and Stability*. New York: McGraw Hill.

——. 1944. *World Commodities and World Currency*. New York: McGraw Hill.

Graham, Frank D. 1942. *Social Goals and Economic Institutions*. Princeton: Princeton University Press.

Graham, William. 1911. *The One Pound Note in the History of Banking in Great Britain*, 2nd. ed. Edinburgh: James Thin.

Gramm, William P. 1974. "Laissez-Faire and the Optimum Quantity of Money." *Economic Inquiry* 12(1) (March).

Greenfield, Robert L., and Leland B. Yeager. 1983. "A Laissez-Faire Approach to Monetary Stability." *Journal of Money, Credit, and Banking* 15(3) (August).

——. 1986. "Money and Credit Confused: An Appraisal of Economic Doctrine and Federal Reserve Procedure." *Southern Economic Journal* 53(2) (October).

Greidanus, Tjardus. 1950. *The Value of Money*, 2nd ed. London: Staples Press.

Griffen, Clarence. 1929. "The Story of the Bechtler Gold Coinage." *The Numismatist* (September).

Gurley, J. G., and E. S. Shaw. 1955. "Financial Aspects of Economic Development." *American Economic Review* 45 (September).

——. 1956. "Financial Intermediaries and the Saving-Investment Process." *Journal of Finance* 11 (May).

——. 1958. "Reply" (to Culbertson). *American Economic Review* 48 (March).

——. 1960. *Banking in a Theory of Finance*. Washington: The Brookings Institution.

Haberler, Gottfried. 1931. "The Different Meanings Attached to the Term 'Fluctuations in the Purchasing Power of Gold' and the Best Instrument or Instruments for Measuring Such Fluctuations." Geneva: League of Nations.

Hall, Robert E. 1982. "Explorations in the Gold Standard and Related Policies for Stabilizing the Dollar." In Robert E. Hall, ed., *Inflation: Causes and Effects*. Chicago: University of Chicago Press.

——. 1984. "A Free-Market Policy to Stabilize the Purchasing Power of the Dollar." In Barry N. Siegel, ed., *Money in Crisis*. San Francisco: The Pacific Institute.

Hammond, Bray. 1957. *Banks and Politics in America from the Revolution to the Civil War*. Princeton: Princeton University Press.

Hancock, Diana. 1983. "The Financial Firm: Production With Monetary and Nonmonetary Goods." *Journal of Political Economy* 93(5) (October).

Hawtrey, R. G. 1932. *The Art of Central Banking*. London: Longmans, Green & Co.

——. 1951. "Money and Index-Numbers." In American Economic Association, *Readings in Monetary Theory*. Homewood, Ill.: Richard D. Irwin.

Hayek, F. A. 1935. *Prices and Production*, 2nd ed. London: Routledge & Kegan Paul.

——. 1939a. "A Note on the Development of the Doctrine of 'Forced Saving.'" In *Profits, Interest and Investment*. London: George Routledge & Sons.

——. 1939b. "Saving." In *Profits, Interest, and Investment*. London: George Routledge & Sons.

——. 1948a. "A Commodity Reserve Currency." In *Individualism and Economic Order*. Chicago: Henry Regnery.

——. 1948b. "The Use of Knowledge in Society." In *Individualism and Economic Order*. Chicago: Henry Regnery.

——. 1975a. "Full Employment at Any Price?" Institute of Economic Affairs *Occasional Paper* no. 45. London: Institute of Economic Affairs.

———. 1975b. *Monetary Theory and the Trade Cycle.* Trans. N. Kaldor and H. M. Croome. New York: A. M. Kelley.

———. 1976. *Choice in Currency: A Way to Stop Inflation.* London: Institute of Economic Affairs.

———. 1978. *Denationalisation of Money—The Argument Refined: An Analysis of the Theory and Practice of Concurrent Currencies.* 2nd ed. London: Institute of Economic Affairs.

Henderson, James M. 1960. "Monetary Reserves and Credit Control." *American Economic Review* 50(3) (June).

Hoff, Trygve J. B. 1981. *Economic Calculation in the Socialist Society.* Indianapolis: Liberty Press.

Holladay, James. 1934. "The Currency of Canada." *American Economic Review* 24(2) (June).

Hoover, Kevin D. 1985. "Causality and Invariance in the Money Supply Process." Dissertation, Oxford University.

Horn, J. E. 1866. "La liberte des banques." Paris: Guillaumin et Companie.

Humphrey, Thomas M. 1975. "The Classical Concept of Lender of Last Resort." Federal Reserve Bank of Richmond *Economic Review* (January/February).

Humphrey, Thomas M., and Robert E. Keleher. 1984. "The Lender of Last Resort: A Historical Perspective." *Cato Journal* 4(1) (Spring/Summer).

Hutt, William H. 1952. "The Notion of the Volume of Money." *South African Journal of Economics* 20.

Jacoby, Neil. 1963. "The Structure and Use of Variable Bank Reserve Requirements." In Deane Carson, ed., *Banking and Monetary Studies.* Homewood, Ill: Richard D. Irwin.

Jastram, Roy W. 1977. *The Golden Constant: English and American Experience, 1560–1976.* New York: John Wiley & Sons.

Jevons, William Stanley. 1882. *Money and the Mechanism of Exchange.* New York: D. Appleton.

———. 1884. "The Frequent Autumnal Pressure in the Money Market, and the Action of the Bank of England." In *Investigations in Currency and Finance.* London: Macmillan.

Johnson, Harry G. 1973a. "Is There an Optimal Money Supply?" In *Further Essays in Monetary Economics.* Cambridge: Harvard University Press.

———. 1973b. "Problems of Efficiency in Monetary Management." In *Further Essays in Monetary Economics.* Cambridge: Harvard University Press.

Johnson, Joseph French. 1910. *The Canadian Banking System.* Washington: National Monetary Commission.

Jonung, Lars. 1985. "The Economics of Private Money: The Experience of Private Notes in Sweden, 1831–1902." Paper presented at the Monetary History Group Meeting, London, September 27.

Joplin, Thomas. 1876. *An Essay on the General Principles and Present Practice of Banking in England and Scotland,* 5th ed. London: Baldwin, Cradock & Joy.

Kane, Edward J. 1983. "A Six-Point Program for Deposit Insurance Reform." *Housing Finance Review* 2 (July).

Kerr, Andrew William. 1884. *History of Banking in Scotland.* Glasgow: David Bryce & Son.

Keynes, John Maynard. 1930. *A Treatise on Money.* London: Macmillan.

———. 1936. *The General Theory of Employment, Interest and Money.* New York: Harcourt, Brace.

King, Peter [Lord]. 1804. *Thoughts on the Restriction of Payments and Species.* (n.p.)

King, Robert G. 1983. "On the Economics of Private Money." *Journal of Monetary Economics* 12 (1) (May).

Kirzner, Israel M. 1984. "Prices, the Communication of Knowledge, and the Discovery Process." In K. Leube and A. Zlabinger, eds., *The Political Economy of Freedom: Essays in Honor of F. A. Hayek.* Munich: Philosophia Verlag.

Klein, Benjamin. 1974. "The Competitive Supply of Money." *Journal of Money, Credit, and Banking* 6(4) (November).

———. 1978. "Competing Monies, European Monetary Union and the Dollar." In M. Fratiani and T. Peeters, eds., *One Money for Europe*. London: Macmillan.

Klein, Lawrence R. 1966. *The Keynesian Revolution*, 2nd. ed. New York: Macmillan.

Kojima, Shotaro. 1943. "The Origination and Extinction of Currency in the World of Circulation." *Kyoto University Economic Review* 18(4) (July).

Koopmans, T. G. 1933. "Zum Problem des Neutralen Geldess." In F. A. Hayek, ed., *Beitrage Zur Geldtheorie*. Vienna: Springer.

Lake, Wilfred S. 1947. "The End of the Suffolk System." *Journal of Economic History* 7(2).

Lavoie, Don. 1985. *Rivalry and Central Planning: The Socialist Calculation Debate Reconsidered*. Cambridge: Cambridge University Press.

Lee, Tuh-Yueh. 1952. "The Evolution of Banking in China." Rutgers University, Graduate School of Banking.

Leijonhufvud, Axel. 1968. *On Keynesian Economics and the Economics of Keynes*. New York: Oxford University Press.

Leslie, J. O. 1950. *The Note Exchange and Clearing House Systems*. Edinburgh: William Blackwood & Sons. Ltd.

Lombra, Raymond E., and Herbert Kaufman. 1984. "The Money Supply Process: Identification, Stability and Estimation." *Southern Economic Journal* (April).

Lombra, Raymond E., and Raymond G. Torto. 1975. "The Strategy of Monetary Policy." Federal Reserve Bank of Richmond *Economic Reveiw* (September/October).

Lopez, Robert S. 1979. "The Dawn of Medieval Banking." In Robert S. Lopez, ed., *The Dawn of Modern Banking*. New Haven: Yale University Press.

Loyd, Samuel Jones [Lord Overstone]. *Tracts and Other Publications on Metallic and Paper Currency*, ed. J. R. McCulloch. London.

Lucas, Robert E., Jr., and Thomas J. Sargent. 1978. "After Keynesian Macroeconomics." In *After the Phillips Curve: Persistence of High Inflation and High Unemployment*. Boston: Federal Reserve Bank of Boston.

Lutz, Friedrich A. 1969. "On Neutral Money." In Erich Streissler, G. Haberler, F. A. Lutz, and Fritz Machlup, eds., *Roads to Freedom: Essays in Honour of F. A. Hayek*. London: Routledge & Kegan Paul.

MacDonald, George. 1916. *The Evolution of Coinage*. Cambridge: Cambridge University Press.

Machlup, Fritz. 1940. *The Stock Market, Credit and Capital Formation*, trans. Vera C. Smith. New York: Macmillan.

Magee. James D. 1923. "Historical Analogy to the Fight Against Par Collection." *Journal of Political Economy* 31(3) (June).

Maisel, Sherman J. 1973. *Managing the Dollar*. New York: W. W. Norton & Co.

Marget, A. W. 1926. *The Loan Fund: A Pecuniary Approach to the Problem of the Determination of the Rate of Interest*. Dissertation, Harvard University.

McCallum, Bennett T. 1984. "Bank Deregulation, Accounting Systems of Exchange, and the Unit of Account: A Critical Review." *Carnegie-Rochester Conference Series on Public Policy* (Autumn).

McCulloch, J. Huston. 1986. "Beyond the Historical Gold Standard." In Colin Campbell and William R. Dougan, eds., *Alternative Monetary Regimes*. Baltimore: Johns Hopkins University Press.

[McCulloch, J. R.] 1826. "Fluctuations in the Supply and Value of Money." *Edinburgh Review* 43 (February).

———. 1831. *Historical Sketch of the Bank of England: with an Examination of the Question as to the Prolongation of the Exclusive Privileges of that Institution*. London: Longman, Ress, Orane, Brown & Green.

McGouldrick, Paul. 1984. "Operations of the German Central Bank and the Rules of the Game, 1879–1913." In Michael D. Bordo and Anna J. Schwartz, eds., *A*

Retrospective on the Classical Gold Standard, 1821–1931. Chicago: University of Chicago Press.

McLeod, Alex N. 1984. *The Principles of Financial Intermediation.* Lanham, Md.: University Press of America.

Meade, J. E. 1933. *The Rate of Interest in a Progressive State.* London: Macmillan.

Melitz, Jacques. 1974. *Primitive and Modern Money: An Interdisciplinary Approach.* Reading, Mass.: Addison-Wesley.

Meltzer, Allan H. 1983. "Monetary Reform in an Uncertain Environment." *Cato Journal* 3(1) (Spring).

Melvin, Michael. 1984. "Monetary Confidence, Privately Produced Monies and Domestic and International Monetary Reform" (unpublished).

Menger, Carl. 1892. "The Origin of Money." *Economic Journal* 2 (June).

———. 1981. *Principles of Economics,* trans. James Dingwall and Bert F. Hoselitz. New York: New York University Press. (Reprint of 1871 ed.)

Merrian, L. S. 1893. "The Theory of Final Utility in its Relation to Money and the Standard of Deferred Payments." *Annals of the American Academy of Political and Social Sciences* 3 (January).

Merrick, John J., and Anthony Saunders. 1985. "Bank Regulation and Monetary Policy." *Journal of Money, Credit, and Banking* 17(4) (November).

Meyer, Paul A. 1986. *Money, Financial Institutions, and the Economy.* Homewood, Ill.: Richard D. Irwin.

Mints, Lloyd. 1930. "The Elasticity of Bank Notes." *Journal of Political Economy* 38(4) (August).

———. 1950. *Monetary Policy for a Competitive Society.* New York: McGraw-Hill.

Mises, Ludwig Von. 1949. *Human Action.* New Haven: Yale University Press. 3rd ed.: Chicago: Henry Regnery, 1966.

———. 1978. "Monetary Stabilization and Cyclical Policy." In Percy Greaves, Jr., ed., *On the Manipulation of Money and Credit,* trans. Bettina Greaves. Dobbs Ferry, N.Y.: Free Market Books.

———. 1980. *The Theory of Money and Credit,* trans. H. C. Batson. Indianapolis: Liberty Classics.

Miskimim, Harry A. 1979. "The Impact of Credit on Sixteenth Century English Industry." In Robert S. Lopez, ed., *The Dawn of Modern Banking.* New Haven: Yale University Press.

Modeste, P. 1866. "Le billet des Banques d'emission et la Fausse Monnaie." *Journal des Economists* 3 (August).

Morawetz, Victor. 1909. *The Banking & Currency Problem in the United States,* 2nd ed. New York: North American Review Pub. Co.

Morley, John [Viscount]. 1898. *On Compromise.* London: Macmillan.

Munn, Charles W. 1981. *The Scottish Provincial Banking Companies, 1747–1864.* Edinburgh: John Donald.

Nataf, Philippe. 1983. "Competitive Banking and the Cycle, 1850–1868" (unpublished).

Noyes, Alexander Dana. 1910. *History of the National Bank Currency.* Washington: National Monetary Commission.

O'Driscoll, Gerald P., Jr., 1985. "Money in a Deregulated Financial System." *Federal Reserve Bank of Dallas Economic Review* (May).

Olivera, J. H. G. 1971. "The Square-Root Law of Pracautionary Reserves." *Journal of Political Economy* 79(5) (September-October).

Paish, Frank Walter. 1950. "Causes of Changes in Gold Supply." In *The Post-War Financial Problem and Other Essays.* London: Macmillan.

Parnell, Henry [Sir]. 1827. *Observations on Paper Money, Banking, and Overtrading.* London: James Ridgeway.

Patinkin, Don. 1965. *Money, Interest, and Prices: An Integration of Monetary and Value Theory,* 2nd ed. New York: Harper & Row.

Perrin, John. 1911. "What Is Wrong with Our Banking and Currency System?" *Journal of Political Economy* 19(10) (December).

Phillips, Chester Arthur. 1920. *Bank Credit.* New York: Macmillan.

Phillips, C. A., T. F. McManus, and R. W. Nelson. 1937. *Banking and the Business Cycle: A Study of the Great Depression in the United States.* New York: Macmillan.

Pigou, A. C. 1933. *The Theory of Unemployment.* London: Frank Cass and Co.

Plumptre, A. F. W. 1938. "The Arguments for Central Banking in the British Dominions." In H. A. Innes, ed., *Essays in Political Economy in Honour of E. J. Urwick.* Toronto: University of Toronto Press.

Poindexter, Carl J. 1946. "Some Misconceptions of Banking and Interest Theory." *Southern Economic Journal* 13(2) (October).

Polakoff, Murray E. 1963. "Federal Reserve Discount Policy and Its Critics." In Deane Carson, ed., *Banking and Monetary Studies.* Homewood, Ill.: Richard D. Irwin.

Powell, Ellis T. 1966. *The Evolution of the Money Market, 1385–1915.* Fairfield, N.J.: A.M. Kelley.

Quiggin, A. Hingston. 1963. *A Survey of Primitive Money: The Beginning of Currency.* London: Methuen.

Reuff, Jacques. 1953. "Influences Regulating the Amount of Currency and the Institutional Problem of Money." *Economia Internazionale* 6.

Richards, R. D. 1965. *The Early History of Banking in England.* New York: A.M. Kelley.

Ridgeway, William. 1892. *The Origin of Metallic Currency and Weight Standards.* Cambridge: Cambridge University Press.

Riefler, Winfield. 1930. *Money Rates and Money Markets in the United States.* New York: Harper & Bros.

Rist, Charles. 1966. *History of Monetary and Credit Theory from John Law to the Present Day,* trans. Jane Degras New York: Augustus M. Kelley. (Reprint of 1940 ed.)

Robertson, D. H. 1926. *Banking Policy and the Price Level.* London: P. S. King & Son.

———. 1964. *Money,* 4th ed. Chicago: University of Chicago Press. (Reprint of 1957 ed.)

Rockoff, Hugh. 1974. "The Free-Banking Era: A Re-Examination." *Journal of Money, Credit, and Banking* 6 (May).

———. 1984. "Some Evidence on the Real Price of Gold, Its Costs of Production, and Commodity Prices." In Michael D. Bordo and Anna J. Schwartz, eds., *A Retrospective on the Classical Gold Standard, 1821–1931.* Chicago: University of Chicago Press.

Rodkey, Robert G. 1928. *The Banking Process.* New York: Macmillan.

———. 1934. "Legal Reserves in American Banking." *Michigan Business Studies* 6(5).

Rolnick, Arthur J., and Warren E. Weber. 1982. "Free Banking, Wildcat Banking, and Shinplasters." Federal Reserve Bank of Minneapolis *Quarterly Review* 6 (Fall).

———. 1983. "New Evidence on Laissez-Faire Banking." *American Economic Review* 73(5) (December).

———. 1985. "Banking Instability and Regulation in the U.S. Free Banking Era." Federal Reserve Bank of Minneapolis *Quarterly Review* (Summer).

———. 1986. "Inherent Instability in Banking: The Free Banking Experience." *Cato Journal* 5(3) (Winter).

Root, L. Carroll. 1894. "Canadian Bank-Note Currency." *Sound Currency* 2(2) (December).

———. 1895. "New York Bank Currency, Safety Fund vs. Bond Security." *Sound Currency* 2(5) (February).

Rothbard, Murray N. 1962. "The Case for a 100 Percent Gold Dollar." In Leland

B. Yeager, ed., *In Search of a Monetary Constitution*. Cambridge: Harvard University Press.

———. 1970. *Man, Economy, and State*. Los Angeles: Nash Publishing Company.

Samuelson, Paul. 1969. "The Non-Optimality of Money Holding under Laissez-Faire." *Canadian Journal of Economics* (May).

Sandberg, Lars G. 1978. "Banking and Economic Growth in Sweden before World War I." *Journal of Economic History* 38(3) (September).

Schlesinger, Karl. 1914. *Theorie der Geld und Kreditwirtschaft*. Munich.

Schumpeter, Joseph. 1983. *The Theory of Economic Development*. Trans. Redvers Opie. New Brunswick: Transaction Books. (Reprint of 1934 ed.)

Schwartz, Pedro. 1984. "Central Bank Monopoly in the History of Economic Thought: A Century of Myopia in England." In P. Salin, ed., *Currency, Competition and Monetary Union*. The Hague: Martinus Nijhoff.

Scott, Kenneth, and Thomas Mayer. 1971. "Risk and Regulation in Banking: Some Proposals for Federal Deposit Insurance Reform." *Stanford Law Review* 23 (May).

Scrope, G. Poulett. 1832. "The Rights of Industry and the Banking System." *Quarterly Review* (July).

Selgin, G. A. 1985. "The Case for Free Banking: Then and Now." Cato Institute *Policy Analysis*, October 21.

———. 1987. "Free Banking in China, 1800–1935" (unpublished).

Selgin, G. A., and Lawrence H. White. 1987. "The Evolution of a Free-Banking System." *Economic Inquiry* (July).

Sharkey, William W. 1982. *The Theory of Natural Monopoly*. Cambridge: Cambridge University Press.

Short, Eugenie D., and Gerald P. O'Driscoll, Jr., 1983. "Deregulation and Deposit Insurance." Federal Reserve Bank of Dallas *Economic Review* (September).

Simons, Henry G. 1951. "Rules versus Authorities in Monetary Policy." In American Economic Association, *Readings in Monetary Theory*. Homewood, Ill.: Richard D. Irwin. Reprinted from *Journal of Political Economy* 44 (1936).

Smith, Vera C. 1936. *The Rationale of Central Banking*. London: P. S. King & Son.

Somers, Robert. 1873. *The Scotch Banks and System of Issue*. Edinburgh: Adam and Charles Black.

Sowell, Thomas. 1980. *Knowledge and Decisions*. New York: Basic Books.

Spencer, Herbert. 1896. *Social Statics*. New York: D. Appleton Co.

Sprague, O. M. W. 1910. *History of Crises under the National Banking System*. Washington: National Monetary Commission.

Stokes, Milton L. 1939. *The Bank of Canada*. Toronto: Macmillan.

Summers, Brian. 1976. "Private Coinage in America." *The Freeman* (July).

Taub, Bart. 1985. "Private Fiat Money with Many Suppliers." *Journal of Monetary Economics* 16 (September).

Tellkampf, J. L. 1867. *Di Prinzipien des Geld-und Bankwesens*. Berlin: J. Springer.

Temple, R. C. 1899. "Beginnings of Currency." *Journal of the Anthropological Institute* n.s. 29(2).

Thornton, Henry. 1802. *An Enquiry into the Nature and Effects of the Paper Credit of Great Britain*, ed. F. A. von Hayek. Fairfield, N. J.: A. M. Kelley, 1978.

Timberlake, Richard H., Jr. 1978. *The Origins of Central Banking in the United States*. Cambridge: Harvard University Press.

———. 1984. "The Central Banking Role of Clearinghouse Associations." *Journal of Money, Credit, and Banking* 16(1) (February).

———. 1986. "Institutional Evolution of Federal Reserve Hegemony." *Cato Journal* 5(3) (Winter).

Tobin, James. 1963. "Commercial Banks as Creators of 'Money'." In Deane Carson, ed., *Banking and Monetary Studies*. Homewood, Ill.: Richard D. Irwin.

Toma, Mark. 1982. "Inflationary Bias of the Federal Reserve System." *Journal of Monetary Economics* 10.

Tooke, Thomas. 1840. *A History of Prices and of the State of Circulation*, vol. 3. London: Longman, Brown, Green, Longmans and Roberts.

———. 1844. *An Inquiry into the Currency Principle*, 2nd Edition. London. (n.p.)

Trivoli, George. 1979. *The Suffolk Bank: A Study of a Free-Enterprise Clearing System*. London: The Adam Smith Institute.

Tsiang, S. C. 1969. "A Critical Note on the Optimum Supply of Money." *Journal of Money, Credit, and Banking* 1(2) (May).

Tussing, A. Dale. 1967. "The Case for Bank Failure." *Journal of Law and Economics* 10 (October).

United States Congress. 1982. *Report of the Commission on the Role of Gold in the Domestic and International Monetary Systems* (March).

Usher, Abbott Payson. 1943. *The Early History of Deposit Banking in Mediterranean Europe*. Harvard: Harvard University Press.

Vaubel, Roland. 1984a. "The Government's Money Monopoly: Externalities or Natural Monopoly?" *Kyklos* 37.

———. 1984b. "International Debt, Bank Failures, and the Money Supply: The Thirties and the Eighties." *Cato Journal* 4 (Spring/Summer).

———. 1984c. "Private Competitive Issue in Monetary History." In P. Salin, ed., *Currency Competition and Monetary Union*. The Hague: Martinus Nijhoff.

———. 1986. "Currency Competition versus Governmental Money Monopolies." *Cato Journal* (Winter).

Viner, Jacob. 1960. "Mr. Keynes on the Causes of Unemployment." In Henry Hazlitt, ed., *The Critics of Keynesian Economics*. New York: D. Van Nostrand.

———. 1962. "The Necessary and Desirable Range of Discretion to be Allowed to a Monetary Authority." In Leland B. Yeager. ed., *In Search of a Monetary Constitution*. Cambridge: Harvard University Press.

Wagner, Richard E. 1977. "Economic Manipulation for Political Profit: Macroeconomic Consequences and Constitutional Implications." *Kyklos* 30(3).

———. 1980. "Boom and Bust: The Political Economy of Economic Disorder." *Journal of Libertarian Studies* 4(1) (Winter).

Wallace, Neil. 1983. "A Legal Restrictions Theory of the Demand for 'Money' and the Role of Monetary Policy." Federal Reserve Bank of Minneapolis *Quarterly Review* (Winter).

Wallich, Henry C. 1981. "Techniques of Monetary Policy." *Financial Analysts Journal* (July/August).

Warburton, Clark. 1981. "Monetary Disequilibrium Theory in the First Half of the Twentieth Century." *History of Political Economy* 13 (Summer).

Warner, John DeWitt. 1895. "The Currency Famine of 1893." *Sound Currency* 2(6) (February).

Watner, Carl. 1976. "California Gold: 1849–65." *Reason* (January).

Wernette, John Philip. 1933. *Money, Business and Prices*. London: P.S. King & Son.

Weston, Rae. 1983. *Gold: A World Survey*. New York: St. Martin's Press.

White, Eugene Nelson. 1983. *The Regulation and Reform of American Banking, 1900–1929*. Princeton: Princeton University Press.

White, Horace. 1896. *Money and Banking Illustrated by American History*. Boston: Ginn & Company.

———. 1897. "National and State Banks." *Sound Currency* 4(10) (May).

White, Lawrence H. 1984a. "Bank Failures and Monetary Policy." *Cato Journal* 4(1) (Spring/Summer).

———. 1984b. "Competitive Payments Systems and the Unit of Account." *American Economic Review* 74 (September).

———. 1984c. "Free Banking as an Alternative Monetary System." In Barry N. Siegel, ed. *Money in Crisis*. San Francisco: The Pacific Institute.

———. 1984d. *Free Banking in Britain: Theory, Experience and Debate, 1800–1845*. New York: Cambridge University Press.

———. 1985. "Depoliticising the Supply of Money" (unpublished).

————. 1987. "Accounting for Non-Interest-Bearing Currency: A Critique of the 'Legal Restrictions' Theory of Money." *Journal of Money, Credit, and Banking* (forthcoming).

Whitney, Caroline. 1934. *Experiments in Credit Control: The Federal Reserve System.* New York: Columbia University Press.

Whitney, D. R. 1881. *The Suffolk Bank and Its Redemption System.* Boston: The Suffolk Bank.

Wicker, E. R. 1960. "Some Loanable-Funds Concepts and Banking Theory." *Journal of Finance* 15(3) (September).

Wicksell, Knut. 1935. *Lectures on Political Economy,* vol. 2. London: George Routledge & Sons.

Withers, Hartley. 1930. *The Meaning of Money.* New York: E. P. Dutton and Company.

Woolridge, William C. 1970. *Uncle Sam, The Monopoly Man.* New Rochelle, New York: Arlington House.

Woolsey, Warren W. 1984. "The Multiple Standard and the Means of Exchange" (unpublished).

————. 1985. "Competitive Payments Systems: Comment" (unpublished).

Yeager, Leland B. 1983. "Stable Money and Free-Market Currencies." *Cato Journal* 3(1) (Spring).

————. 1985. "Deregulation and Monetary Reform." *American Economic Review* 75 (May).

————. 1986. "The Significance of Monetary Disequilibrium." *Cato Journal* 6(2) (Fall).

Yohe, William P. 1974. "Federal Reserve Behavior." In William J. Frazer, ed., *Crisis in Economic Theory.* Gainesville, Fla.: University of Florida Press.

Zawadski, W. 1937. "Changes in the Price Level and the Influence of Maladjustment of Supply and Demand." *Economica* n.s. (14) (May).

Index